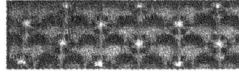

CHINA
2002

WTO entry
and world recession

Ross Garnaut and
Ligang Song (editors)

Australian
National
University

E PRESS

ANU
E PRESS

Published by ANU E Press
The Australian National University
Canberra ACT 0200, Australia
Email: anuepress@anu.edu.au
This title is also available online at http://epress.anu.edu.au

---

National Library of Australia Cataloguing-in-Publication entry

Title: China 2002 : WTO entry and world recession / edited by Ross Garnaut
            and Ligang Song.

ISBN: 9781922144522 (pbk.) 9781922144539 (ebook)

Notes: Includes bibliographical references.

Subjects: World Trade Organization--Membership.
            China--Economic conditions.

Other Authors/Contributors:
            Garnaut, Ross.
            Song, Ligang.

Dewey Number: 382.920951

First published by Asia Pacific Press, 2002
This edition © 2012 ANU E Press

Contents

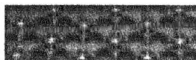

Figures		vi
Tables		vii
Boxes		viii
Symbols		viii
Abbreviations		ix
Contributors		x
1	Catching up with America	1
	Ross Garnaut	
2	Cyclical growth rebound and secular consumption patterns	17
	Yiping Huang	
3	State-owned enterprise reform in China: has it been effective?	29
	Xiaolu Wang	
4	WTO accession and regional incomes	45
	Tingsong Jiang	
5	Competition, ownership diversification and industrial growth	63
	Mei Wen	
6	The WTO challenge to agriculture	81
	Xiaolu Wang	
7	Entry to the WTO on the domestic private economy	97
	Ligang Song	
8	Services driving growth	111
	Christopher Findlay and Mari Pangestu	
9	The impact of WTO accession on FDI	123
	Chen Chunlai	
10	Insurance sector following WTO accession	149
	Ken Waller	
11	Securities market development: assessing and improving market efficiency	159
	Michael Hasenstab	
12	Radical economic reform and income distribution	171
	Xin Meng	
References		183

Figures

2.1	Impact on GDP growth of a 10 per cent devaluation in the yen	18
2.2	Rapid slowdown of the Chinese economy	19
2.3	Decline of industrial production growth and producer prices	20
2.4	Relatively strong income growth	21
2.5	Relatively strong consumer spending	22
2.6	Government spending on capital construction	22
2.7	Growth of FDI inflow	23
2.8	Growth of industrial profits	24
2.9	Changing composition of GDP	24
3.1	Return rate in the industrial sector	33
3.2	Price margin in the industrial sector	34
3.3	Liability rate	35
3.4	Rate of return and state shares in industrial branches	36
3.5	Price margin and state shares in industrial branches	37
3.6	Changing return rate relating to the state share	40
4.1	Coefficient of variation of regional per capita GDP	46
4.2	Gini coefficient of per capita GDP	46
4.3	Theil index of regional disparity	47
4.4	Gini coefficient within and between regions	49
4.5	Gini coefficient within and between regions	50
5.1	Proportion of investment in fixed assets ownership	73
5.2	Proportion of gross industrial output value by ownership	73
7.1	Transitional paths toward the private economy	99
7.2	Ownership shares in China's GDP	101
7.3	Reform, marketisation and changes in private gains and costs from informality	103
7.4	Assets distribution of financial institutions	107
9.1	Regional distribution of accumulated FDI inflows into China	133
9.2	Sectoral distribution of accumulated FDI inflows into China	136
9.3	Composition of FIEs by industry groups of factor intensity	139
12.1	Change in dispersion of real per capita household income in urban China	173
12.2	Lorenz curves for real per capita household disposable income	175
12.3	Average per capita income distribution	176
12.4	Distribution of households with unemployed members across income deciles	178

Tables

2.1	China's contingent liabilities	26
2.2	Rising fragility of China's banking sector	27
3.1	Shares of SOEs an other enterprises in gross industrial output	30
3.2	Shares of SOEs and other enterprises in urban employment	31
3.3	Shares of SOEs and other enterprises in total investment	31
3.4	Performance measures of state and non-state enterprises	36
3.5	How much profit growth can be explained by the interest rate reduction	38
3.6	Analysing sources of profit growth in SOEs and NSEs	40
4.1	Beta convergence of per capita GDP	48
4.2	Selected estimation of factors affecting regional growth	51
4.3	Macroeconomic effects of tariff cuts	53
4.4	Income distribution effects of tariff cuts	54
4.5	Regional distribution of foreign investment	55
A4.1	Regional income disparity	59
A4.2	China's tariff rates after WTO accession	61
5.1	Output of some industrial consumption goods	67
5.2	Average size of industrial enterprises with independent accounting systems	69
5.3	Barriers to foreign entry	71
5.4	Barriers to domestic private entry	72
5.5	Effects of competition and ownership on total factor productivity	78
6.1	Rural labour, TVE employment and rural–urban migration	83
6.2	Real price changes: state and market	86
6.3	Comparison of the rural market prices with C.I.F. prices	86
6.4	Tariff quotas for grains	88
6.5	Estimation of the volume of non-traded grain	88
6.6	Estimating the size of the domestic grain market	90
6.7	The direct impact of grain imports	93
7.1	Growth of private and other enterprise	100
7.2	Bank lending to private enterprises	106
9.1	Key provisions of TRIMs agreement and China's current FDI policy	127
9.2	FDI inflows into China	128
9.3	Estimation of future FDI inflows into China	130
9.4	Accumulated FDI inflows into China by source economies	131

11.1 Chronology of key financial market reforms   160
11.2 Evaluation of China's securities markets   164
12.1 Various inequality measures of income   174
12.2 Decomposition of the contributing factors to the change in the gini 180
     coefficient

Box

8.1   Universal service obligations in telecommunications   120

Symbols

..   not available
n.a.   not applicable
-         zero
.   insignificant

Abbreviations

AIA	American International Assurance
AIU	American International Assurance operation in Shanghai and Guangzhou
AMC	asset management companies
BOC	Bank of China
CD	certificate of deposit
CIRC	China Insurance Regulatory Commission
DIGEM	dynamic intertemporal general equilibrium model
FDI	foreign direct investment
FEC	Foreign Exchange Certificate
FIE	foreign-invested enterprise
GATS	General Agreement on Trade in Services
GDE	Guandong Enterprises
GITIC	Guandong International Trust and Investment Company
M&As	mergers and acquisitions
MFN	most-favoured nation
MNE	multi-national enterprise
MOF	Ministry of Finance
MOFTEC	Ministry of Foreign Trade and Economic Cooperation
NBS	National Bureau of Statistics
NIE	newly-industrialised economy
NPL	non-performing loans
NSE	non state-owned enterprise
PBC	People's Bank of China
PPP	purchasing power parity
SAIC	State Administration for Industry and Commerce
SOB	state-owned bank
SOE	state-owned enterprise
TIC	Trust and Investment Company
TRIMs	trade-related investment measures
TRIPs	trade-related aspects of intellectual property rights
TVE	town and village enterprise
UNCTAD	United Nations Conference on Trade and Development
WTO	World Trade Organization

Contributors

Chen Chunlai is a lecturer at The National Centre for Development Studies, Asia Pacific School of Economics and Management at The Australian National University.

Christopher Findlay is Professor of Economics in the Asia Pacific School of Economics and Management at The Australian National University.

Ross Garnaut is Professor of Economics at the Research School of Pacific and Asian Studies, The Australian National University, and Chairman of the China Business and Economy Program.

Michael Hasenstab is Portfolio Manager, Franklin Templeton.

Yiping Huang is the Chief Economist for Greater China at Citigroup

Tingsong Jiang is a Postdoctoral Fellow at The National Centre for Development Studies at The Australian National University.

Mari Pangestu works with the Centre for Strategic and International Studies, Jakarta and is Adjunct Professor at the Australia–Japan Research Centre at The Australian National University.

Ligang Song is a Fellow at The Australia–Japan Research Centre, Asia Pacific School of Economics and Management at The Australian National University.

Ken Waller is an economic advisor for the Commonwealth Bank of Australia.

Xiaolu Wang is a Visiting Fellow at The National Centre for Development Studies, Asia Pacific School of economics and Management, The Asuatralian National University.

Mei Wen is a Research Fellow with the Division of Economics, in the Research School of Pacific and Asian Studies at The Australian National University.

Xin Meng is a Fellow with the Department of Economics at the Research School of Pacific and Asian Studies at The Australian National University.

1

Catching up with America

Ross Garnaut

THE HURDLES OF 2002 IN CHINA'S RACE TO CATCH UP

In *Australia and the Northeast Asian Ascendancy*, I noted that the powerful sustained growth that had propelled first Japan and then Hong Kong, Singapore, Taiwan and Korea from poverty into the ranks of the medium or high-income economies seemed inexorable only in retrospect (Garnaut 1989). Along the way, the path of growth was strewn with barriers, many of which at the time had seemed as if they might be the one that brought the whole process to an end. In the end, at each hurdle the domestic interests that favoured growth turned out to be strong enough to break through, and rapid growth continued until the productivity and income frontiers of the reasonably rich countries had been reached, first of all by Japan in the early 1970s. So it was likely to be with China. And in China's case, too, there would be great challenges to sustained growth along the way. No-one could be sure in advance that a particular hurdle would not turn out to be too great for the polity and the society to overcome, although each time there would be be powerful tendencies for continuity in the growth process.

China is at present above what an informed observer would see as one of the biggest hurdles—or two big hurdles piled on top of each other. The first of the joined hurdles has been recession in China's main trading partners and sources of investment in 2001, amidst fears that it would stretch an indefinite period into the current

1

year. The second, piled on top, is China's entry into the World Trade Organizaton (WTO) in December 2001.

The rapid expansion in China's external trade and investment has been a major factor in its sustained growth. Continued growth has underpinned far-reaching and increasingly radical reform to convert an inward-looking centrally planned economy into an internationally-oriented market economy. Mainland China's external trade and investment is concentrated strongly in the Asia Pacific region—with its immediate neighbours in East Asia, and across the Pacific in North America, particularly the United States. In the Asia Pacific region as a whole, the year just passed, 2001, has been the weakest for growth in output and trade since China's reform era began in 1978 (PEO 2001). The Asia Pacific downturn is deeper than in the depths of the East Asian financial crisis in 1998 because, this time, it extends to the United States and its North American partners. Indeed it has had its centre in the United States. The effects of United States recession have been expanded by its being focused first of all in the high technology and wider electronics industries, inputs into which had become the major export commodities of a number of East Asian economies, most notably Taiwan, Singapore and Malaysia. Recession elsewhere has compounded Japan's continuing economic weakness.

At this difficult time for China's external trade and investment, China was at last admitted into the WTO in December 2001. This concluded a long process of China exploring the possibility of, and then seeking, membership of the WTO, stretching back to discussions between the then Ministry of Foreign Trade and Technical Co-operation and the Australian Government, and the Australian provision of technical assistance on what was involved, in 1986. As described in chapters 6, 8, 9 10 and 11 of this book, China's entry into the WTO is no mere formality. China's accession agreements embody commitments to further far-reaching trade and investment liberalisation. On a number of important matters, the commitments go beyond those of any other member at the time of WTO entry or in the Uruguay Round. The implementation of these commitments, commencing immediately and continuing over a number of years, would intensify structural change throughout the economy (see especially chapters 2, 5 and 7). These changes compound the ongoing challenges to the viability of the surviving state-owned enterprises (chapter 3), of unemployment (chapter 12), and dispersion in income distribution (chapters 4 and 12).

Is the hurdle of WTO entry in an Asia Pacific recession so high that 2002 becomes the year in which the sustained strong growth since reforms began in 1978 comes to an end or, as in Southeast Asia with the financial crisis in 1997–98, moves to a lower trajectory? How should we see the 2002 hurdles in the long process of China's catching up with the productivity and incomes of its more prosperous neighbours in East Asia and of its other economic partners amongst the developed countries?

This chapter outlines the long-term path of growth in China and some of the hurdles that could bring it to a conclusion before the frontiers of global productivity and incomes have been reached. It explains why, if the hurdles can be cleared and the process continues for a long period, catching up with the world's advanced countries takes less time than would be suggested by the application of growth rate differentials to current per capita incomes as measured conventionally in the national accounts and converted into a common currency at current exchange rates. It then outlines the ways in which subsequent chapters expand understanding of the contemporary challenge to growth.

HURDLES IN A LONG RACE

What are the natural end points of the rapid growth that was established in China by the beginning of internationally-oriented reform in 1978 and sustained after that by the deepening of reform and integration into the international economy? What are the hurdles that would have to be cleared if growth were to be sustained until China's average productivity and living standards were near the global frontiers?

Deng Xiaoping in 1980 laid out what then seemed to all foreign observers to be an unrealistically ambitious goal, to quadruple Chinese output by the end of the century. Perhaps it should not have been seen as unrealistic, as this feat had been achieved in the preceding decades by four of China's Northeast Asian neighbouring economies, commencing with Japan in the 1960s and 1970s. But then again, China in the immediate aftermath of the Cultural Revolution was not an obvious candidate for membership of the group of high-growth East Asian economies that had been attracting international attention and some admiration.

A while later Deng added that the next goal, after the first quadrupling of production, would be to take China to the living standards of the middle-income countries half way into the twenty-first century. In 1986, in Beijing, I asked Deng what he

3

meant by China catching up with the middle-income countries half way through the next century. Did he mean reaching the levels in the 1980s of the middle-income countries (then conventionally including Northeast Asia's newly industrialised economies, Hong Kong, Taiwan and Korea)? Or did he mean the levels in the mid twenty-first century of what were then the middle-income economies? Deng said that it was the former that he had in mind. By 2050, China would have the standard of living of Taiwan, Hong Kong and Korea in the 1980s. He added that he hoped that by then the Chinese people would be satisfied.

That was high ambition for a country which had until a short time before contained a majority of the world's poor people, and which was then only a few steps down the uncertain path onto which it had been led by the durable elder statesman. But in a way it was also a very low ambition, for, if the quadrupling goal were met on time, it would mean that by the mid twenty-first century, China, unlike the other Northeast Asian economies, would have experienced the cessation of rapid growth long before it had reached the global economic frontiers. The second goal as elaborated by Deng in 1986 also ascribed low ambition to the Chinese of the twenty-first century, for it contemplated their satisfaction with living standards that were way below the levels of the most prosperous parts of the world community at that future time.

Deng's high ambitions for the first twenty years of reform were realised several years ahead of time. It now seems that, barring a fall at one of the hurdles in China's path, the long-term goals were wildly and unrealistically low.

Why would we expect the end point of economic growth in China to be significantly below the average incomes in the world's most successful economies? The average ability of the Chinese people in matters related to economic performance is not obviously lower than the average of Australians or Americans. Nor is there any reason to expect the material ambitions of Chinese to falter a long way short of Americans' ambitions. It would be surprising if one day China did not have about the per capita income of the United States, give or take one quarter or one third to take account of differences in preferences, demographic structures, and the myriad institutional detail that can affect productivity at the margin. (The qualification on demographic differences is far from trivial, as the sharp decline in fertility in China after 1978 means that the Chinese population will age more and more quickly than that of the United States through the middle decades of the twenty-first century.) The difference in population

4

size means, of course, that the Chinese economy will be larger when its per capita income is only one quarter or (given the stronger twenty-first century population growth that is anticipated in America) one third that of the United States.

How long it takes to get there is a different matter. I suggest that it will not take as long to catch up as most observers would expect, so long as China continues to meet the demanding conditions for sustained strong growth that I describe in this section.

Chinese output, as measured by the official agencies and accepted by the Washington-based international institutions, has averaged a bit below 9 per cent per annum over the reform period. This is above the 7.2 per cent per annum that doubles output each decade, which was the focus of Deng's early exposition and has continued *de facto* as something like an official target. Growth could ease a bit from the high average levels of the past quarter century without quibbles about its continuation at a rapid rate. It has become conventional to query the Chinese growth statistics, but they are not wildly misleading. Problems of measurement outside the main centres and of valuation elsewhere raise some doubts at the margin, as they do in all developing countries. But there is not much doubt that real output has been growing at a rate that doubles output each decade.

What will it take to maintain strong growth, at something approaching the average rate of the past quarter century? It takes high levels of investment, and in a country as large as China a high proportion of investment will need to be funded from domestic savings. This seems a relatively easy condition for China to meet, with its extraordinarily high domestic savings rate, supported by its attractions to foreign direct investment. It takes flexibility in the structure of the domestic economy and the allocation of resources to productive uses, which in turn require effective markets for labour, capital, goods and services. This is the core agenda of past and prospective economic reform, and the subject of a majority of the chapters in this book.

The most important requirement for increased flexibility in the Chinese economy in the early stages of reform, and at the beginning apparently the most politically demanding and technically complex, was to change fundamentally the institutions of production. At the beginnings of reform these were overwhelmingly the People's Communes in the countryside and large state-owned enterprises (SOEs) in the cities. Reform of collective agriculture and state-owned businesses was the hurdle at which reform to promote economic growth fell in most of the once centrally-planned economies. In the event, strong growth in the first two decades of reform in rural China, home in the late 1970s to 80 per cent of the Chinese population, was underpinned by two huge, rapid institutional transformations, both emerging spontaneously from rural communities and reinforced but not initiated by the central authorities: the replacement of the People's Communes by the household responsibility system (HRS) in agriculture; and the emergence of township and village enterprises as the main focus of industrial and services activity in the countryside. The SOEs have been more strongly resistant to reform, although, as discussed in chapter 3, there has been greater success in the period of more radical reform since the mid 1990s. The persistent problems of large dimension in the SOEs have not had fatal consequences for growth, however, because of one third dramatic transformation: the emergence of a large, dynamic private sector in an unfavourable regulatory environment from the mid 1990s (Garnaut et al. 2001; chapter 7, this volume). This powerful recent development shows promise of providing the structural flexibility for the next demanding stage of rapid growth in China, with the Government now giving some attention to the removal of artificial impediments to private sector development.

Sustained rapid growth requires a reasonable degree of economic stability supported by sound fiscal and monetary policy. The requirement is not perfect stability, but at least the avoidance of persistent high inflation and balance of payments and domestic financial crises. This condition cannot be met without the exercise of good judgment by people who understand complex macroeconomic relationships, at some distance in their day to day work from people whose main expertise is in the accumulation and exercise of political power. The analytical requirements to support sound judgment are considerable at times of change. There is also an element of good luck behind sustained macroeconomic stability, as the institutional underpinnings of a rapidly changing economy and society themselves change rapidly, in ways that affect unpredictably the influence of particular policy interventions on the economy. Cautious fiscal policy reduces the risk that ill fortune will lead to a major fracture in economic growth performance.

Sustained strong growth requires in high degree openness to foreign ideas, technology, management practices and trade. These can all be assisted by high levels of direct foreign investment. China so far has met this test. The requirements of openness (like the requirements of structural flexibility and efficiency in resource

6

allocation that have already been discussed) are more and more demanding as successful growth takes the economy closer to the international productivity frontiers. Openness is two-sided, with the requirements extending to access to other economies' markets for goods, services, capital, management practices and technology. Both sides of the requirements of openness are addressed substantially by China's entry into the WTO, which is a second main focus of the following chapters of this book.

Of the essential conditions for sustained growth, two others are more complex, and further from conventional economic analysis. Sustained strong growth requires political stability at home and in China's relations with its neighbours and with the world's superpower, the United States.

Deng Xiaoping famously saw political stability through the stress of radical economic reform coming first of all from the continued internal discipline and political hegemony of the Chinese Communist Party. This was the basis on which he secured the dismissal from high office of the two key leaders through the first and crucial decade of reform: General Secretary Hu Yaobang in the wake of the student demonstrations in Shanghai and elsewhere late in 1986; and former Premier and then current General Secretary Zhao Ziyang (together with Politbureau Standing Committee member Hu Qili) in the midst of the crisis focused on Tiananmen in 1989. This was the basis on which he proposed decisively the imposition of martial law on 17 May 1989 (contemporary communications corroborated in Nathan and Link 2001:175).

The authority of Deng Xiaoping and the then old leaders, and through them of the Chinese Communist Party, derived from their roles in the revolution that brought the Communist Party to power, in the defeat of the radical Maoist leadership after the death of Mao Zedong, and then in the early success of economic reform. Political legitimacy cannot forever depend on events that pass rapidly into history, through a new leadership that was not associated directly with them. The maintenance of political stability requires the continued delivery of rising living standards widely distributed through the population. It requires, as well, timely responses to the increased emphasis that Chinese, like people everywhere, place on personal freedoms and opportunity to influence policy decisions that affect their welfare, through the extension of education and knowledge, information about the realities of life in China and the rest of the world, and awareness of their own value as individuals that accompanies sustained economic growth over long periods.

This book is not about the domestic political conditions for sustained economic growth, but its discussion of inequality of income distribution between regions and individuals (especially chapters 4, 6, 9 and 12) are closely relevant to assessment of its prospects.

On international political stability, Chinese are much more aware than foreigners of the challenges of China's geographic location. China shares a long border with Russia, which still possesses the world's second most formidable military capacity, built around nuclear capacity. After a difficult first decade following the collapse of the Soviet Union, in which descent into domestic political instability and economic anarchy at times seemed possible, Russia now seems to be making progress on strengthening domestic political and economic institutions. But there is a sense in which the risk of instability in Russia remains a risk to China. To the east of the Russian border is the world's last surviving Stalinist state, with considerable conventional military capacity and nuclear aspirations, recently described by the President of the United States as a source of terrorist threat to the international community. On its borders to the west there is Mongolia, and then Chinese provinces with large Islamic communities adjacent to Islamic communities in Kazakstan, Uzbekistan, Tajikistan, Kyrgyzstan, Afganistan and Pakistan. On the Southern border is India, whose size inevitably makes it a rival for influence in the mainland of Asia, as well as Vietnam, Myanmar, Laos, Bangladesh, Nepal and Bhutan. And then close across the waters to the east are the economically strong countries of Japan and Korea. Taken together these are the world's most difficult frontiers, demanding at the best of times, and thought provoking at a time when state-backed terror is seen as a challenge to domestic order all over the world. China has seldom had less troubled relations than it has now with countries on its borders taken as a whole, but Chinese at least will continue to see risks to stability in their immediate international environment.

China's size and growing economic weight mean, inevitably, that its interests will from time to time bump into those of the United States, with its global interests. The risks of a destructive stand-off between China and the United States seemed large a year ago, but have been eased with sensible resolution to immediate problems. China's entry into the WTO provides a helpful international context for resolution of bilateral conflicts over trade. For the time being, the United States' identification of the war against terrorism as its greatest strategic challenge and China's support on these matters has eased tensions.

Maintenance of productive working relations with the United States is necessary for continued economic as well as political liberalisation in China, and for sustained growth in China, as it is for world peace. The greatest tests will continue to arise over the status of Taiwan, where the formula for the outcome that is most satisfactory for Chinese on both sides of the Taiwan Straits remains unchanged through all the political noise of recent times. China can live with the formal *status quo* for a long time, so long as there is continued movement towards functional integration of the communities and economies across the Straits, as there has been since 1987. However, an overt move towards international recognition of Taiwan as an independent entity would destabilise any mainland leadership that was seen within China as being inclined to accept it, which would make military confrontation inevitable. There would be no overt movement towards Taiwan independence unless the Taiwan leadership thought that it had unlimited and unconditional support from the United States. This is why seven US Presidents, and Chinese leaders from Mao to Jiang, have in the end settled on the acceptance of an untidy formal *status quo*. It is important that they continue to do so until political and economic change on both sides of the Straits has created opportunities that cannot now be readily envisaged.

Finally, the environmental challenge to sustained economic growth in China should be acknowledged. Chinese, like people everywhere, have been giving higher priority to domestic environmental amenity as incomes have increased. China's capacity to deal with accumulating domestic environmental problems has been expanding with economic growth, and, with the usual lags in human political response to new challenges, China are using this capacity with increasing effect. The higher environmental hurdles in the path to sustained growth are global, with the raising of Chinese living standards towards those of the developed countries. Economic prosperity everywhere will require China to contribute its part to workable global management regimes.

CATCHING UP TAKES LESS TIME THEN YOU THINK

If China continued to clear the many hurdles in the path of sustained rapid growth, how long would it take for it to reach the productivity levels and living standards of

the developed economies? This section explains why, in other East Asian economies, it has taken less time than would be expected from simple comparison of
growth rate differentials and differences in average output at the starting point. It
then discusses the relevance of these comparisons to China.

When Deng Xiaoping was defining ambitions for future Chinese living standards
in terms of those in East Asian middle-income economies in the mid 1980s, the
comparators were at the beginning of an extraordinary period of rapid catching up
with the world's advanced countries.

In 1985, Korea's per capita income in constant 1992 US dollars was around $3,000.
In 1996, on the eve of the East Asian financial crisis, it was almost $11,000 in 1992
US dollars. Singapore moved from around US$8,000 to the vicinity of US$28,000
over the same period. For Hong Kong, the lift was from around US$8,000 to the
vicinity of US$24,000. A minor part of these large gains in Singapore and Hong
Kong, and more in Korea, was lost in recession and currency adjustments in the
financial crisis. Part of the large relative expansion of the rapidly growing East
Asian economies over this period can therefore be seen as reflecting unsustainable
speculative boom conditions, but the major part has to be explained in other terms.

This was the most spectacular but not the only period of accelerated catching up
with the world's developed economies. In Hong Kong, per capita incomes expressed
in 1992 US dollars doubled between 1971 and 1973, from around US$3,000 to about
US$6,000. Korean per capita GDP expressed in the same terms roughly doubled to
US$3,000 in three years from the mid 1970s. Singapore moved from around US$4,000
to over US$7,000 between 1971 and 1974.

These are the periods of most rapid catching up with the developed economies.
They would be uninteresting if they were matched by other periods in which there
were similarly spectacular relative declines. They could then be said to reflect merely
the vagaries of the foreign exchange markets.

But they were not so matched. From 1971, when Singapore's per capita income
expressed in 1992 US dollars was about US$4,000, to 1998, when the effects of the
financial crisis were strongest, Singapore per capita income converted into constant 1992 US dollars at the exchange rates of the day grew at almost one and a
half times the average rate of growth of GDP in constant domestic prices. Between
1968 when Hong Kong's per capita income expressed in 1992 US dollars was about

US$2,500, and 1998, Hong Kong's per capita income converted into constant US dollars at the exchange rates of the day grew almost 1.9 times the average rate of growth of GDP in constant domestic prices. In Korea the deviation between the two measurements of rates of growth is between those of Hong Kong and Singapore over the long period from 1965–98. Similar patterns can be found in the experience of Taiwan and, earlier, Japan.

The general story is that an economy that sustains rapid growth over a long period reaches a point or points at which its GDP converted in the US dollars of the day rises much more rapidly relative to the developed economies than the differentials in real growth rates would suggest.

Why is this so? And is it relevant to assessments of how many years of sustained rapid growth it would take for China to reach the world's frontiers of average output and living standards?

The resolution of a big part of the statistical puzzle lies in the manner in which standard ways of measuring GDP systematically underestimate the 'real' incomes of low-income countries. The standard way of calculating GDP in US dollars is simply to take national output as measured in the domestic currency in the national accounts, and to convert it into US dollars at the exchange rates of the year under consideration. In a poor country, while the prices of goods that enter international trade generally bear a reasonably close relationship to international prices in international currency, this is not the case for goods and services which are only traded within the country. The prices of 'non-tradables' tend to be lower in low-income developing countries where wages are low.

Wages of low-skill workers remain low for as long as labour remains abundant. In this early stage of development, rapid economic growth is associated with strong expansion in production and export of simple, labour-intensive products, and with expansion of modern sector employment. More and more people are attracted from agriculture into industrial and later services employment. This process continues until most of the economically surplus labour in the farm economy has been absorbed into the modern economy. At this point when labour begins to become scarce, the 'turning point in economic development', real wages begin to rise, sometimes rapidly. In East Asia this point has sometimes occurred at around US$3,000 in 1992 US dollars, although it seems to have occurred at below this level in Korea.

There seems to have been further acceleration at higher incomes, perhaps US$8,000.

Beyond the 'turning point', there is rapid structural transformation, with the old labour-intensive industries being replaced by more capital-intensive and technologically complex activities as the main loci of growth. Per capita income in international prices rises more rapidly than standard growth rates of real GDP would suggest. The rapidly growing middle-income economy catches up even more rapidly with the high-income countries.

Conventionally measured GDP converted to US dollars is a reasonable indication of the international purchasing power of domestic incomes. For other purposes, however, conventional GDP tells us less than the 'purchasing power parity' or 'real purchasing power' measure of GDP. The 'purchasing power parity' measure does not systematically underestimate output of low-income countries. Therefore there is no accelerated catch-up with developed countries as real wages rise beyond the turning point in economic development. Neither is it affected artificially by policy-induced or temporary market-induced exchange rate mis-valuation.

How do we apply these insights to assessment of the period of sustained rapid growth that would be required for China to catch up with the developed economies?

To begin, we should use purchasing power parity measures of GDP as the starting point. China's purchasing power parity per capita income in 2000 was US$3612. On the latest available World Bank data, per capita income in China is about one fortieth that of the United States in conventional terms (US$856 compared with US$35,101 in 2000), compared with one tenth in terms of real purchasing power (US$3,612 compared with US$35,101). The corresponding figures for Japan are US$36,894 by conventional measures and US$28,992 for real purchasing power (World Bank 2002).

The period of sustained 4.5 per cent differentials in growth in per capita income that would be required for China to catch up with average incomes in the United States is about 50 years when we, appropriately, use the purchasing power measure as the starting point.

Incidentally, in terms of conventional national income accounting, the sum of all Chinese incomes is now 11 per cent of American, and 23 per cent of Japanese. In purchasing power terms, the ratios are 46 per cent and 124 per cent.

It is not clear that the accelerated catching up with developed country incomes in conventional terms after labour becomes scarce will occur over a relatively short period in China, as it did in Japan, Hong Kong, Taiwan, Singapore and Korea. China's huge population and land area and the geographic, policy and institutional barriers to internal trade and factor movements are causing labour to become scarce and wages of unskilled labour to rise rapidly in the advanced coastal provinces long before there are signs of labour shortage in central and western regions. The structural transformation that follows and then accompanies sustained rapid growth is occurring in the coastal regions while other parts of China retain strong comparative advantage in labour-intensive products.

China's accelerated catch-up can be expected to commence at a relatively low level of conventionally defined average incomes. There is no sign of it yet in the data if we compare only China and the United States, largely because the United States dollar, against which the Chinese yuan is pegged, has been exceptionally strong against almost all other countries over the last several years. But China's per capita income ranking against third countries has been rising more rapidly than is indicated by conventional growth rate differentials.

The same regional disparities that generate large differentials across Chinese regions and provinces in rates of growth and economic structure are discussed in chapters 4 and 12 as sources of widening income inequalities. This is a challenge for political cohesion around reform policies that support continued rapid growth. At the same time, the regional disparities cause Chinese growth to place less pressure for structural change on China's trading partners, which are faced by less concentrated competition and more widely differentiated opportunities for export to China than would be the case if China, like its smaller East Asian neighbours, were more deeply integrated domestically.

GETTING OVER 2002

So is 2002 possibly the year in which the hurdle is too high?

Huang in chapter 2 suggests not. He notes that this is a year of generational leadership change, which exacerbates uncertainty but is likely to lead to leadership that is more closely knowledgeable about the necessary economic and political reform in the period ahead. Continued growth in urban incomes is essential to political stability at a time of uncertainty, and will be delivered. China's macroeconomic environment is holding up well to the severe external shocks. Growth is slower, but not dramatically so. The greater risks are in the longer term, related mainly to domestic financial fragility. Deeper financial reform is the remedy, much hangs on whether the Chinese government implements the necessary change in time to forestall a major problem. Huang's views on the short-term are reinforced by recent evidence of early recovery in the US economy.

Other chapters highlight the extent of the long-term challenge to continued strong growth and to equitable income distribution that is inherent in recent economic trends and in the WTO commitments.

Wang in chapter 3 discusses the history of SOE reform, and notes the failure in the early reform years. There has been more progress in recent years of radical reform. SOE performance has been helped considerably by improvements in economic conditions beyond the firm, but there are improvements too from improved incentive structures, greater profit orientation leading to reduction in numbers of redundant employees and generally more efficient operations. Joint ventures with foreign and private enterprises have lifted performance.

Jiang in chapter 4 notes that regional disparities contracted in the early years of reform, but have widened again since. The early reductions in inequality were associated with the concentration of early gains in agriculture. WTO entry will raise total incomes and, at first sight surprisingly, by more in rural than in urban areas. But the rural gains are mostly in industry in the richer, coastal provinces. The model used to draw these conclusions does not take account of the effects of WTO entry in encouraging capital inflow, the gains from which are also likely to be concentrated in the coastal provinces. The result is a worrying widening of the distribution of income between regions. This requires an effective policy response, which can be built around improving infrastructure for trade between coastal and inland areas, acceleration of reform in Central and Western provinces including in ways that would support off-farm development in the inland provinces, as well as resource transfers from wealthier provinces

Mei Wen in chapter 5 makes the important point that it takes time to build the institutional base for market exchange that is taken for granted in the long-developed economies. The development of markets had to start with changes in the ideological environment between 1985 and 1991, with accelerated improvement of market institutions themselves from the early 1990s. The internet has been important in reducing transaction costs in market exchange. Diversification of ownership types, with township and village industries and then private firms playing important roles, has been important in improvement in markets. A significant component of productivity growth has come from the diversification of ownership. A level playing field between types of ownership is required to get the most out of this institutional change.

Wang in chapter 6 takes a closer look at the effects of WTO entry commitments on the agricultural sector. Commitments to liberalisation are expected to result in displacement of over 9 million farm workers in the land-intensive grain sector. Wang doubts that township and village enterprises can expand enough to absorb them. Overall consumer gains will be large, but to different people. The later discussion in chapter 9 suggests that the strong focus in chapter 6 on land-intensive agriculture in which China's comparative disadvantage is strongest has affected perceptions of the outlook for employment.

Song in chapter 7 observes how WTO entry will reinforce recent trends towards strong growth in the private sector. The reforms that have facilitated this growth have been modest in extent but considerable in their effect. There would be a large return from deeper reform, amongst other things to raise efficiency in the financial sector. More efficient financial markets are required to establish a more level playing field for different types of business ownership. The flourishing private sector has been a major force for improvement in markets and economic institutions more generally.

Findlay and Pangestu in chapter 8 describe the WTO commitments to truly radical liberalisation and internationalisation in the services sector. This will spur the development of more efficient community service obligations and regulatory arrangements, weaknesses in which have caused important problems.

Chen in chapter 9 examines how WTO entry is likely to expand further the high levels of inward direct foreign investment flows that have been a feature of Chinese development over the past decade. Chen throws a different light on some of the pessimism about the agricultural sector after WTO entry, noting the prospects for expansion of labour-intensive agricultural exports and for market pressures after WTO entry to push more labour-intensive industries inland.

Waller in chapter 10 and Hasenstab in chapter 11 examine the role of WTO entry in ongoing reform in the financial sector. For the liberalisation of foreign entry to the insurance sector to generate the potential benefits that are available to China, there will need to be regulatory reform and more generally an expanded role for the private sector. Hasenstab looks at Chinese financial reforms in a long perspective, seeing them as capable of moving Chinese financial markets to a place in the global big three. But major market imperfections remain. These require timely correction, and in the meantime China should take care with capital account liberalisation.

Finally, Meng addresses in detail the tendencies in income distribution over the period of reform There have been two distinct periods. Reform was more gradual until the early 1990s. More radical reform since then has been associated with large increases in inequalities. The emergence of households with more than one person unemployed is a feature of recent structural change, that warrants priority in policy response.

Taken as a whole, the reviews of contemporary developments in subsequent chapters suggest that China is not going to be knocked off course by the challenges of 2002. This, through a period of great external weakness, will boost confidence in China's capacity to sustain growth over long periods, perhaps even to catch up with America.

The review has highlighted the growing challenges from widening income inequalities of many kinds, exacerbated by WTO entry. It has also identified the financial sector as requiring timely efforts in reform if it is not to be a source of risk to economic stability as well as a drag on efficiency in other parts of the economy. Tardiness on financial sector reform would, amongst much else, hold back the development of the private sector that has become important to wider economic and political development in many ways.

The clearing of the more conventionally economic hurdles would make more prominent the long-term challenges of internal and external political stability. Dealing with the long-term issues of income inequality and financial sector weakness would contribute to management of these wider challenges.

2

Cyclical growth rebound and secular consumption patterns

Yiping Huang

THE YEAR OF UNCERTAINTY

2002 is a critical year for the Chinese economy not only because the growth trajectory may reverse its trend but also because a number of key events will take place during the year.

First, the fourth generation of the leadership is ready to take over from the third at the forthcoming 16th Party Congress in September and the 10th National People's Congress in March 2003. The transition is likely to be smooth despite the inevitable power struggles and infighting. Candidates from the younger generation are similar to those that they will succeed, but tend to be better educated, more open-minded, and have a better understanding of Western-style economy and society. Uncertainties related to the leadership transition will be mainly reflected in the areas of policymaking and implementation. There are already signs that the current government intends to postpone some tough decisions for the next government. Most senior officials are currently busy seeking critical appointments in the next government rather than pushing through reforms now. As a consequence, there may be a vacuum in policy reforms over the next few months.

Second, China has already begun implementing WTO reforms since joining the organisation in early December 2001. The Chinese version of the WTO agreement was published just before Christmas—a delay which has caused difficulties for the public in gauging the implications of the WTO reforms accurately and for government officials in implementing these changes. An important area of reform is the financial sector. With foreign banks, insurance companies and asset management firms moving into China and expanding their scope there, serious doubts are emerging about whether the domestic financial institutions will be able to survive the competition. The financial policy conference in early February 2002 laid the groundwork for reforms, but much more needs to be done. The recently revealed Bank of China (BOC) scandals provide an illustration of the seriousness of the problems in the banking sector. Non-performing loans (NPLs) in the banks and the asset management companies (AMCs) are now believed to constitute nearly 50 per cent of total outstanding loans.

Finally, the pattern of global economic recovery will also affect the performance of the Chinese economy in 2002, particularly through trade links. It is now widely believed that the US economy will emerge from recession in 2002. But there is still a heated debate about the timing and extent of the recovery. A more critical factor is the future movement of the Japanese yen. The yen has weakened significantly since the end of 2001, stirring anxiety in the region as well as in China. However, the impact of yen depreciation on the Chinese economy is assessed as being limited. A weaker yen puts some pressure on China's export sector because Japan

FIGURE 2.1 **IMPACT ON GDP GROWTH OF A 10 PER CENT DEVALUATION IN THE YEN**

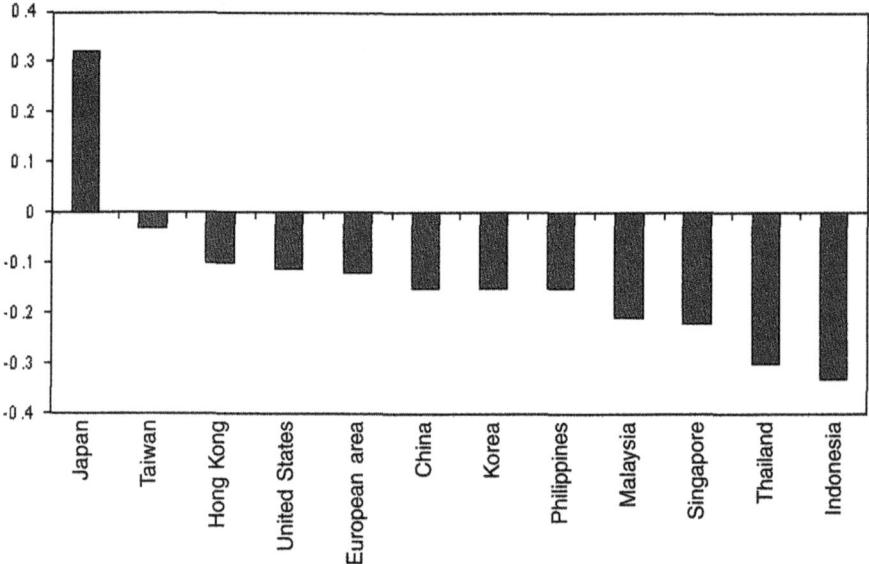

Source: Citigroup estimates applying the Oxford Macroeconomic Model.

18

FIGURE 2.2   **RAPID SLOWDOWN OF THE CHINESE ECONOMY**

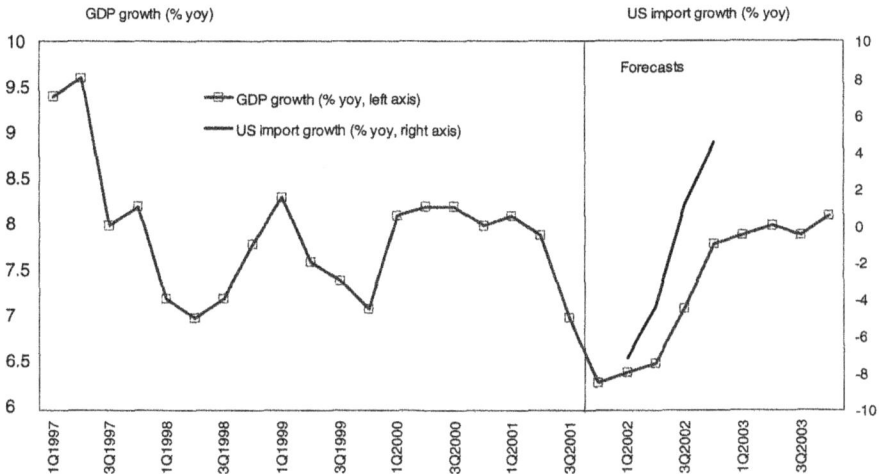

Source: CEIC.

accounts for about 17 per cent of China's export market. This is particularly difficult at the moment because China's export companies have been severely affected by the global recession. China, however, does not compete directly with Japan in third export markets as export similarities from the two countries are quite low.

The Oxford macroeconomic model was applied to assess the impact of yen depreciation on Asian growth. A 10 per cent yen devaluation reduced China's GDP growth by 0.15 percentage points. This is rather small compared to 0.5 percentage gain in China's growth if US growth is lifted by one percentage point. The Chinese yuan will remain stable even if the exchange rate of the yen slides further.

GROWTH REBOUND

Growth of the Chinese economy slowed rapidly in 2001, from 8.1 per cent in the first quarter and 7.8 per cent in the second quarter to 7 per cent in third quarter and 6.3 per cent in the fourth quarter. The slowdown was mainly attributable to the recession of the global economy, and especially the US economy.

The pace of the growth deceleration surprised many market economists who argued that the Chinese economy would not be affected by external changes because of China's relatively small export sector and its aggressive counter-cyclical fiscal measures. Nonetheless, China still outperforms most of its East Asian neigbours. In 2001, Singapore, Hong Kong and Taiwan recorded negative GDP growth,

19

FIGURE 2.3   **DECLINE OF INDUSTRIAL PRODUCTION GROWTH AND PRODUCER PRICES**

Industrial growth (%)   PPI (%)

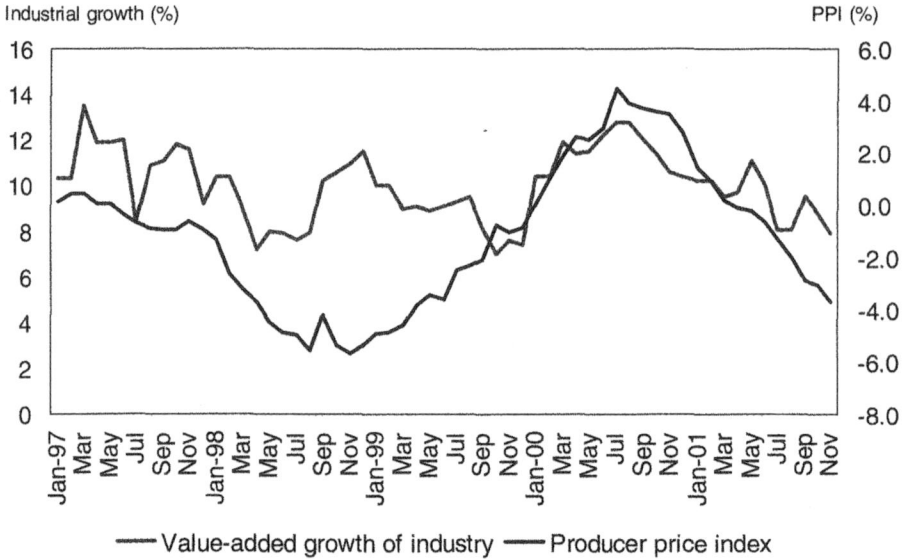

——— Value-added growth of industry ——— Producer price index

Source: CEIC.

while China achieved positive growth of 7.3 per cent.

China has felt the pain of global recession. After all, the export sector still accounts for 22 per cent of GDP according to official statistics, and export growth collapsed from 28 per cent in 2000 to 7 per cent in 2001. This had most visible impact on the coastal provinces, which happen to be the engine of the Chinese growth. As a result, growth of industrial production was dragged down.

The economy is likely to stay sluggish in the first half of 2002, but domestic demand is probably enough to support GDP growth of 6–7 per cent. WTO membership is likely to deliver significant benefits in a few sectors. Chinese growth will probably rebound in the second half of 2002. This prediction rests on the assumptions about the US economic recovery—although recent data suggest that a US recovery is already well underway, we believe a significant surge of imports into the United States will take place in the third and fourth quarters of 2002.

FIGURE 2.4   **RELATIVELY STRONG INCOME GROWTH**

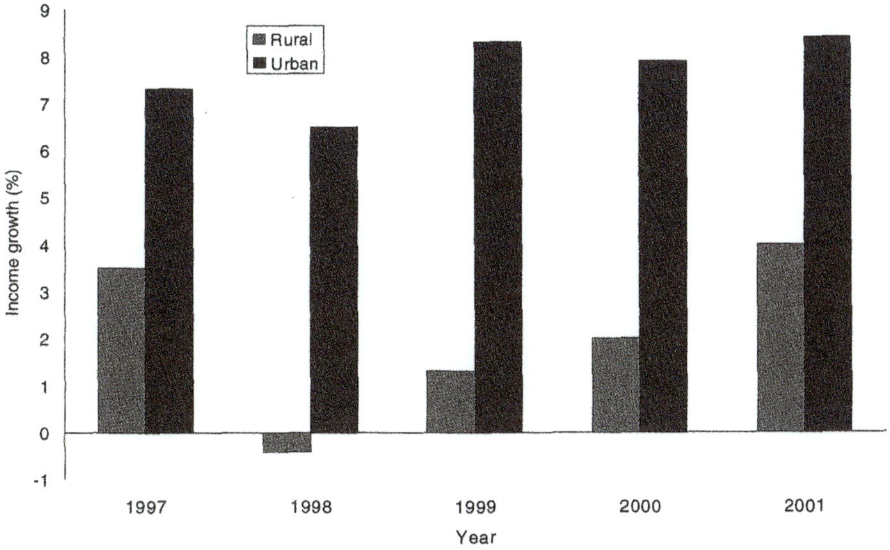

Source: CEIC and Citigroup.

CONSUMPTION PATTERNS

Before an export-led rebound takes place, Chinese growth in the first couple of quarters in 2002 will have to be supported by domestic demand. This will be influenced by relatively strong urban consumption alongside a weakening investment trend.

The stability of consumer confidence in recent months has been underpinned by rapid income growth. In 2001, urban per capita income increased by 8.4 per cent and rural disposable income was up by 4 per cent. Both rates of growth were higher than in the previous year, although GDP growth was slower. The rapid growth in urban incomes was caused by the government's pay rise policy—a 30 per cent increase in base salary plus year-end bonus equivalent to one month's salary.

Growth in incomes drove consumer spending strongly. Retail sales consistently grew by more than 9.5 per cent every month in 2001, except February (which was

21

FIGURE 2.5 **RELATIVELY STRONG CONSUMER SPENDING**

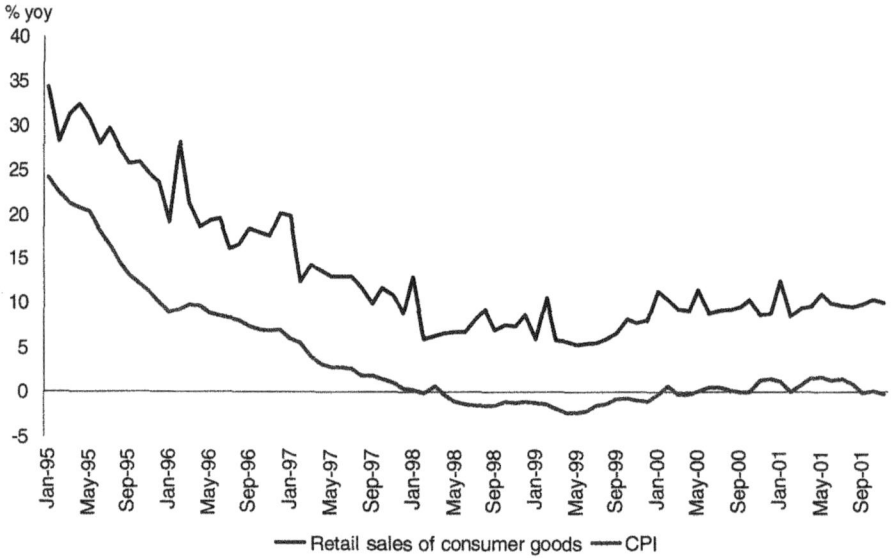

% yoy

Retail sales of consumer goods — CPI

Source: CEIC and Citigroup.

FIGURE 2.6 **GOVERNMENT SPENDING ON CAPITAL CONSTRUCTION**

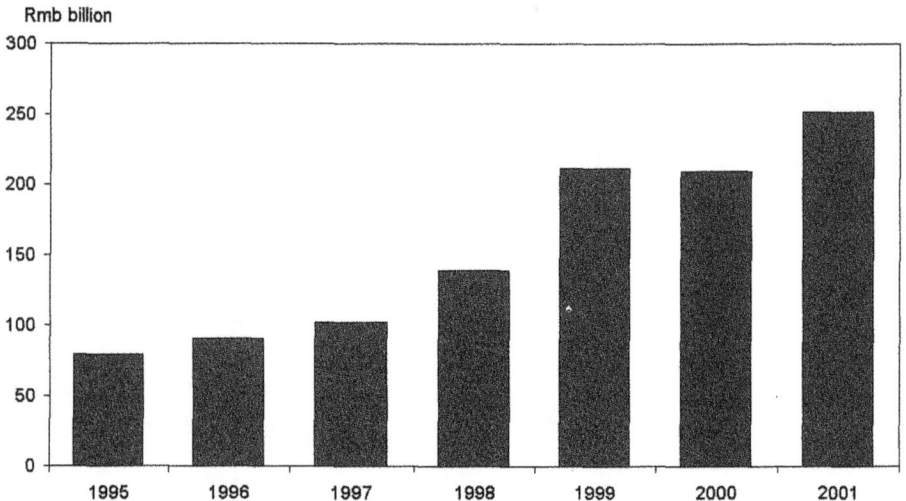

Rmb billion

Source: CEIC and Citigroup.

22

mainly caused by the special effect of the Chinese New Year). The government has recently committed to continuing the pay rise policy in 2001. Urban consumer spending will remain steady, but the strength of rural consumption has been questionable for some time.

Investment may be relatively weak. We examine three types of investment activities—public investment, foreign direct investment (FDI) and corporate sector investment. Government spending has been a major driver for GDP growth in the last couple of years, and the spending program has concentrated mainly on infrastructure projects in western provinces. But the proportion of government spending on capital construction in GDP stabilised during the period 1999–2001. In 2002, the government committed another 150 billion yuan to infrastructure projects, exactly the same amount as in 2000 and 2001. This means that the contribution of the spending program to economic growth will probably be smaller this year.

The inflow of FDI surged in 2001, growing by 15 per cent, owing to China's expected accession to the WTO. On average, FDI contributed about 0.6 percentage points to GDP growth. In 2002, strong capital inflow is likely to continue but the

FIGURE 2.7   **GROWTH OF FDI INFLOW**

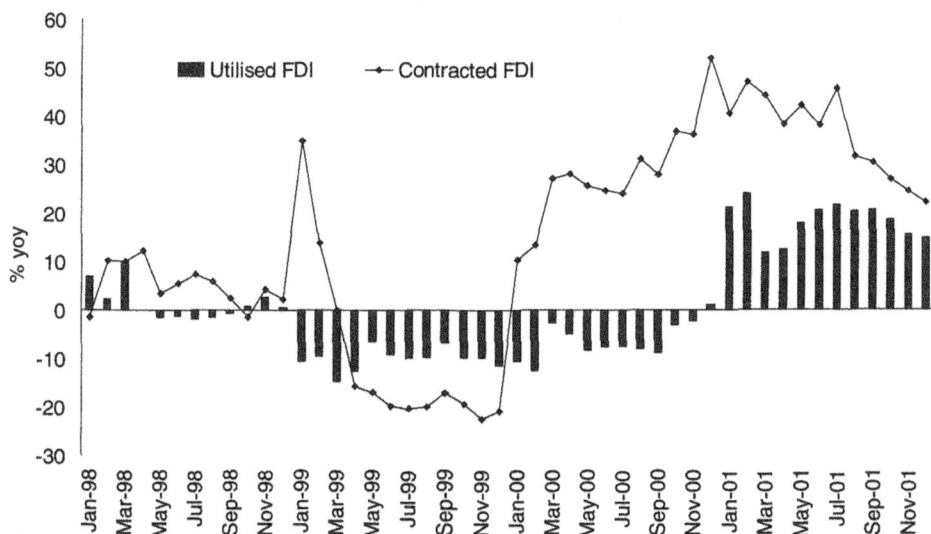

Source: CEIC and Citigroup.

FIGURE 2.8   **GROWTH OF INDUSTRIAL PROFITS**

Growth of profits %

■ Growth of industrial profits ■ Growth of industrial SOE profits

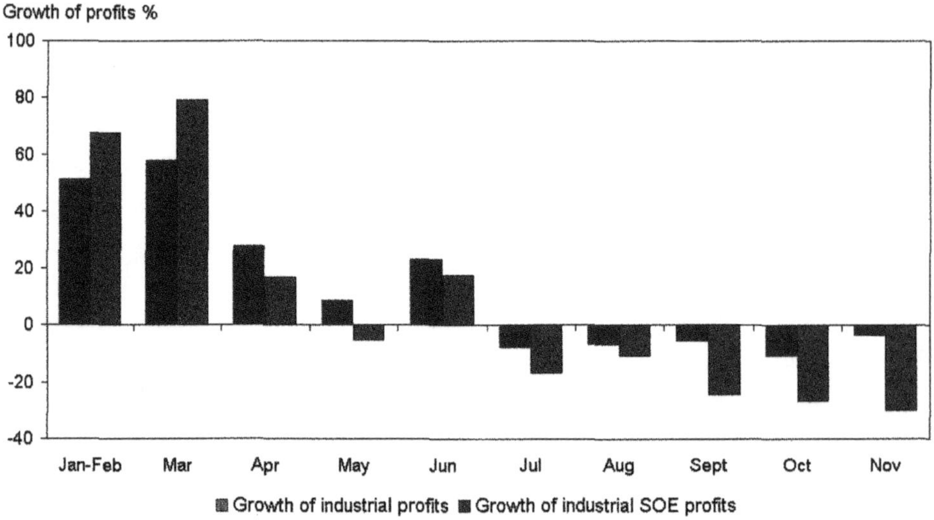

Source: CEIC.

FIGURE 2.9   **CHANGING COMPOSITION OF GDP**

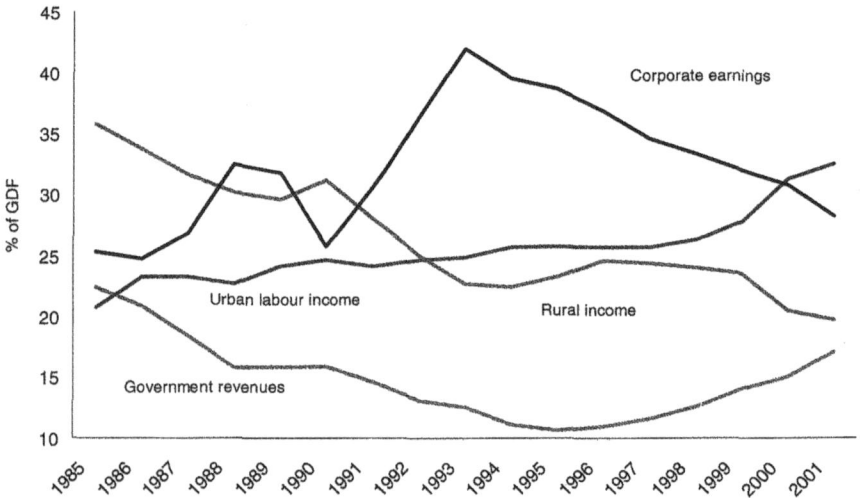

Source: CEIC and Citigroup.

growth rate of FDI will probably fall, mainly because global FDI is likely to fall due to recession.

Corporate sector investment may also weaken somewhat. Total industrial profits have been declining since mid 2001, probably because of three key factors—increased competition triggered by weakening export demand and illustrated by a rapid fall in producer prices; increases in the collection of government revenue; and a rapid rise in household income caused by the pay rise policy. Meanwhile, the real interest rate in China is rising again because the government has not changed its nominal interest rate since June 1999 but price deflation has also re-emerged. A combination of declining profits and rising real interest rates does not imply a bullish outlook for corporate investment in the short term.

Of course, the investment outlook, especially that of FDI and corporate sector investment, may improve significantly once an overall macroeconomic upturn starts. The outlook could be further improved by two possible policy changes currently under consideration—the interest rate cut in late February 2002, and expected reduction of corporate tax from 33 per cent to 25 per cent.

But the changing composition of GDP overall does not favor investment activity. Since the mid 1990s, the proportions of corporate earnings and rural income have been squeezed by those of government revenues and urban income. Such changes were driven by government policies to raise urban income and increase government revenue, but they could be bad news for investors, both direct investors and share holders in the Chinese companies.

Efforts to raise urban income are partly aimed at stimulating domestic demand after the East Asian crisis but are also partly a characteristic of China's gradual reform approach. Because reform is gradual, continuous compromises have to be made in order to keep the reform process alive. It is thus important to win the support of politically important constituencies or at least reduce their opposition. At present, this means raising urban incomes. Increases in government revenue are also a response to the declining government influence experienced during the early stages of reform as a result of decentralisation and liberalisation. Revenue growth in recent years has been realised through better collection of taxes, especially personal income tax and private sector tax, rather than increases in tax rates.

Over the longer term, even stronger consumer spending expansion can be expected. The foremost reason for optimism is the expected strong income growth. The government has estimated that the total size of the middle-class population

25

TABLE 2.1   CHINA'S CONTINGENT LIABILITIES, END OF 2000

	Amount (billion yuan)	Share in GDP (%)
Accumulated public debt	1367	15.3
Debt for recapitalisation in 1998	270	3.0
Costs on policy bank bonds	154	1.7
Bank restructuring	4467	50.0
External debt US$145.7 billion	1210	13.5
Total	7468	83.5

Source: Citigroup estimate.

may rise to 200 million by 2010. Improvements in investment efficiency will also make more resources available for consumption. With the further reforms and liberalisation prompted by WTO accession, a steady improvement in productivity is expected. China's demographic transition will also accelerate in the coming decade because of the one-child policy. According to the World Bank, the proportion of young workers in the Chinese population will fall from 61 per cent in 1990 to 45 per cent in 2010, while the proportion of aged population will rise from 9 per cent to 1 per cent during the same period. Population aging usually results in a decline of the saving ratio (which is currently around 40 per cent in China).

An obvious qualification for the bullish consumption story is rural income. As the government focuses increasingly on the urbanisation program, however, rural productivity and income may start to pick up again.

FISCAL SUSTAINABILITY A KEY CHALLENGE

China will be a main source of growth in the global economy in the coming decades. Even after another two decades of rapid growth, China's official per capita income level will probably still be around US$4000–US$5000. The gap between China and the advanced economies will be significant and the potential for further catch up will be huge. But China is already the world's sixth largest economy in the world, because of its vast population. In 20–30 years, China will definitely become the third or even second largest economy.

Growth sustainability is dependent on effective control of some of the key problems in the economy and society, including unemployment, the non-performing loans, corruption, regional disparities. The most significant challenge, however, is the maintenance of fiscal sustainability.

TABLE 2.2   **RISING FRAGILITY OF CHINA'S BANKING SECTOR**

	end 1996	end 1998	end 2001
Proportion of NPLs (%)			
Big four banks	40.0	48.0	35.0
Ten joint-stock banks	-	13.5	15.5
Average CAR (%)	4.4	8.0	6.6

Notes: NPLs: non-performing loans; CAR: capital adequacy ratio. Proportion of non-performing loans for the four major banks for 1996 and 1998 are re-estimated based on new information made available at the beginning of 2001. The proportion for 2001 excluded the Rmb1.4 trillion transferred to the Asset Management Companies in the previous year.
Source: Citigroup estimates.

Current fiscal programs do not pose serious problems as fiscal deficits have ranged between 2.5 per cent and 2.8 per cent of GDP in recent years. Government's massive spending on infrastructure to stimulate economic growth caused some side effects because most of those projects were implemented inefficiently by the SOEs and public spending crowded out more efficient private investment. But active fiscal policies during the past years still do not add up to significant fiscal risks. Public debts currently account for a little over 15 per cent of GDP. However, if all the contingent liabilities are counted, they already amount to nearly 84 per cent of GDP. This is already quite high. If the rising trend of contingent liabilities is not contained quickly, then the chances of fiscal crisis will increase quickly.

The key to averting a fiscal crisis lies in the effective control of the banking problems and the successful development of the pension fund. The newly established pension fund suffers from significant and growing deficits, rising from Rmb30 billion in 2000 to Rmb70 billion in 2001. It is estimated to reach around Rmb200 billion in five years. These shortfalls are not counted in the calculation of the contingent liabilities as the government as already decided to finance the pension fund by selling State shares in stockmarkets. However, this policy has not yet developed as speculation about sales of State shares has already led to a significant downward correction of the market. Should stockmarkets fail to come up with the needed funds, then the state budget will have to shoulder pension fund shortfalls.

Problems in the banking sector are more serious. The average proportion of non performing loans (NPLs) of the big four banks is around 35 per cent while their average capital adequacy ratio is about 6.6 per cent. What is even more worrisome is that there is limited evidence of improvement in the banking sector, even after several years of reform. Although the proportion of NPLs declined from its record high at 48 per cent in 1998, the reduction was mainly because the transfer of the NPLs to Asset Management Companies (AMCs). The majority of that portion of NPLs still needs to be disposed of, and is thus still the responsibility of the banks or the Ministry of Finance. Worse still, most of the problem SOEs stay with the parent banks and continue to create new NPLs. This is the reason the quality of banking assets has deteriorated rapidly during past years, with the capital adequacy ratio falling from above 8 per cent in late 1998 to around 6.6 per cent. Banks are in need of another round of recapitalisation.

The pace of China's banking reforms has accelerated recently. This is partly because China committed to open up the banking system completely within five years of joining the WTO. The Central Financial Works Conference in early February 2002 called for significant improvement in bank supervision through both reorganisation of the central bank and capacity building. It also confirmed a three-step reform approach for the banks—improvement of internal management system, corporatisation and public listing. The authorities now also permit foreign strategic investors to take equity interests in domestic banks. All these are positive and important steps toward eventual resolution of the banking problems. With the reform tasks lying ahead the Chinese government is anxious to avoid a fiscal crisis.

3

State-owned enterprise reform: has it been effective?

Xiaolu Wang

THE QUESTION TO BE ANSWERED

Economic reform in China in the past two decades has significantly accelerated economic growth and increased people's income. However, reform of state-owned enterprises (SOEs) during the major part of this period has basically been ineffective. The rapid economic growth in China during the reform period was mainly led by the rapidly growing non-state-owned enterprises (NSEs)—or later privately-owned or collective-owned enterprises, shareholding corporations, and foreign-invested enterprises. Meanwhile, the performance of the SOE sector has generally been unsatisfactory. Due to their lower growth rate, partly caused by the serious financial problems faced by many of them, the SOEs' share in the economy has fallen dramatically. This chapter focuses on analysing which reform measures have been relatively more effective, and uses that to develop a view on future priorities.

REFORMS AND PERFORMANCE OF SOEs TO DATE

SOE reform in the 1980s and early 1990s was mainly focused on government–enterprise relations and enterprise management. This included increasing the autonomy of, and reducing government interventions in, SOEs by allowing enterprise managers to make more decisions with respect to production, pricing, marketing, investment, and more or less, employment. Production plans, price controls, and government distribution of inputs and outputs were basically abandoned. The old

29

requirement for SOEs to surrender a proportion of turnover was abolished; instead, value-added tax and profit tax systems were introduced. The direct government finance to SOEs was replaced by bank loans. There were also partial changes to the incentive system in enterprises with the Enterprise Contract System to SOEs.

It was expected that these changes would enable SOEs to survive growing market competition and be able to develop themselves. However, the strategy was not very successful until the late 1990s. Initially, the financial situation of SOEs worsened. Non-performing loans built up rapidly. Statistical data show that the SOE share in gross industrial output dropped from 76 per cent in 1980 to only 28 per cent in 1999 (see Table 3.1).[1] The statistical definition of gross industrial output changed in 2000 to exclude small NSEs with an annual sale of 5 million yuan or less. However, under the original definition, the SOE share further dropped from 48.9 per cent to 47.3 per cent in 2000. Contribution by either SOEs or NSEs to GDP are unavailable in published statistics. The author estimates that the share of SOEs in GDP fell from a dominating position of around 60 per cent to 36 per cent of GDP in 1999 (Wang, forthcoming).[2]

While the SOE share in total output was dropping rapidly, the share in inputs (labour and investment) fell much more slowly, remaining quite high throughout the 1980s and early 1990s. The SOE share in urban employment was 76 per cent in 1980—it was still 59 per cent in 1995. The reduction of the SOE share in total investment in fixed assets was also slow. It only fell from 66 per cent in 1985 to 54 per cent in 1995 (see Tables 3.2 and 3.3). The allocation of bank loans has been biased towards SOEs throughout the reform period. Take as an example the state-owned Industry and Commerce Bank, the largest commercial bank in China. In mid

TABLE 3.1   **SHARES OF SOEs AND OTHER ENTERPRISES IN GROSS INDUSTRIAL OUTPUT (PER CENT)**

	SOE	Collective	Self-employed	Others, including private	Total
1980	76.0	23.5	-	0.5	100.0
1985	64.9	32.1	1.9	1.2	100.0
1990	54.6	35.6	5.4	4.4	100.0
1995	34.0	36.6	12.9	16.6	100.0
1999	28.2*	35.4	18.2	18.2	100.0

Note: Including the shareholding corporations with controlling shares owned by the state.
Source: Calculated from National Bureau of Statistics (NBS), 1994, 1999, 2000 and 2001. *China Statistical Yearbook*, China Statistics Press, Beijing.

1999, 79.1 per cent of its short-term loans were extended to SOEs, and only 20.9 per cent to NSEs. Of the latter, collectively-owned enterprises received the major part (Wang 2000).[3] Non-performing loans in the state banks, (loans mainly extended to SOEs) accumulated sharply and the government had to write off a large proportion in the late 1990s. In general, SOEs have been characterised by high inputs and low rates of return, reflecting inefficient use of resources.

SOE reform changed direction in the mid and late 1990s, particularly after 1998, when a large number of workers were made redundant. Another significant change occurred to ownership structure. Restrictions on privatisation were lifted for small SOEs. Many small SOEs have been privatised or rented to private managers. The recent fall in SOEs' share in the economy was in part a result of this privatisation. Shareholding systems were introduced to a large number of medium and large SOEs, although the state still holds a controlling proportion of shares in many of them. Some SOEs have been converted to joint ventures with foreign investment.

According to an enterprise survey carried out in 19 provinces, 75 per cent of the

TABLE 3.2 **SHARES OF SOEs AND OTHER ENTERPRISES IN URBAN EMPLOYMENT (PER CENT)**

	SOE	Collective	Self-employed	Others, including private	Total
1980	76.2	23.0	0.8	-	100.0
1985	70.2	26.0	3.5	0.3	100.0
1990	70.2	24.1	4.2	1.5	100.0
1995	59.0	16.5	8.2	16.4	100.0
2000	38.1	7.0	10.0	44.8	100.0

Source: Calculated from National Bureau of Statistics (NBS), 1994, 1999, 2000 and 2001. *China Statistical Yearbook*, China Statistics Press, Beijing.

TABLE 3.3 **SHARES OF SOEs AND OTHER ENTERPRISES IN TOTAL INVESTMENT (PER CENT)**

	SOE	Collective	Self-employed	Others, including private	Total
1985	66.1	12.9	21.0	-	100.0
1990	65.6	11.9	22.5	-	100.0
1995	54.4	16.4	12.8	16.3	100.0
2000	50.1	14.6	14.3	21.0	100.0

Source: Calculated from National Bureau of Statistics (NBS), 1994, 1999, 2000 and 2001. *China Statistical Yearbook*, China Statistics Press, Beijing.

small and medium SOEs had been subject to fundamental change by the end of 1999, including ownership changes. Another survey indicates that, of the 520 large SOEs that the survey covered, 70 per cent had been transformed to corporations with a multi-owner system by the end of 1999 (Lu 2001). According to the statistics, by the end of 2000, pure SOEs only contributed 49.7 per cent of SOEs' gross industrial output. This implies that half of the current SOEs have already become share-holding companies or joint ventures with mixed shares of state and private owners (although the state still holds a controlling share). The state also tightened the monitoring system on large SOEs by appointing special auditors to these firms.

These measures were observed to have improved the resource allocation in SOEs. SOE employment, which has long included a high proportion of supernumaries, decreased from 113 million to 81 million during the period 1995–2000. SOEs' share in urban employment fell from 59 per cent to 38 per cent over the same period. Their share in total investment fell, though less dramatically, from 54 per cent to 50 per cent (see Tables 3.2 and 3.3).

To date, NSEs have dominated or at least been very important in the labour-intensive industries such as light industry, construction, road transport, retail, catering, and daily services. Meanwhile, SOEs still play a dominant role in some heavy industries such as oil, power generation, metal smelting and chemical materials. They also dominate in some service sectors, such as finance, insurance, rail and air transport, telecommunications, and medical services. Thus, the performance of SOEs still has important impact on China's overall economic performance.

THE EFFECT OF RECENT SOE REFORMS

SOEs' profits fell continuously between 1993 and 1997–98.[4] But the trend changed during the period 1998–2000, when SOEs profits in the industrial sector increased from 53 billion yuan to 241 billion.[5] Total profits in non-state industrial enterprises also increased dramatically, from 93 to 199 billion,[6] although the improvement was less impressive than for the SOEs. Figures 3.1–3.3 compare three indicators of SOE performance with different groups of NSEs for the period 1998–2000. They are the rate of return on assets (defined as the ratio of total profit to the value of total assets), price margin (defined as the ratio of total profit to total sales) and liability rate (defined as total liability as a proportion of total assets). A higher rate of return indicates higher productivity of capital; a higher price margin shows generally higher profitability; a higher liability rate indicates, all other things being equal, higher

FIGURE 3.1   **RETURN RATE IN THE INDUSTRIAL SECTOR, 1998–2000**

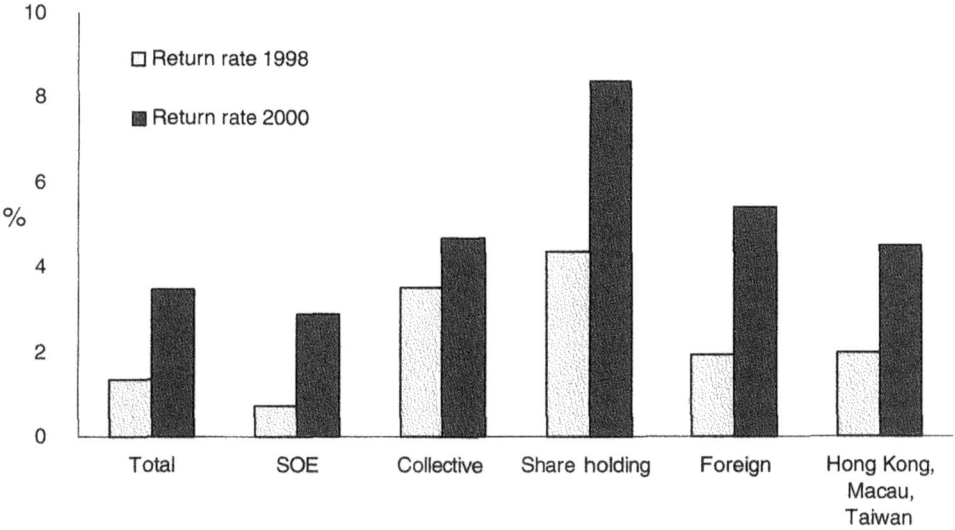

Note: Data of the NSEs are 'non state-owned above designed size industrial enterprises', defined by NBS.
Source: Calculated from National Bureau of Statistics (NBS), 2001. *China Statistical Yearbook*, China Statistics Press, Beijing.

operating risk of enterprises.

There were substantial increases in the return rate and price margin of SOEs as well as NSEs, except collective enterprises which only showed a minor improvement (Figures 3.1 and 3.2). There was also a slight reduction in the liability rate of SOEs and other NSEs (Figure 3.3). All three indicators show improvement in the efficiency of SOEs, although they still have the lowest return rate and a relatively high liability rate compared with NSEs.

Furthermore, using the year 2000 data for 37 industrial branches for an efficiency analysis, negative relations are found between the return rates and the share of SOEs in the value-added of branches, and between price margin and the SOE shares (Figure 3.4). There is a clear trend of decreasing return rate when the percentage share of SOEs in the value-added of the corresponding branches is increasing. A similar trend is apparent in the price margin, although it is less obvious (Figure 3.5). This indicates that, in spite of their improved efficiencies, SOEs are generally less efficient than NSEs.

33

FIGURE 3.4 **RATE OF RETURN AND STATE SHARES IN INDUSTRIAL BRANCHES, 2000**

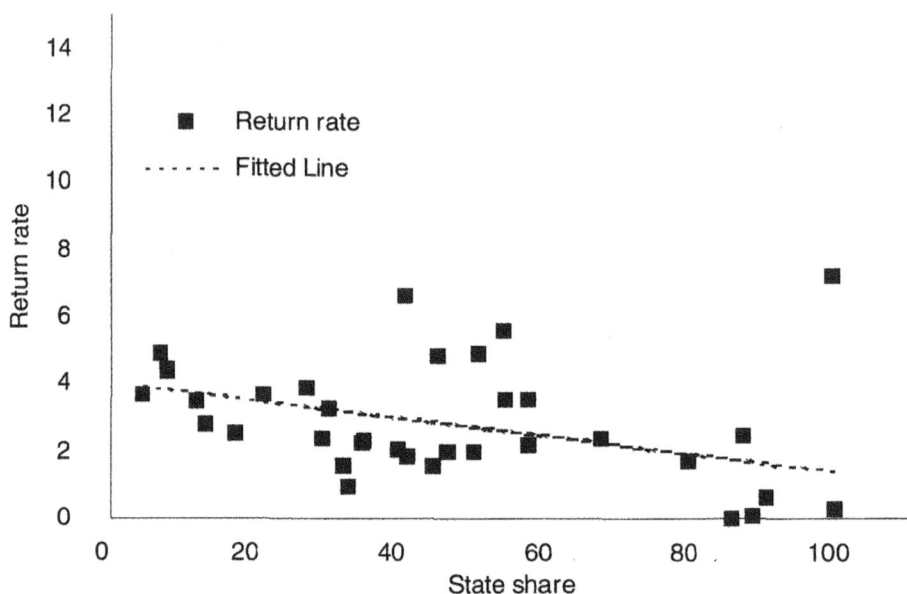

Source: Calculated from National Bureau of Statistics (NBS), 2001. *China Statistical Yearbook*, China Statistics Press, Beijing.

TABLE 3.4 **PERFORMANCE MEASURES OF STATE AND NON-STATE ENTERPRISES, 2000 (PER CENT)**

	Return rate	Price margin	Liability rate
SOE	2.9	5.7	60.3
Collective-owned	4.7	4.2	64.7
Share-holding	8.4	12.7	48.8
Foreign funded	5.4	6.0	55.5
Hong Kong, Macau, Taiwan-funded	4.5	5.3	57.2
Others (estimate)	1.3	0.9	70.4
Total	3.5	5.2	60.1

Source: Calculated from National Bureau of Statistics (NBS), 2001. *China Statistical Yearbook*, China Statistics Press, Beijing.

FIGURE 3.5   **PRICE MARGIN AND STATE SHARES IN INDUSTRIAL BRANCHES,** 2000

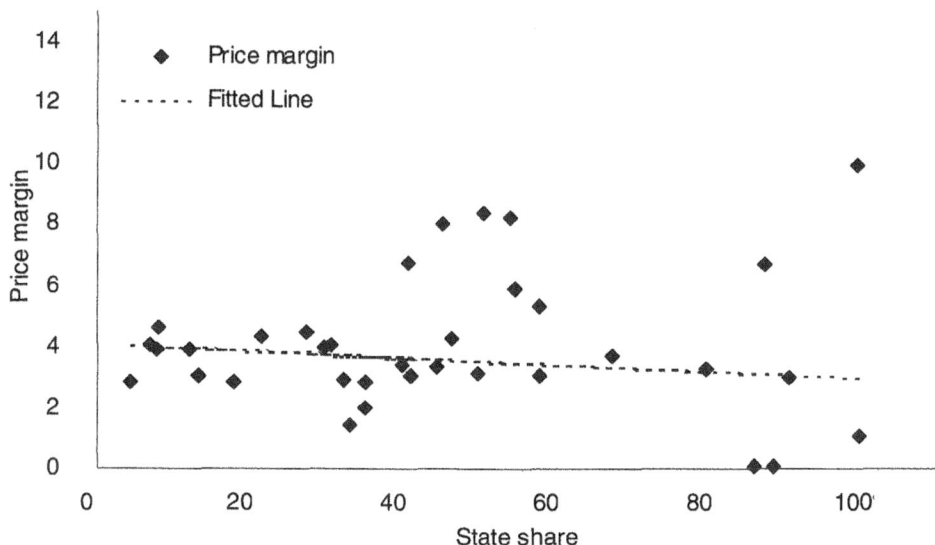

Source: Calculated from National Bureau of Statistics (NBS), 2001. *China Statistical Yearbook*, China Statistics Press, Beijing.

During the period 1998–2000, 148.7 billion yuan of non-performing loans in SOEs were written-off (Li 2001). An estimated 30 billion was converted to the share-holdings of four state agencies.[8] This should reduce SOEs' interest payments by 10 billion yuan, which explains 5.4 per cent of the profit growth of SOEs.

Thus, 75 per cent of the dramatic increases in SOEs' profits can be explained by changing external factors. The remaining 25 per cent—or 47 billion yuan—can be attributed to the higher profitability caused by internal factors in SOEs; this resulted in an 89 per cent real increase in profit from 53 to 99 billion yuan between 1998 and 2000. During the same period, NSEs' real profit increased by 117 per cent, from 93 to 203 billion yuan (after deduction of the positive and negative effects of the external factors; that is, lower interest rates and higher oil prices). If we calculate the return rates in 2000 using the profit and deducting the effects of these external factors, they increased from 0.7 per cent to 1.2 per cent for SOEs during the 1998–2000 period, and from 2.8 per cent to 4.8 per cent for NSEs during the same period (Table 3.6). The above calculation suggests an improvement in the performance of

37

TABLE 3.5   **HOW MUCH PROFIT GROWTH CAN BE EXPLAINED BY THE INTEREST RATE REDUCTION? (PER CENT, 100 MILLION YUAN)**

	Industry total			Industry SOE		
	Short term	Long term	Total	Short term	Long term	Total
Bank loans 2000 (%)	34423.0	27931.0		3224.0	1846.0	
Interest 1998 (%)	6.9	8.1		6.9	8.1	
Interest 2000 (%)	5.6	5.7		5.6	5.7	
Interest rate reduction (%)	1.4	2.4		1.4	2.4	
Benefit	472.0	351.0	823	300.0	223.0	523.0
Total profit increase per cent			2935			1883.0
Per cent explained			28			27.8

Notes: Bank loans to industrial enterprises are estimated, derived from the following procedure:
1) Assuming the following categories of short-term loans are lent to industrial enterprises: short-term loans to industry, town and village enterprises, private enterprises and self-employed persons, and to foreign-invested enterprises.
2) The ratio of the above loans to total classified short-term loans is derived as 52.4 per cent (Total classified short-term loans accounted for 78 per cent of the total short-term loans and 51 per cent of total loans lent by all financial institutions).
3) Apply this ratio to unclassified short-term loans and medium and long-term loans to derive total loans to industrial enterprises.
Loans to industrial SOEs is calculated as short-term loans to industry (SOE share = 100 per cent) + unclassified short-term loans x (SOE share) + medium and long-term loans x (SOE share). The SOE share is derived from the share of SOE loans in total classified short-term loans. Interest rates are based on the regulated rates of short-term loans and medium and long-term loans. The interest rate differences are calculated as the differences of the average rates in 1998 and 2000, respectively, for the two categories of loans
Source: Calculated from National Bureau of Statistics (NBS), 1999 and 2001. *China Statistical Yearbook*, China Statistics Press, Beijing.

SOEs (though not as dramatic as it first appears) implying that SOE reforms since 1998 have been effective.

To further investigate the performance of SOEs, return rates are calculated for the 37 industrial branches from 1998–2000. The relationships between the changes in return rate (2000 return rate minus 1998 return rate) and the shares of SOEs in all branches are plotted in Figure 3.6.[9] It illustrates an inverse U-shape relation between changing return rate and the share of SOEs, with predominantly a downward slope. The fitted curve indicates that industrial branches with both a low and medium level of state shares had a greater improvement in efficiency. The branches with a medium level of state shares are even better. However, those branches dominated by SOEs had only a minor improvement, implying that the improvement in

38

SOEs' efficiency was not mainly an effect of policies that favoured SOEs.

Thus we can conclude that the significant increase in returns to SOEs from 1998 to 2000 have resulted mainly from external factors—falling interest rates, increases in oil prices and the write-off of bad loans. However, SOEs' profitability has also increased, most likely as a result of recent reforms relating to changes in their ownership structure. In many industries, SOEs compete with NSEs, thus inducing greater efficiency in the SOE sector.

LESSONS FROM PAST SOE REFORMS

The early reform measures (mainly decentralisation) were necessary for SOEs while the economy was moving from a central planing to a market system. However, experience has shown that establishing a competitive market environment via de-regulation has not been enough to revive SOEs, as a major residual problem within SOEs is a lack of incentive to win market share. In addition, the government, as the owner of SOEs, has failed in its role as a monitor of enterprise management. However recent reforms, which have relieved SOEs of the burden of redundant employment, and more importantly, allowed changes in the ownership structure of SOEs by accepting private ownership, appear to have been more effective. To further understand this issue, a review of the major problems faced by SOEs in the past is necessary.

Government intervention

Excessive government controls and interventions in SOEs caused low efficiency. However, this was addressed via deregulation during the reform period. Most SOE managers now have substantial freedom in decision making and operate in the market.

Incentives

Payment to both managers and workers in SOEs was regulated and usually unrelated to work performance. Wage determination in SOEs has become more flexible following reform, although many SOE managers are either still underpaid compared with those who work for private or foreign companies, or well paid but not in a way that relates to their contribution to the firm. The situation differs from region to region. According to a survey by NBS in 1999, the highest CEO salary of SOEs was 200 times the average workers' wage rate in Sichuan province, whereas it was

CHANGING RETURN RATE RELATING TO THE STATE SHARE, 1998–2000

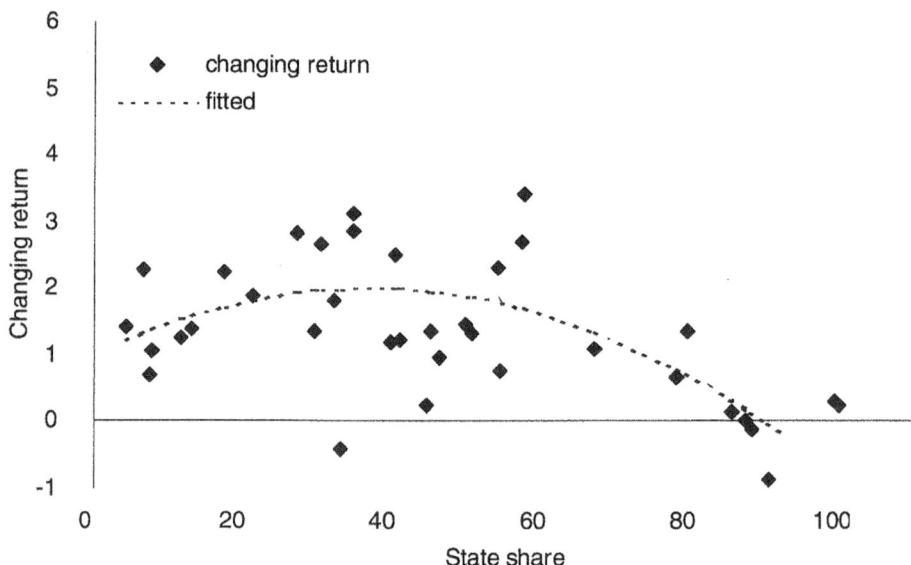

Note: Changing return rate means the percentage point changes in return rate from 1998–2000.
Source: Calculated from National Bureau of Statistics (NBS), 2001. *China Statistical Yearbook*, China Statistics Press, Beijing.

TABLE 3.6   **ANALYSING SOURCES OF PROFIT GROWTH IN SOES AND NSES, 1998–2000** (100 MILLION YUAN)

| | SOE | | | | NSE | | | |
	1998	2000	Change	Exp	1998	2000	Change	Exp
Total profit per cent	525	2408	1883	(100.0)	933	1985	1052	(100.0)
From								
Interest rate reduction			523	(27.8)			300	(28.5)
Changing oil price			791	(42.0)			-341	(-32.4)
Written-off bad loans			101	(5.4)				
Own profitability growth			468	(24.8)			1093	(103.9)
Real return rate	0.7	1.2	0.5		2.8	4.8	2.0	

Notes: Data in parentheses under 'Exp' are share of contribution by different factors to total profit changes. 'Real return rate' for 2000 is calculated as the ratio of total profit, excluding that resulting from the three external factors, to total assets.
Source: Calculated from National Bureau of Statistics (NBS), 1999 and 2001. *China Statistical Yearbook*, China Statistics Press, Beijing.

only five times that in Henan province. As another example, a company listed in the stockmarket made 553 million yuan net profit in 1998, of which its CEO's annual salary was only 33,000 yuan. In comparison, another stock company incurred 97 million yuan of losses in the same year, but its CEO salary was 430,000 yuan, far higher than the average. A correlation analysis shows that the salaries of directors and CEOs of the 919 companies listed in the stockmarket in 1999 that there is no statistically significant correlation to the performance of these companies (Zhang 2001).

Punishment

Jobs were guaranteed for SOE workers and managers in the past. This made them unconcerned with their work performance or the future of their firms. This has changed in recent years following the layoff of large numbers of SOE workers. However, there is still little real risk of poor management leading to loss of a manager's job, and this encourages irresponsible behaviour. Due to the lack of a punishment mechanism, the performance of SOEs relies mainly on the managers' personal characteristics.

Monitoring problem

Along with the process of deregulation during the reform period, monitoring of SOE management was also relaxed and this has encouraged corruption and dereliction of duty amongst managers. There are several reasons for this. First, there is a lack of standard and effective procedures and regulations of auditing and monitoring. Second, there is insufficient information on SOE management for the government as owner (Lin and Cai 1997). This also relates to whether the number of SOEs was beyond the government capacity for effective supervision. Third, unlike private owners, government officials in charge of SOEs do not have any personal interests relating to the performance of the SOEs under their supervision. Fourth, rent-seeking behaviour of government officials is undermining SOEs' competitiveness. This raises the question of how the government should conduct itself as a conscientious owner of SOEs, and how best to monitor government officials.

Investment behaviour of governments

The poor performance of SOEs has been largely due to excessive government investment in many areas of manufacturing. Local governments, from provincial to county level, were fond of investment in manufactures and tended to compete with each other with little care for investment risks. This resulted in a serious surplus of production capacity. According to the third national industrial census in 1995, for over half of the 900 industrial products, the producers' capacity–utilisation rate (total output to total production capacity) was below 60 per cent. In 1998, there were 120 automobile manufacturers in China—mostly SOEs—with total annual output of 1.6 million automobiles. Of these manufacturers, only one achieved a minimum economically efficient scale of 150,000 cars per year. In the same year, there were 3,500 steel and iron smelters in China, also mostly SOEs, and only five achieved the economically efficient scale of 4 million tonnes of output capacity (Liu 2001). The serious over-capacity and sub-economic scale in production of manufactures indicates that, compared with private investors, government investors are likely to be more adventurous in investment and less concerned about risks and efficiency.[10] It also indicates the lack of mechanisms for bankruptcy of SOEs, and for mergers of SOEs under the administration of different provincial, municipal and county governments, or between SOEs and NSEs.

These problems can be summarised as two major issues: the need to establish a better supervision system for correctly assessing the performance of SOE management and implementing incentive and punishment accordingly; and the need for correcting the behaviour of the owners of SOEs. Within an environment of market competition, SOEs can be revitalised if these needs are met. However, past experience has shown little achievement in these areas within the existing ownership framework. In this case, a third need becomes crucial: to replace the sole state ownership of SOEs by either a mixed multiple ownership structure, or full privatisation. This will convert more SOEs to shareholding companies, joint ventures, cooperatives and private firms. The improvement in SOE efficiency that has been identified in this paper indicates that these reform measures appear to be successful.

Privatisation also has difficulties and costs. In particular, in privatising large SOEs, a common problem is the lack of domestic buyers; alongside the political unacceptability of foreign control of many large enterprises. A dispersed shareholding system by all small owners may help to overcome this difficulty, but may not solve the monitoring problem. In practice, state assets were often sold to SOE managers or others at very low prices. This may be one of the solutions to the efficiency problems, although is not a fair redistribution of public assets, and therefore could easily cause social conflicts and government corruption. In addition, privatisation is not an option for those SOEs that produce public goods or have substantial externalities. To avoid the problems, a mixed ownership structure may be still a better option in reforming some large SOEs.

So long as public ownership exists—even if private ownership is introduced to the SOE ownership structure—a better supervision system from the government side and well-disciplined government representatives for public ownership are still necessary. The 'state–assets–authorisation–operation system' (see Chen 2001) that was introduced in recent years could be helpful if the role of the organisations being authorised is clearly defined, and the assessment system is transparent.

While ownership structure reform in SOEs appears to have had some initial success, there is no simple solution for SOE reform. A 'big bang' measure cannot solve the problem overnight. 'To cross the river by groping the stones', an analogy to past reform experience in China, with careful consideration of all the economic and social impacts, is still the best strategy for SOE reform in the future.

Notes

[1] This included shareholding corporations and joint ventures with controlling shares owned by the state. This definition holds throughout unless otherwise specified. However, this figure might be understated to some extent because the gross industrial output of the non-state sector, especially of rural collective and small private enterprises, was over-reported in the 1990s. See Meng and Wang (2000).

[2] Data used in this paper are from the National Bureau of Statistics (NBS), various years, unless otherwise specified.

[3] Surveys reveal that small private enterprises suffer more from the financial restrictions, whereas larger private enterprises, share-holding companies, foreign enterprises, and previously, collective enterprises, are relatively more able to obtain bank loans.

[4] The figures are not comparable between 1997 and 1998 due to inconsistencies in the statistical definition. Profit was likely lower in 1998.

[5] Profits were 43 billion yuan in 1997.

[6] This excludes small NSEs, with 5 million yuan in sales, or less.

[7] According to the 2000 data, final oil consumption by industry accounts for 53.7 per cent of total oil production. This can be partially attributed to industrial SOEs according to their share in industrial value-added (34.8 per cent); thus the final oil consumption by industrial SOEs accounted for 18.7 per cent of total oil production. This proportion is used to calculate the increases in oil cost to SOEs as a proportion of the increases in oil profit. Meanwhile, the oil effect on NSEs should be a negative 35 per cent of the oil profit growth, or -34.1 billion yuan.

[8] To mid 2001, 483 SOEs were allowed to conduct the loan–share conversion, and a

total of 294 billion bank loans were involved. Of these SOEs, 60 have completed the conversion (Department of Industry, the State Economic and Trade Committee 2001). The converted loans were therefore roughly estimated by the author as 36.5 billion, on the basis of the ratio between the number of SOEs that completed conversion and the number of permitted SOEs, and further reduced to 30 billion for the period to the end of 2000.

[9] Due to unavailability of information, the effects of external factors on profit change for the industrial branches could not be deducted from their profits. However, since one can assume that the distribution of these effects is not systematically biased among the other 36 industrial branches except the oil industry, analysing the relationship between changes in the 'gross' return rate and the SOE shares is still useful.

[10] In recent years the government has substantially reduced its investment in manufactures and redirected its investment to infrastructure construction. This has been a good step towards reducing the problems mentioned above.

4

WTO accession and regional incomes

Tingsong Jiang

As observed by many authors (Wu 1999, Sun 2000, Sun and Parikh 2001), the income gap between China's coastal and inland regions has widened since economic reforms began in 1978. The literature on regional income disparity in China has concentrated on two aspects: the measurement and pattern of regional disparity (Wu 1999) and its sources (Sun 2000, Bao et al. 2001, Démurger et al. 2001). Few authors have discussed the impact of WTO accession on regional incomes. This chapter discusses this issue explicitly, in addition to the exploration of new trends and sources of regional income disparity, using the most recent statistics.

REGIONAL INCOME DISPARITY IN CHINA

A set of regional income disparity indicators are calculated using the regional per capita GDP data from 1978 to 2000: the unweighted and population-weighted standard deviations (STDUW, STDPW), coefficients of variance (CVUW, CVPW), Gini coefficients (GUW, GPW) and the Theil index (T).[1] The per capita GDP data are evaluated at both current and 1978 prices (Table A4.1 and Figures 4.1–4.5).

The gap in per capita GDP between rich and poor provinces has been widening since 1978, as evidenced by the standard deviation series in Table A4.1. However, the values of relative indicators (coefficient of variance, Gini coefficient and Theil index) in 2000 are more or less the same as in 1978. This suggests that regional income disparity in China is mainly driven by overall economic development (higher average per capita GDP).

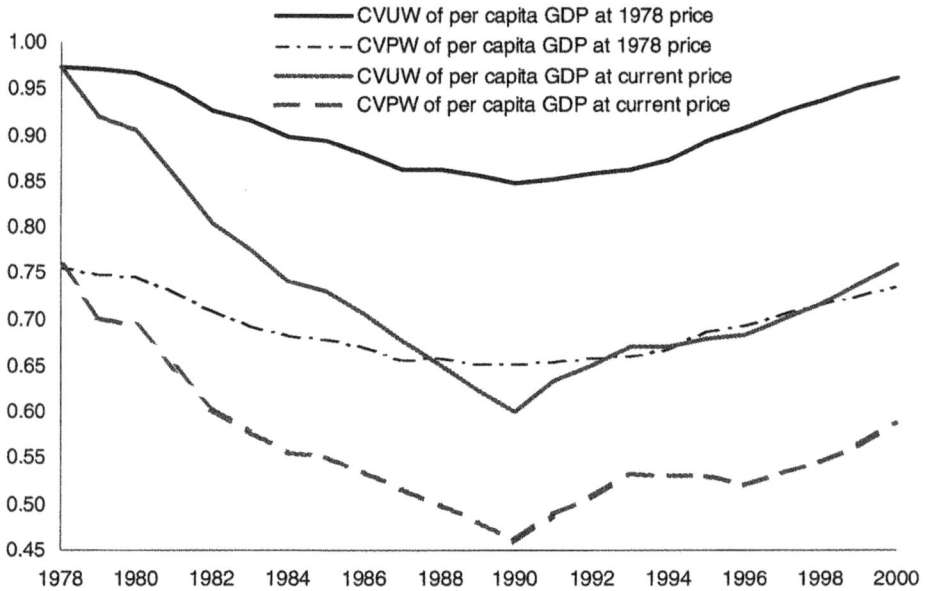

FIGURE 4.1   **COEFFICIENT OF VARIATION OF REGIONAL PER CAPITA GDP**

- CVUW of per capita GDP at 1978 price
- CVPW of per capita GDP at 1978 price
- CVUW of per capita GDP at current price
- CVPW of per capita GDP at current price

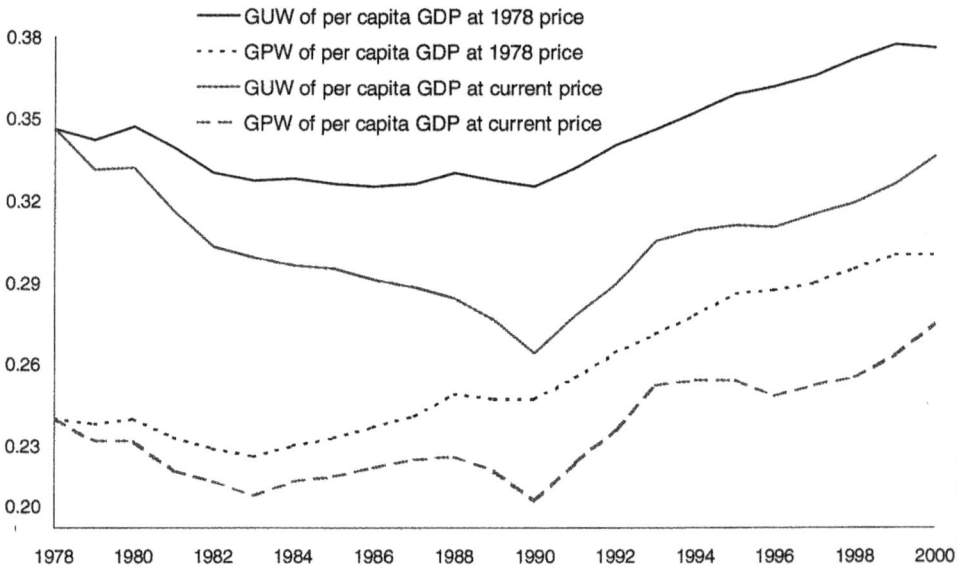

FIGURE 4.2   **GINI COEFFICIENT OF PER CAPITA GDP**

- GUW of per capita GDP at 1978 price
- GPW of per capita GDP at 1978 price
- GUW of per capita GDP at current price
- GPW of per capita GDP at current price

FIGURE 4.3   THEIL INDEX OF REGIONAL DISPARITY

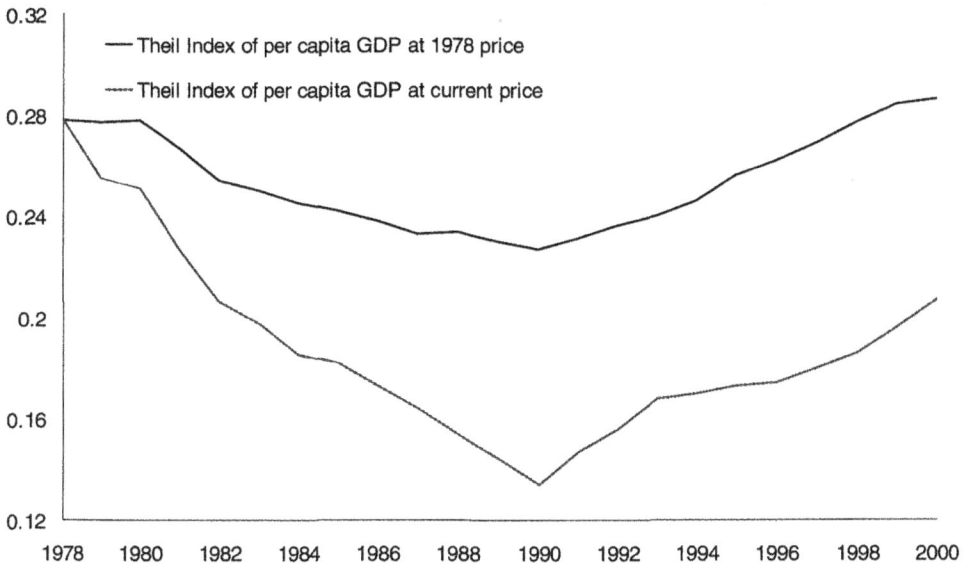

Theil Index of per capita GDP at 1978 price
Theil Index of per capita GDP at current price

The disparity pattern changed significantly during the period between 1978 and 2000. The path of disparity indicators shows that the whole period can be divided into two sub-periods: 1978–90 and 1990–2000. The degree of regional disparity remained unchanged during the first sub-period or even decreased for some indicators, but it increased significantly during the second sub-period. This pattern of change in regional income disparity seems to be closely related to the economic reforms and the development process in China.

During the first half of the first sub-period (1978–84), China successfully implemented agricultural reform and, consequently experienced high economic growth in the agricultural sector. Because the poorer provinces have higher agricultural shares in their economic structure than the richer, the boom in agriculture helped to reduce regional income gaps. During the second half of the first sub-period, China began urban economic reforms and the opening up of the coastal regions for foreign investment. But these reforms did not have an immediate impact on regional growth disparity.

During the second sub-period (1991–2000), the urban reforms initiated in the late 1980s were broadened and the effects have become evident. The most important

47

TABLE 4.1　　　　**BETA CONVERGENCE OF PER CAPITA GDP, 1978–2000**

Period	National		Eastern region[#]	Central region[#]	Western region[#]
	without dummy	with dummy[+]			
1978–2000	0.254	1.077	0.882	2.122	1.786
	(0.589)	(0.002)	(0.107)	(0.006)	(0.030)
1978–90	0.690	1.242	1.077	1.739	2.270
	(0.131)	(0.008)	(0.133)	(0.084)	(0.066)
1978–84	0.956	1.493	1.136	2.637	3.649
	(0.103)	(0.018)	(0.190)	(0.100)	(0.064)
1985–90	0.330	1.079	0.907	1.023	3.158
	(0.609)	(0.125)	(0.287)	(0.429)	(0.335)
1991–2000	-0.935	0.845	0.506	3.452	1.945
	(0.177)	(0.089)	(0.428)	(0.020)	(0.225)
1991–95	-1.239	1.896	1.595	5.496	1.714
	(0.273)	(0.016)	(0.141)	(0.012)	(0.510)
1995–2000	-0.723	-0.378	-0.709	1.648	1.936
	(0.072)	(0.477)	(0.307)	(0.402)	(0.253)

Notes: Beta convergence ratio is in percentage, numbers in parentheses are p-values. [+] The dummies include one each for the central and western regions. [#] Please see note 3 for the classification of regions.
Source: Author's computations.

effect was the decline of the state-owned economy. Because the central and western regions have a higher share of SOEs in their economy, their growth has been hindered. On the other hand, the eastern region has benefited from the rapid growth of foreign investment and non-state-owned enterprises.

This pattern is confirmed by the estimation of beta convergence which measures how fast poorer regions catch up with richer [2] (Table 4.1). There was weak beta convergence during the period 1978–90, while divergence was observed for the period 1991–2000.

Because of significant differences in their natural and economic circumstances, mainland China's 31 provinces, autonomous regions and municipalities are often grouped into three regions: the eastern coastal, central and western regions.[3] The degree of income disparity decreases within each of these regions while it increases between them. Relative disparity indicators display this pattern, among which the unweighted Gini coefficients are reported in Figures 4.4 and 4.5.

These figures also show that the degrees of disparity in the two inland regions are similar, while the level of income disparity in the eastern coastal region is much

FIGURE 4.4   GINI COEFFICIENT WITHIN AND BETWEEN REGIONS

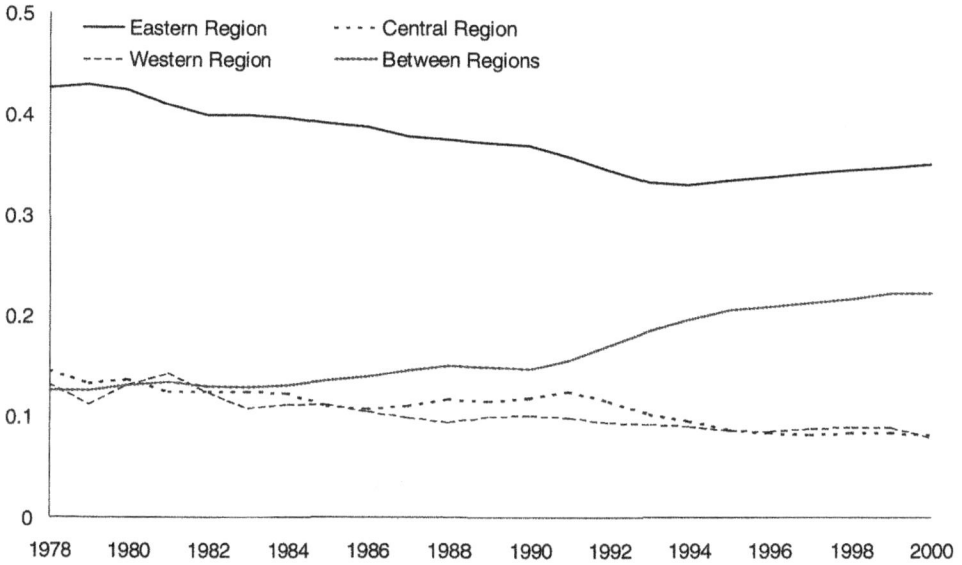

higher. This is not surprising because the grouping is mainly based on geographical location. The eastern region includes the three richest municipalities which some authors claim are outliers (Wu 1999, Démurger et al. 2001) and the most dynamic economic areas in the country, as well as poor provinces like Guangxi and Hainan. They are grouped together purely because they are located along the coast.

FACTORS AFFECTING REGIONAL GROWTH

The literature has suggested over 60 factors affect economic growth (Sala-i-Martin 1997). As regards regional development and income disparity in China, geography, economic policy, economic structure, education and infrastructure are the most frequently mentioned factors (see Bao et al. 2001, Démurger 2001 Démurger et al. 2001, Sun 2000 and Wu 2000). This issue is reinvestigated using the data from 1978 to 2000. The growth rate of per capita GDP during different periods is regressed against different factors. Some of the estimation results are reported in Table 4.2. The following factors are identified as being important, either positively or negatively, for regional growth rates.

FIGURE 4.5   **GINI COEFFICIENT WITHIN AND BETWEEN REGIONS**

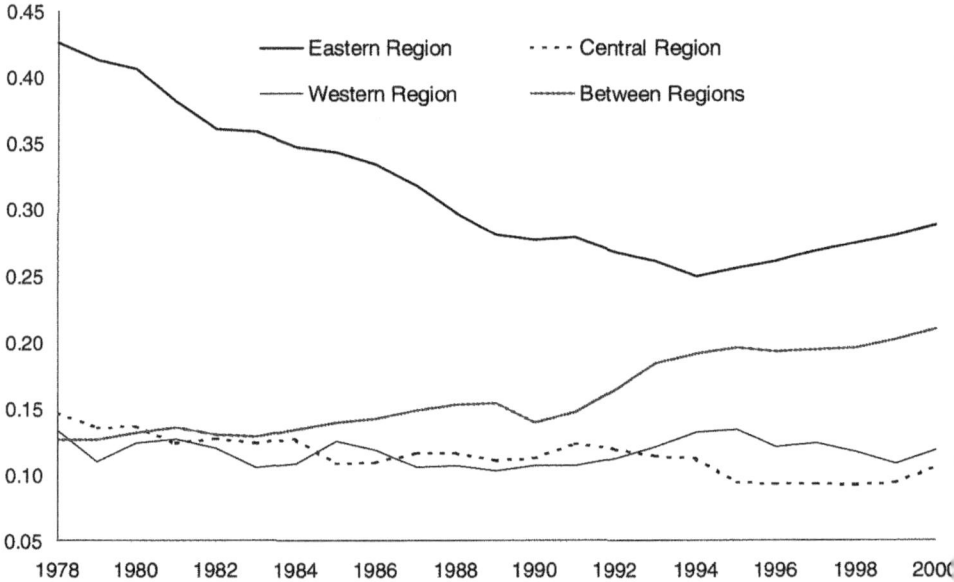

Economic structure and ownership

In all estimations, the share of SOEs in total industrial output value has a significant negative coefficient. This is understandable because SOEs have become a
symbol of low efficiency and poor competitiveness. On the other hand, the share of
the primary sector in total GDP (PRIM) has different impacts over time. It has a
significant positive coefficient before 1996. This seemingly paradoxical result arises
from the fact that about 70 per cent of Chinese people live in rural areas and most
of them are engaged in primary industries, and thus the primary sector plays an
important role in the growth of per capita GDP. As pointed out above, the rapid
growth of the Chinese econmy was initially boosted by the rural economic reforms.
Therefore, PRIM is significant during this period. However, as the economy grows,
the share of primary sector has been declining and its importance diminishes. This
explains why it was insignificant or had a negative impact on income growth during
the most recent years (1996–2000).

TABLE 4.2   **SELECTED ESTIMATION OF FACTORS AFFECTING REGIONAL GROWTH**

| | 1978–90 | 1991–95 | 1996–2000 | | | |
			Model 1	Model 2	Model 3	Model 4
GDP0	-5.2E-05	-0.67E-05	-4.62E-06	-5.50E-06		
	(0.231)	(0.270)	(0.139)	(0.075)		
EDU	0.15607				5.36E-02	4.19E-02
	(0.039)				(0.016)	(0.059)
RAIL	-0.09423		0.53868	0.49868		
	(0.109)		(0.050)	(0.070)		
WATER		0.049019	9.55E-02	0.10216		
		(0.358)	(0.068)	(0.048)		
HIGH	0.028022	0.064809				
	(0.453)	(0.038)				
PRIM	0.000898	0.001028	-5.14E-04	-5.90E-04		
	(0.037)	(0.005)	(0.155)	(0.100)		
SOE	-0.00099	-0.001283	-3.15E-04		-4.34E-04	
	(0.047)	(0.000)	(0.008)		(0.000)	
OPEN	0.012761	0.010365				
	(0.038)	(0.059)				
MARKET				3.78E-03		5.16E-03
				(0.007)		(0.000)
EAST	-0.02167	0.025126				
	(0.092)	(0.026)				
CENTRAL	-0.01504	0.012148				
	(0.096)	(0.054)				
R^2	0.5846	0.9300	0.6232	0.6263	0.4945	0.5004

Notes: Numbers in parentheses are p-values
Source: Author's computations.

Infrastructure

Infrastructure is another factor contributing to the economic growth. It is represented in estimations by the intensity of railway (RAIL), navigable waterways (WATER) and highways (HIGH). HIGH in 1991–95 and RAIL and WATER in 1996–2000 had a significant positive impacts on regional growth.

Education

Education (EDU), measured by the proportion of people receiving education of junior secondary school and above, has a significant positive relationship with per capita GDP growth as evidenced by estimations for the periods 1978–90 and 1996–2000 (models 3 and 4). [4]

Economic policy

During the period 1978–95, economic policy is represented by the OPEN index developed by Démurger et al. (2001), constructed according to the type and number of various special economic zones in each province. The coefficient of OPEN is significant during the periods 1978–90 and 1991–95, indicating the opening-up policy contributed to the economic growth. However, as the policy was developed, special economic zones were established in almost every region. As a result, the OPEN index became an inappropriate indicator for economic policy as the index in different regons became similar. To better approximate economic policies, a marketisation index (MARKET) developed by Fan and Wang (2001) is used in the regression for the period 1996–2000. The MARKET index considers the relationship between government and firms, development of non state-owned sectors, development of product and factor markets, and regulations. The estimation indicates a positive significant relationship between marketisation and economic growth.

Geographical location

Regional dummies are significant in most estimations even if the above variables are included. This suggests that geographical location is an important factor. The negative sign and magnitude of EAST and CENTRAL during the period 1978–90 confirm the previous finding that regional per capita income was converging in that period. By contrast, the coefficients of EAST and CENTRAL during the period 1991–95 indicate divergence.

IMPACT OF WTO ACCESSION

The impact of WTO accession on regional development is analysed using a general equilibrium model of the Chinese economy developed by Yang and Huang (1997). The model includes six representative households: three rural and three urban households. The three categories of rural households are classified in broad concordance with the eastern, central and western regions (note 3). This feature makes it suitable for analysing the regional impacts of WTO accession.

There are 50 commodities in the economy, of which 20 are agricultural and 30 are industrial. The agricultural commodities are produced solely by the rural sector. The industrial commodities are produced by both the rural and urban sectors. Therefore, there are a total of 80 sectors in the model. The breakdown of rural and urban industries is necessary because rural industries tend to be labour-intensive and segregated from their urban counterparts.

The analysis is focused on the tariff cuts required by China's WTO commitments as they are the most important and obvious part of the requirements. The necessary tariff cuts are reported in Table A4.2. Tariff rates are only roughly consistent with the requirements in Annex 8: Schedule CLII of Protocol on the Accession of the People's Republic of China because the detailed import data for recent years are not available.

The results of simulating the tariff cuts are reported in Tables 4.3 and 4.4. Real GDP increases by 2.6 per cent, and welfare as measured by equivalent variation increases by 80 billion yuan. The economy is invigorated by cheaper inputs on the supply side and higher real income on the demand side. Following the tariff cuts and higher demand for imported goods, China's terms of trade deteriorate and the trade balance declines by about 12.1 billion yuan.

Although the whole economy benefits from the tariff cuts, its impacts are not uniform. Two patterns of income distribution can be observed from the simulation results. First, the real income of rural households increases to a larger degree than for urban households. This is attributed to the fact that rural output increases while urban output declines. The differential impact on rural and urban sectors helps to reduce rural–urban inequality.

TABLE 4.3   **MACROECONOMIC EFFECTS OF TARIFF CUTS**

Real GDP (%)	2.6
Equivalent variation (billion yuan)	79.6
GDP deflator	-5.4
CPI	-4.9
Total savings (nominal, %)	-2.9
Government revenue (nominal, %)	-2.9
Change in trade balance (billion yuan)	-12.1
Terms of trade	-1.1
Rural output (%)	0.9
Farm output (%)	0.2
Non-farm output (%)	1.2
Urban output (%)	-0.5
Total non-farm output (%)	0.1

Source: Author's computations.

TABLE 4.4   INCOME DISTRIBUTION EFFECTS OF TARIFF CUTS

Household	Equivalent variation (billion yuan)	Real income after tax (%)	Real consumption (%)
Rural household 1	21.0	2.7	2.9
Rural household 2	10.4	1.8	1.9
Rural household 3	3.5	2.1	2.2
Urban household 1	16.5	2.2	2.3
Urban household 2	6.0	1.5	1.6
Urban household 3	2.9	1.0	1.1

Source: Author's computations.

Second, the real income of the wealthiest households (household 1) in rural and urban areas increases the most. As households 1, 2 and 3 represent the eastern, central and western regions, respectively, this result suggests that regional income disparity will deteriorate after WTO accession. This pattern can be explained as follows. Rural households in the eastern region have greater access to the non-farming sectors which grow faster than the farming sectors, and therefore benefit more than other households. The urban economy in the eastern region is more open than the other regions; for example, it has a higher proportion of non state-owned enterprises, and its level of technology, management and thus, competitiveness, is higher than other regions. As a result, it benefits more from China's WTO accession.

However, these results should be interpreted with caution as only the WTO tariff cuts are considered in the analysis. For example, the simulation suggests that farming output will increase by 0.2 per cent, which may not be consistent with the prediction that WTO accession has an adverse impact on China's agricultural sector. The simulation results can be justified by the following arguments. First, in recent years the domestic prices of rice and wheat have been significantly lower than the world price as measured by CIF prices (Wu 2001). Second, the current tariff rates for grains within TRQ (0–3 per cent) already meet the WTO requirements. Therefore, the tariff cuts will not negatively affect agricultural production. However, as China's agricultural production costs are higher than the world level (Huang and Ma 2001) and, consequently, the domestic equilibrium prices of agricultural products are higher (Wang 2002), it is inevitable that WTO accession will have a negative effect on China's agricultural sectors. From the finding in the previous section,

TABLE 4.5   **REGIONAL DISTRIBUTION OF FOREIGN INVESTMENT (PER CENT)**

Year	Eastern	Central	Western
1990	86.2	10.9	2.9
1991	83.5	12.7	3.8
1992	84.4	10.1	5.5
1993	86.5	9.9	3.6
1994	84.3	12.0	3.6
1995	83.5	12.5	4.0
1996	84.2	12.3	3.5
1997	82.6	13.0	4.4
1998	82.9	13.0	4.1
1999	88.0	9.2	2.8
2000	88.1	9.0	2.9

Source: Author's computations.

this will widen the regional income gap further.

Another effect that the simulation does not capture relates to capital flows. It is expected that there will be a large increase in foreign investment in China (Chen 2001). Because of the higher returns in the eastern coastal region, over 80 per cent of foreign capital has been invested in this area, and the share has been rising since 1997 (Table 4.5). If this trend persists, regional income disparity will deteriorate further.

CONCLUSION

Regional income disparity in China fell between 1978 and 1990. However, it has been increasing since 1991. The widening of the regional gap is mainly due to the regional differences in economic structure, notably the share of SOEs, infrastructure, geographical location and economic policies.

As the eastern region has a higher share of non-farming industries in the rural economy and a more efficient urban economy than other regions, WTO accession will tend to widen the existing regional income gap.

To mediate the adverse impact of WTO accession on regional growth, the following strategies could be considered.

First, the policies implemented in the coastal region could be extended to the inland regions with a more 'favourable' context. These policies could be divided into two categories. Policies in the first category could be 'true' preferential policies—for example, lower tax rates and cheaper land prices lower than market prices, or just let the market work to reflect lower opportunity cost of land—which could offset to some degree the geographical disadvantage of the central and western regions. Other policies could be better described as 'market-oriented' rather than 'preferential' policies. These policies—for example, lifting the government's control and support to SOEs—could help to create a favourable market environment for all players in the economy.

Second, economic structure plays an important role in regional development. Because of the significant differences in resource endowments, it is inevitable that labour and resource-intensive sectors will be relocated from coastal to inland regions. The government should acknowledge this process and make sure it is a smooth adjustment. At the same time, the government should promote the development of the private sector in the inland regions.

Third, the role of large cities should be given more attention in regional development. It has been an implicit policy to control the development of large cities in China because of the lack of administerial capacity and funds to be invested in infrastructure. However, the success in the coastal region has demonstrated the important role of large cities, which have economies of scale and assist the development of surrounding areas. Moreover, large cities in the western region like Chongqing and Xi'an, have equivalent fundamental economic factors (for example, the number of higher education and research institutions, infrastructure, economic structure, and so on) to big cities in the coastal region. Making full use of these factors may well foster regional development.

Fourth, as the CGE model predicts, rural non-farm output will increase faster than farm output (1.18 versus 0.21 per cent). Consequently, there will be a large amount of labour moving from farming to the non-farming sectors. The degree of movement may be higher if the comparative disavantage of some agricultural products is fully considered. The government should provide training and information services to farmers to foster this movement.

Finally, economic success in coastal regions raises the cost of labour and land, which in turn increases inland provinces' competitiveness in supplying labour and land-intensive goods and services to the most developed provinces. Therefore, infrastructure and regulation affecting inland-coastal trade becomes more important. As the whole economy gains from WTO accession, the central government may be able to increase transfer payments to improve infrastructure in the central and western regions. Such improvement in infrastructure could also be achieved through the deregulation of the electricity, railway transportation and telecommunication sectors.

Acknowledgments

The author wishes to acknowledge the assistance of Professors Ron Duncan and Ross Garnaut, Drs Chunlai Chen, Ligang Song, Xiaolu Wang, Yongzheng Yang and Yiping Huang in the preparation of this chapter.

Notes

[1] See Appendix for the formula for calculating these indicators. The Theil index is calculated without using population as a weight because the index's upper limit is $\ln N$, where N is the number of individuals or regions. If the population weight is used, the upper limit would not be fixed and the index is not comparable over time.

[2] Beta convergence can be estimated by $\ln Y_{iT} - \ln Y_{i0} = c - (1 - e^{-\beta T}) \ln Y_{i0} + \varepsilon_i$, where Y_{iT} and Y_{i0} are, respectively, per capita GDP at time T and time 0; β is the beta convergent coefficient; and ε is the error term. Clearly, a positive (negative) β indicates convergence (divergence).

[3] It is commonly accepted that the eastern coastal region includes Beijing, Tianjin, Hebei, Liaoning, Shanghai, Jiangsu, Zhejiang, Fujian, Shandong, Guangdong, Guangxi and Hainan; the central region includes Shanxi, Inner Mongolia, Jilin, Heilongjiang, Anhui, Jiangxi, Henan, Hubei and Hunan; and the western region includes the remaining six provinces, three autonomous regions and one municipality. This paper adopts this classification.

[4] EDU is not included in some estimations because it is highly correlated with other variables, for example, the correlation coefficient between EDU and initial per capita GDP level (GDP0), RAIL, HIGH and PRIM are, respectively 0.75, 0.81, 0.63 and 0.83 during the period 1991–95.

APPENDIX

Formula for calculating regional disparity indicators

$$STDUW = \sqrt{\frac{\sum_i (Y_i - \bar{Y})^2}{N}}$$

$$STDPW = \sqrt{\frac{\sum_i P_i (Y_i - \hat{Y})^2}{\sum_i P_i}}$$

$$CVUW = \frac{STDUW}{\bar{Y}}$$

$$CVPW = \frac{STDPW}{\hat{Y}}$$

$$GUW = \frac{\sum_i \sum_j |Y_i - Y_j|}{2N^2 \bar{Y}}$$

$$GPW = \frac{\sum_i \sum_j |Y_i - Y_j| P_i P_j}{2 \left(\sum_i P_i \right)^2 \hat{Y}}$$

$$T = \sum_{i=1}^{N} \frac{Y_i}{N\bar{Y}} \ln \left(\frac{Y_i}{\bar{Y}} \right)$$

TABLE A4.1   REGIONAL INCOME DISPARITY, 1978–2000 (GDP PER CAPITA)

1978 PRICES

	STDUW	STDPW	CVUW	CVPW	GUW	GPW	Theil
1978	449.47	276.54	0.974	0.757	0.346	0.240	0.278
1979	474.67	292.76	0.971	0.749	0.342	0.238	0.277
1980	508.03	313.09	0.968	0.747	0.347	0.240	0.278
1981	520.59	320.61	0.951	0.731	0.339	0.233	0.267
1982	543.62	335.79	0.926	0.709	0.330	0.229	0.254
1983	583.21	360.26	0.915	0.694	0.327	0.226	0.250
1984	652.87	404.29	0.896	0.683	0.328	0.230	0.245
1985	724.89	451.42	0.893	0.679	0.326	0.233	0.242
1986	753.03	472.58	0.879	0.670	0.325	0.237	0.238
1987	800.99	507.79	0.863	0.657	0.326	0.241	0.233
1988	872.61	558.37	0.862	0.658	0.330	0.249	0.234
1989	886.99	567.07	0.855	0.652	0.327	0.247	0.230
1990	911.30	585.76	0.848	0.651	0.325	0.247	0.227
1991	979.76	632.55	0.852	0.653	0.332	0.255	0.231
1992	1119.94	730.68	0.857	0.659	0.340	0.264	0.236
1993	1281.61	844.65	0.862	0.661	0.346	0.271	0.240
1994	1464.37	971.69	0.872	0.668	0.352	0.278	0.246
1995	1669.15	1121.15	0.893	0.687	0.359	0.286	0.256
1996	1873.43	1251.24	0.908	0.693	0.362	0.287	0.262
1997	2099.15	1401.95	0.924	0.705	0.366	0.290	0.269
1998	2325.57	1550.79	0.937	0.715	0.372	0.295	0.277
1999	2555.02	1704.24	0.951	0.727	0.377	0.300	0.284
2000	2780.32	1912.47	0.960	0.736	0.376	0.300	0.286

CURRENT PRICES

	STDUW	STDPW	CVUW	CVPW	GUW	GPW	Theil
1978	449.44	276.52	0.973	0.757	0.346	0.240	0.278
1979	463.52	286.82	0.919	0.701	0.331	0.232	0.255
1980	501.01	310.64	0.905	0.690	0.332	0.232	0.251
1981	503.52	312.87	0.856	0.645	0.316	0.221	0.227
1982	514.64	322.45	0.804	0.604	0.303	0.217	0.206
1983	542.93	340.95	0.776	0.577	0.299	0.212	0.197
1984	607.00	386.02	0.741	0.555	0.296	0.217	0.185
1985	713.63	456.72	0.731	0.550	0.295	0.219	0.182
1986	754.55	491.95	0.705	0.534	0.291	0.222	0.173
1987	832.91	555.17	0.677	0.515	0.288	0.225	0.164
1988	984.48	669.24	0.650	0.499	0.284	0.226	0.154
1989	1049.24	722.35	0.624	0.481	0.276	0.221	0.144

	STDUW	STDPW	CVUW	CVPW	GUW	GPW	Theil
1990	1112.46	762.14	0.601	0.461	0.264	0.210	0.134
1991	1324.71	911.80	0.634	0.489	0.278	0.224	0.147
1992	1638.81	1148.74	0.649	0.508	0.289	0.236	0.156
1993	2191.63	1573.33	0.671	0.533	0.305	0.252	0.168
1994	2848.15	2055.30	0.671	0.530	0.309	0.254	0.170
1995	3577.53	2586.25	0.679	0.530	0.311	0.254	0.173
1996	4178.85	2972.95	0.682	0.521	0.310	0.248	0.174
1997	4789.92	3385.53	0.700	0.532	0.315	0.252	0.180
1998	5266.62	3705.09	0.715	0.544	0.319	0.255	0.186
1999	5755.56	4041.93	0.738	0.564	0.326	0.263	0.196
2000	6522.64	4707.79	0.759	0.587	0.336	0.275	0.207

Source: Author's computations.

TABLE A4.2   CHINA'S TARIFF RATES AFTER WTO ACCESSION

Commodity	Baseline rate	WTO rate	Tariff change (%)
Rice	-	-	n.a.
Wheat	-	-	n.a.
Corn	-	-	n.a.
Other grains	17.7	3.0	-83.04
Cotton	12.5	1.0	-92.00
Oil crops	-	-	n.a.
Sugar crops	49.3	20.0	-59.43
Vegetables	47.5	13.0	-72.63
Fruits and tea	62.2	25.0	-59.81
Other crops	116.7	30.0	-74.29
Forestry	26.3	10.0	-62.02
Pork	51.5	20.0	-61.17
Beef	50.0	20.0	-60.00
Mutton	50.0	20.0	-60.00
Poultry	50.0	20.0	-60.00
Egg	64.9	23.0	-64.56
Milk	45.8	21.0	-54.15
Other livestock	54.5	20.0	-63.30
Other agriculture	32.1	12.8	-60.00
Fishing	36.1	15.0	-58.45
Energy mining	7.7	5.0	-35.47
Ore ming	2.0	1.0	-50.42
Other mining	29.6	3.0	-89.86
Grain mills	37.0	25.0	-32.43
Meat and dairy process	56.0	21.0	-62.49
Fishing (processed)	41.5	18.0	-56.63
Sugar refining	49.3	20.0	-59.43
Other food	60.3	28.0	-53.59
Beverage and wine	57.0	45.0	-21.07
Forage manufactures	22.0	6.0	-72.73
Textiles	57.6	20.0	-65.28
Clothing	82.1	25.0	-69.55
Wood and cultural products	39.8	10.0	-74.86
Electricity and water	3.0	1.0	-66.67
Energy refinery	26.4	7.0	-73.48
Chemical fertilisers and pesticides	6.3	4.0	-36.24
Other chemicals	29.7	5.5	-81.48
Rubber and non-metal Products	41.1	20.0	-51.33
Metal manufactures	16.7	7.0	-58.02

Commodity	Baseline rate	WTO rate	Tariff change (%)
Machinery	23.5	11.0	-53.15
Motor vehicles	81.6	40.0	-50.98
Other transport equipment	13.2	5.0	-62.26
Electrical equipment	34.5	15.0	-56.56
Electronical equipment	38.7	15.0	-61.19
Other manufactures	31.2	15.0	-51.85
Construction	-	-	n.a.
Transportation	-	-	n.a.
Trade and storage	-	-	n.a.
Real estate	-	-	n.a.
Service	-	-	n.a.

5

Competition, ownership diversification and industrial growth

Mei Wen

The rapid economic development of China, with an average annual GDP growth rate of 9.7 per cent for more than two decades, has been attracting worldwide attention. In particular, among all sectors, China's industry has achieved the highest average annual growth rate of 11.9 per cent from 1978 to 2000. The fast industrial growth has not only provided Chinese people with abundant manufactured goods and raised living standards, but has also enriched the world market with more variety of commodities at low prices. What makes China's industrial growth so phenomenal?

As market transaction, private ownership and freedom of contracts are the base for an advanced market economy, the transition of a centrally planned economy to a market-oriented economy must experience formation, enlargement and perfection of the market; introduction and strengthening of industrial competition; and ownership diversification or reform of industrial enterprises in the distribution of the rights to claim residual income and control. Since China's economic reform, a market system has been gradually established and continues to improve, industrial competition has been gradually strengthening, and enterprises of diversified ownership types have been emerging and developing.

The market, a basic institution for free trading and free contracting, has to be established gradually in transitional economies. Its size—determined by industrial structure, national purchasing power, transportation and transaction conditions—increases endogenously with industrial growth. Industrial policies and legal regulations regarding enterprises' behaviour can improve the functioning of the market in

63

the provision of information, a level playing field for competition, efficiency of resources and product allocation. Imperfection of the market in transitional economies is a major institutional shortcoming for achieving efficiency, which is easily neglected by economists who take such basic conditions of market economies for granted.

While the market provides a common place for enterprises within an industry to compete with each other, industrial competition increases the market by increasing production, increasing derived demands for factors, improving production efficiency, and therefore increasing industrial GDP. Competition provides incentive mechanisms and additional industrial information for firms to improve their production efficiency. It can either force managers to make more effort to reduce production costs, or drive inefficient firms out of business. It enlarges industrial output with more efficient production, hence improves social surplus.[1] The efficiency implication of industrial competition is evident in other transitional economies including Mongolia (Carlin et al. 2001; Anderson, Lee and Murrell 2000).

Privatisation has been used as a mechanism to improve firms' internal efficiency since the 1980s in advanced market economies, developing market economies as well as transitional economies. One striking feature of China's transition is the fast industrial growth without large-scale direct privatisation in the first 17 years of reform. But this does not mean that there was no large-scale change in the relative importance of ownership components in industries, and in ownership arrangements within firms. Many studies summarised in Jefferson and Singh (1999) indicate that changes in ownership arrangements within firms and the entry of firms with new ownership types may have made a large contribution to China's rapid industrial growth. In this chapter, the author reviews China's reforms in the light of market competition and ownership diversification, and investigates their contributions to industrial growth.

HOW HAS CHINA ESTABLISHED ITS MARKET SYSTEM?

China gradually established and developed a market system in three stages. During the first stage, from 1979–84, the Chinese had a 'taste' of the market. During this period, free markets were allowed for trading agricultural products. With the great success of radical agricultural reform—the gradual adoption of the household responsibility system nationwide—markets for agricultural products were activated. Free wholesale and retail markets for small industrial consumption goods were then allowed. Gradually, the government reduced the number of industrial products under central planning, raised the procurement prices of agricultural products according to the degree of shortage, adjusted the prices of some light industrial products according to market demand, and let the price of small consumption commodities be determined by the market.

Although establishment of the markets for intermediate goods and primary industrial inputs was not on the reform agenda during this period, due to the necessity for agricultural products and small consumption industrial goods, all Chinese were more or less involved in market transactions. People started to learn how the market works and gain the benefits of the market in product allocation. From purchasing most necessities through quota and queuing at fixed prices, people began to compare different qualities and prices of consumption goods, and learnt to bargain for better quality at a lower price. Although the prices of some necessities increased due to shortages in the early years of economic reform, consumers realised that the market brought them the convenience of purchasing daily necessities, more variety of consumption goods and better-quality products as well as a higher income level.

The second stage was from 1985 to 1991. This was an important period for ideological change towards a market system. Due to the ideology of socialism that dictated the state ownership of capital goods and land, most intermediate goods, labour, capital and land were still under central planning up to 1985. In 1984, the introduction of the dual-track system—which required output under the plan to be sold at the planned price, while output beyond the plan could be sold at floating prices within a 20 per cent difference of the planned price—allowed state firms in more and more final product industries to transact with non-state marketised firms. In addition, the Central Governmental Decision on the Reform of the Economic System, passed in October 1984 at the third plenary session of the twelfth congress of the Chinese Communist Party, initiated the establishment and development of a market for intermediate goods from 1985–91.

Although high inflation rates during 1988 and 1989 caused suspicion and dispute about the market system,[2] markets for capital, labour, technology, information and housing were gradually established during this period. Most banks were restructured under state ownership. Workers in SOEs, especially new employees, were shifted to the contract system. Free contracting for the application of most research and development results was allowed. Some departments, such as transportation, power, meteorology and banking, started to establish businesses and networks to share information.[3] With the reform of SOEs towards independent economic entities and the growth of collectives and individuals during this period, the market played a more important role in the economy for the efficient allocation of products and resources.

Comprehensive development for a sound market system occurred in the third stage—from 1992 to the present. Not only were the dual tracks merged to the market prices in 1992 and most intermediate goods opened to market competition, the reform of the housing system towards a semi-commercial system was also executed nationwide. Two stock exchanges were also established in 1992 in Shanghai and Shenzhen. After Deng Xiaoping's southern tour, the fourteenth congress of the Chinese Communist Party, held in October 1992, officially declared that the aim of China's economic reform was to establish a socialist market system.

With the networking of product markets, the introduction of future markets and the adoption of the Internet, a hierarchical network market system was gradually establishing. Adoption of the Internet accelerated development of the product market, while reducing transaction costs and extending the size of the market through e-commerce. It also promoted the development of service markets. The introduction of future markets facilitated inter-temporal optimisation of economic agents.

In 1996, less than 10 per cent of commodity categories were under government control. Over 90 per cent of retail prices and 80 per cent of agricultural and producer good prices (as a proportion of output value) were determined by the market. The number of production factors under central planning fell from 256 in 1979 to less than 20 in 1996. The number of consumption goods under central control declined from 188 in 1978 to 14 in 1996. More importantly, by June 1998, there was no shortage of any of the 610 commodities within state domestic trade statistics.[4] Shortage had been a common feature of the centrally planned economies (Kornai 1980). After two decades of market-oriented reforms, China eliminated shortages and a buyers' market emerged. However, this does not mean that there are no institutional constraints restricting China's market from functioning more efficiently. In fact, due to the existing household registration system, which limits labour mobility and official interference in banks' lending decisions due to state ownership of most banks, functioning of labour and the capital market is limited, which causes distortions in resource allocation. Although markets for housing and land-use rights exist, they are still immature due to the lack of relevant service agents.

TABLE 5.1   OUTPUT OF SOME INDUSTRIAL CONSUMPTION GOODS, SINCE 1978

	Salt	Sugar	Dairy products	Beer	Cigarettes	Household refrigerators	Domestic air conditioners	Household washing machines	Colour television sets	Garments	Leather shoes	Bicycles	Watches
	(10,000 tons)	(10,000 tons)	(10,000 tons)	(10,000 tons)	(10,000 cases)	(10,000)	(10,000)	(10,000)	(10,000)	(10x8 pieces)	(10,000 pairs)	(10,000)	(10,000)
1978	1953	227	4.7	40	1182	2.8	0.02	0.04	0.4	6.7	10053	854.0	1351.1
1979	1477	250	5.4	52	1303	3.2	0.86	1.81	1.0	7.4	11608	1009.5	1707.0
1980	1728	257	6.3	69	1520	4.9	1.32	24.5	3.2	9.5	15745	1302.4	2215.5
1981	1832	317	7.9	91	1704	5.6	1.40	128.1	15.2	10.1	20239	1754.3	2872.4
1982	1638	338	10.0	117	1885	10.0	2.44	253.3	28.8	9.9	18661	2420.0	3301.0
1983	1613	377	11.2	163	1938	18.9	3.45	365.9	53.1	10.0	18361	2758.2	3469.0
1984	1642	380	13.0	224	2132	54.7	6.12	578.1	134.0	11.1	19676	2861.4	3798.2
1985	1479	451	16.4	310	2370	144.8	12.35	887.2	435.3	12.7	23162	3227.7	5431.1
1986	1766	525	22.9	413	2596	225.0	9.65	893.4	414.6	27.0	26440	3568.3	7317.4
1987	1764	506	27.2	540	2881	401.3	13.22	990.2	672.7	23.0	30910	4116.7	6142.4
1988	2264	461	29.5	656	3096	757.6	25.91	1046.8	1037.7	29.1	34720	4140.1	6661.6
1989	2829	501	28.7	643	3195	670.8	37.47	825.4	940.0	30.0	35433	3676.8	7275.6
1990	2023	582	31.4	692	3298	463.1	24.07	662.7	1033.0	31.8	43770	3141.6	8352.6
1991	2410	640	37.7	838	3226	469.9	63.03	687.2	1205.1	36.3	53592	3676.8	7595.5
1992	2838	829	41.3	1021	3285	485.8	158.03	708.0	1333.1	42.7	77068	4083.6	8610.5
1993	2943	771	41.7	1192	3376	596.7	346.41	895.9	1435.8	63.7	115059	4149.6	15183.0
1994	2996	592	42.5	1415	3432	768.1	393.42	1094.2	1689.2	79.4	154284	4364.9	45393.7
1995	2978	559	52.6	1569	3485	918.5	682.56	948.4	2057.7	180.0	320207	4472.2	24480.0
1996	2904	640	50.4	1682	3402	979.7	786.21	1074.7	2537.6	126.6	237528	3361.2	29628.6
1997	3083	703	56.5	1889	3377	1044.4	974.01	1254.5	2711.3	136.7	247343	2999.3	25482.7
1998	2243	826	n.a.	1988	3374	1060.0	1156.87	1207.3	3497.0	..	..	..	..
1999	2812	861	n.a.	2099	3340	1210.0	1337.64	1342.2	4262.0	..	..	..	..
2000	3128	700	n.a.	2231	3397	1279.0	1826.67	1443.0	3936.0	..	..	..	..

Source: State Statistics Bureau of the PRC, *Statistical Yearbook of China 2000*, China Statistical Publishing House, Beijing, for products with data from 1978–2000; State Statistics Bureau of the PRC, 1988. *Industrial Statistical Yearbook of China 1988*, China Statistical Publishing House, Beijing, for products with data from 1978–97.

Nevertheless, the development of a market system enabled firms with different ownership types to compete with each other.

During the past two decades, opening up to the world market to increase exports is another means through which China developed its market. With policy encouragement and a firm market-oriented reform environment, the large amount of FDI flowing into China since 1993 has increased China's exports. The endeavour to increase exports has not only made Chinese enterprises participate in rigorous international competition and learn about the market, but also increased the market size tremendously. In 1978, China had net imports of US$1.14 billion. Since 1995, however, China's net exports have surged to new levels, reaching US$24.1 billion in 2000.

INDUSTRIAL COMPETITION AND OWNERSHIP DIVERSIFICATION

The general trend in industrial competition

Although the market is far from perfect and relationships (*guanxi*) still play an important role in conducting business, after two decades of gradual introduction and strengthening of market competition, output has increased for most consumption good industries as shown in Table 5.1. Opportunities emerged from the product shortages and the profits made by enterprises in the early period of reform attracted many entries into various industries. The number of enterprises with the independent accounting systems in each of the 12 industries in Table 5.1 increased from 1978–88. Although the demand contraction policies that began in 1989 drove some small firms out of business, the number of industrial firms continued to increase from 1993–95.

Firms adopted output as a competition strategy in many industries before 1998 due to several reasons. SOEs pursued profits outside state-planning quotas before 1992. On the one hand the central government introduced the policy of a 40 per cent income tax rebate for re-investment from enterprise-retained funds to encourage enterprise investment in fixed assets before 1995. On the other hand, competition among provinces led to severe redundant investment, such that excess production capacity was observed in most industries in the Third National Industrial Census in 1995. Even though the 'excess' market competition drove small enterprises and severe loss-making SOEs out of business, the average size of industrial firms kept

TADLE 5.2   **AVERAGE SIZE OF INDUSTRIAL ENTERPRISES WITH INDEPENDENT ACCOUNTING SYSTEMS, 1989–1997**

Million yuan of net value of fixed assets per enterprise.

Industry	1989	1990	1991	1992	1993	1994	1995	1996	1997
Food	0.9	1.1	1.3	1.5	1.84	2.1	2.7	3.5	4.4
Beverage manufacturing	1.3	1.5	1.9	2.2	2.9	3.3	3.8	4.6	6.6
Tobacco processing	19.2	25.5	33.5	41.6	45.9	50.6	64.6	105.4	108.0
Textiles	2.7	3.2	3.8	4.4	5.2	6.0	7.2	8.9	10.5
Garments and other fibre products	0.4	0.5	0.6	0.9	1.2	1.5	1.7	2.1	2.7
Leather, furs, down and related products	0.6	0.7	0.8	1.0	1.4	1.7	2.0	2.6	3.1
Timber processing, bamboo, cane, palm fibre and straw products	0.5	0.5	0.7	0.8	0.9	1.0	1.1	1.4	1.9
Furniture manufacturing	0.3	0.3	0.4	0.4	0.6	0.7	0.8	1.0	1.3
Papermaking and paper products	1.3	1.5	1.7	2.0	2.5	2.6	3.2	4.2	5.3
Printing and record medium reproduction	0.6	0.7	0.8	0.9	1.2	1.3	1.5	1.9	2.2
Cultural, educational and sporting goods	0.5	0.6	0.7	0.9	1.2	1.5	1.8	2.2	2.7
Medical and pharmaceutical products	2.9	3.4	4.4	5.2	5.8	6.4	6.7	8.5	10.6
Chemical fibre	28.9	29.5	33.2	38.8	34.1	35.7	42.1	47.7	53.7
Rubber products	1.8	1.9	2.2	2.7	3.0	3.4	4.2	5.6	7.2
Plastic products	0.8	1.0	1.2	1.4	1.7	2.0	2.3	2.8	3.5
Non-metal mineral products	1.0	1.1	1.3	1.5	1.9	2.4	2.9	3.8	4.4
Smelting and pressing of ferrous metals	20.8	23.1	26.8	31.2	25.5	24.3	29.5	39.8	48.2
Smelting and pressing of non-ferrous metals	8.5	9.3	10.3	11.2	12.4	10.9	13.3	17.8	21.4
Metal products	0.5	0.6	0.7	0.8	1.1	1.4	1.8	2.2	2.8
Electronic and telecommunications equipment	3.5	3.9	5.3	6.0	6.3	7.3	8.6	10.8	14.4

Source: Calculated from State Statistics Bureau of the PRC, 1990–98, *Statistical Yearbook of China*, China Statistical Publishing House, Beijing.

increasing (Table 5.2). Although the Asian financial crisis, which started in 1997, caused international markets to weaken and diminished export opportunities, the output of most industrial products has continued to increase while prices decreased consecutively since 1998. Since then, price games have become common in many industries.

Distinctions among industries

New entries. Due to the gradual character of China's market formation, the conditions of the market for different products varied during the reform period. The schedule of opening for free trading in the market varied for different products and, hence, the size of different product markets differed at any timepoint during the reform period. In addition, regulations on foreign and domestic private entry,[5] legal and bank-lending discrimination against domestic private agents, and variations in industrial fixed costs have all meant that the conditions for new entries differed from industry to industry. Subsequently, FDI flowed into each industry, and exports and the strength of competition also varied from industry to industry.

Since the four special economic zones were established in Guangdong and Fujian in 1980, foreign investment has been encouraged in broad manufacturing areas focused on technology introduction and export promotion. Measures adopted to attract FDI include tax redemption and reduction; flexible investment forms such as joint ventures, cooperation, and pure foreign enterprises; gradual extension of open cities and areas; gradual extension of open industries; formal bank-lending policies to joint ventures and foreign enterprises; and legal protection of private properties of foreign agents. Since 1995, these active measures have triggered billions of annual FDI inflow and brought about a technology spillover effect to domestic industry, as well as significantly changing the structure of many industries. For example, after many years of competition, the major players in the automobile industry are all joint ventures. The colour television industry is also dominated by joint ventures. Joint ventures are permitted in most manufacturing industries.

In contrast, domestic private agents were not given enough opportunities to develop large enterprises, making it impossible for them to have their own accumulation of applied research and product development.[6] Due to the slow accumulation of legalised private property and the lack of formal bank-lending documents supportive of domestic private production investment in the first two decades of the reform, the financial constraints were barriers to domestic private entry into high fixed-cost industries. In addition, domestic private economic entities were not given legal support during the early years of the economic reform, until 1996 when the *Law of Township and Village Owned Enterprises of the People's Republic of China* provided equal legal backing to collective and private TVEs. Furthermore, without the technological advantage that foreign investors brought in, domestic private entry was not encouraged in many industries because of quality and safety concerns. Unfortunately, this seems to have created a vicious cycle: slow legalised private capital accumulation led to low levels of private research and development, low technology led to less opportunities for private agents to enter high-tech areas, less business in high-tech areas led to fewer chances for high capital return, and low capital return led to slow private capital accumulation. Hence, domestic private agents have been facing different barriers to entry than foreigners. Tables 5.3 and 5.4 provide some representative product industries according to fixed costs and barriers to foreign and domestic private entry, respectively, where x of (x,y) stands for fixed costs and y stands for barriers to entry; H is high and L is low. Differences between the entry barriers faced by foreign and domestic private agents can cause the industrial structure to vary substantially from industry to industry.

Unlike private economic entities, however, collective enterprises were legal when economic reform was initiated. This ideological advantage enabled the government to promote the development of industrial collectives, especially industrial township village enterprises, to absorb surplus labour released from the agricultural sector under the institutional constraints of the household registration system and state land ownership in urban areas.[7] Therefore, the number of industrial township village enterprises increased from 794,000 in 1978 to 7,570,000 in 1996. Although there

TABLE 5.3 **BARRIERS TO FOREIGN ENTRY, (FIXED COSTS)**

(H,H) Representative industries
Tobacco, air-conditioners, mining and processing of Celestine, etc.

(H,L) Representative industries
Civic airplanes; car and motorcycle moulds, textile and paper-making machinery with new technology, etc.

(L,H) Representative industries
Colourful light-sensitive material, salt, musk, hand-made carpets, processing of tiger bone, etc.

(L,L) Representative industries
Soft drinks, garments, plastic products, new micro-electronic products, small parts for cars, etc.

was no formal barrier to the entry to collectives in most industries, and bank-lending policies are more favourable to collectives than to domestic private entities, the collectives lack technological and locational advantage compared with most foreign-invested enterprises. Therefore, the difference between the industrial structure of high-tech and low-tech industries in terms of different ownership types (hence exports) depended on the effectiveness of the reform of SOEs.

Ownership diversification. Ownership diversification since the economic reform can be seen in Figures 5.1 and 5.2. In 1978, the three existing ownership types were state ownership, collective ownership and individuals, with collectives and individuals as a whole only having a share less than 0.2 in both investment in fixed assets in the whole economy and in the gross industrial output value. But after more than two decades of market-oriented reform—with a large amount of FDI inflow and the development of industrial collectives—investment in fixed assets through SOEs in the economy dropped to 50 per cent of the total investment in 2000, while all industrial SOEs and state-controlled share companies produced only 28.2 per cent of gross industrial output value.

Although collectives have been the major industrial producers since 1994, their investment in fixed assets was much less than SOEs. Meanwhile, the contribution of individuals and enterprises with other ownership types (mainly foreign and overseas Chinese related) to gross industrial output value has been accelerating. However, the difference between the development of individuals and enterprises of other ownership types lies in the definition of an 'individual'. Individuals are small domestic economic entities that usually have less than eight employees. Hence, they are usually in the retail or service sectors of manufacturing industries. However,

TABLE 5.4   **BARRIERS TO DOMESTIC PRIVATE ENTRY, (FIXED COSTS)**

(H,H) Representative industries	(H,L) Representative industries
Cars, televisions, telecommunications, spacecraft, power-transmission equipment, nuclear power stations, etc.	Computers, timber, silk garments, furniture, tyres, etc.
(L,H) Representative industries	**(L,L) Representative industries**
Cigarettes, coal mining, ergot, ergotamine, etc.	Wool jumpers, garments, food processing, software, small plastic products, wine, CDs, handcraft, kitchen utensils, etc.

FIGURE 5.1   PROPORTION OF INVESTMENT IN FIXED ASSETS OWNERSHIP, 1980–2000

FIGURE 5.2   PROPORTION OF GROSS INDUSTRIAL OUTPUT VALUE BY OWNERSHIP, 1978–1999

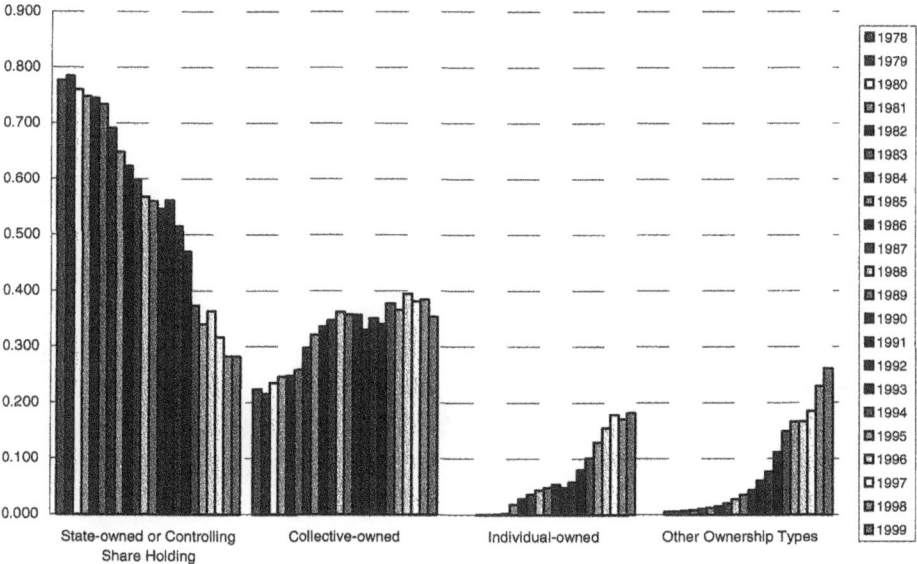

enterprises of other ownership types including many large foreign-funded enterprises were usually found in the production sector. Due to state ownership of most banks and bank-loan policies favouring SOEs (profit-making enterprises are often not strictly distinguished from loss-making ones when banks loan to them), the financial disadvantage of collectives and domestic private agents can make them weaker in current and future industrial competition. In these circumstances, China's accession to the World Trade Organization will further change the ownership structure of many industries towards a larger foreign-funded sector.

Competition in different industries. This analysis is limited to two-digit industries, as data on product market are not available. Fixed costs, number of firms and the strength of competition varied from industry to industry. For example, there were 82 enterprises above the designated size in the petroleum and natural gas-extraction industry and 14,540 in the non-metal mineral products industry in 2000.[8] Generally speaking, there is strong competition in most manufacturing industries, while competition in extraction industries is mainly oligopolistic. Within manufacturing industries, only the competition in the tobacco industry is restricted mainly among SOEs. In the other manufacturing industries, major players include collectives and foreign-funded enterprises.

Although the percentage of foreign-funded enterprises was very small in the six extraction industries and the gas, water and power-supply industries, foreign-funded enterprises occupied a large share (among all enterprises above the designated size) in some manufacturing industries such as 0.72 in the gross industrial output value of the electronic and telecommunications equipment industry, 0.57 in the instruments, meters, and office-machinery industry, 0.60 in the cultural, educational and sports-goods industry, 0.56 in the leather, furs, down and related products industry and 0.49 in the garments and other fibre products industry in 2000.[9]

More importantly, according to the *Statistical Yearbook of China 2001*, the average size of foreign-funded firms (in terms of annual average balance of net value of fixed assets per firm) is bigger than the average size of all enterprises above the designated size in 23 out of the 28 manufacturing industries. Only in the chemical fibre industry and three industries that have higher fixed costs and few foreign entries (the share of the foreign-funded sector is less than 10 per cent), the average size of foreign-funded firms is smaller than the average size of all enterprises above the designated size.

Quantity games were common in consumption-good industries in the earlier years of the economic reform. But in the 1990s, with FDI inflow and the development of joint ventures, price games started in many household electrical items such as television sets, fridges and air-conditioners. Since there was excess production capacity in many industries in 1995, price games were common in industries with severe excess capacity. Due to the SOEs' soft budget problem and a lack of effective exit for insolvent SOEs, competition from big foreign-funded enterprises drove SOEs to make more losses. As foreign-funded enterprises usually had advanced technology, better management and easy access to licences for exports in industries where there was export licence management, the foreign-funded sector occupied an even larger share in sales revenue and total profits. But due to policies favourable to foreign direct investment through tax exemption or reduction, the total tax payable by the foreign-funded sector was less than by the domestic sector. The larger firm size in the foreign-funded sector, the further release of restrictions on foreign direct investment after China's WTO accession, and taxation policy changes towards foreign-funded enterprises will affect major players in many industries in the near future. There could also be capacity games for entry deterrence against domestic private agents.

Efficiency implications of industrial competition and ownership diversification

It is believed that private ownership can make firms more efficient than state ownership due to clearly defined property rights, hence lower agency costs, when information and contracts are incomplete and transaction costs are not negligible. Hence, privatisation will improve production efficiency and social surplus in industries not benefiting from economies of scale. Although China has never had large-scale privatisation, reforms within SOEs gave managers more control and more rights to claim residual income. As studies comparing technical efficiency among enterprises of different ownership types in China's economy have found that SOEs are less internally efficient than enterprises of other ownership types on average, the introduction and development of a variety of ownership types in the economy must have improved efficiency (see Zhang, Zhang and Zhao 2001; Wen, Li and Lloyd forthcoming).

Competition makes firms run more efficiently through both the incentive effect and the information effect. Increases in the number of firms and industrial output force managers to put more effort into cost reduction for achieving the same amount of profit. Although this effect may not be strong for firms facing a soft budget, competition makes firms' inefficiency apparent as they make losses. This can provide the government with information about the ability of SOEs' managers, or about managers' attempts to improve internal efficiency. For example, in 1996, the Chinese government observed the successful performance of Handan Steel Company and made it a well-managed and cost-cutting model for other SOEs to emulate. Although examples such as the Handan Steel Company are a very small fraction of SOEs and many loss-making SOEs can still get bank loans, market competition drives relatively inefficient firms with the same ownership types in the non-state sector out of business. Furthermore, competition squeezes the cost–price margin and forces firms to have stronger incentives to develop new products and explore new markets. Therefore, gradually strengthened industrial competition, introduction of more efficient ownership types and development towards more flexible ownership types in China's industry may have improved industrial efficiency.

The exact extent to which competition and ownership diversification can improve industrial efficiency is unknown, especially in transition economies. Some economists argue that transfer of ownership is more important for efficiency gain in transitional economies while others claim competition is essential. Hence, further quantitative research is required.

CONTRIBUTION OF COMPETITION AND OWNERSHIP DIVERSIFICATION TO INDUSTRIAL GROWTH

Measurement of the strength of industrial competition is a very difficult task, especially in transitional economies where the market is not perfect. Historical statistics for rough ownership classification exist in China. As many statistics before 1998 used state ownership, collective ownership, individuals and the other ownership types as the four big categories of ownership groups, this classification is adopted to study the effect of ownership diversification on industrial total factor productivity. As the sum of the shares across all ownership groups is a constant [10]—and individuals are relatively less important in the industrial production sector, the shares of SOEs—collectives and enterprises of other ownership types in the gross industrial output value will be used as explanatory variables in the following regression of the production function.

Due to limited data availability, this chapter evaluates the contribution at an industry level only (as a subsection of a secondary industry parallel with the construction industry). As the number of firms within a product industry can approximately reflect the degree of industrial competition,[11] and the development of substitutes usually increases the total number of industrial firms as new product, industry may emerge. The number of industrial enterprises will be used to approximately measure the effect of competition on total factor productivity.

Annual data from 1978–97 are used to evaluate the competition and ownership effects. After trying both the translog and the Cobb–Douglas production functions, it is found that the Cobb–Douglas production function provides a better fit of the data (see Table 5.5).

In the regression, the number of industrial firms, the share of collectives and the share of enterprises with other ownership types are significant at the 0.05 level while capital, which is roughly measured by the annual balance of the net value of fixed assets, is significant at the 0.01 level (Table 5.5). Labour input (total number of employees) and share of SOEs are not significant even at the 0.50 level.

The insignificance of labour input is not surprising as both SOEs and collectives have been overstaffed. The share of SOEs is not significant, indicating that the disembodied improvement of total factor productivity in the state sector is negligible. However, there is significant disembodied technology improvement in the collective sector and the other ownership types sector. Furthermore, the total factor productivity of enterprises with other ownership types is higher than collectives.

Although the majority of studies found that the reforms of SOEs did improve the internal efficiency of SOEs (Jefferson and Singh 1999), efficiency improvement may be mainly through investment in fixed assets. According to the regression, competition and capital inputs significantly contribute to industrial growth.

From the regression and the historical data, approximately 10 per cent of average annual industrial growth is due to disembodied total factor productivity improvement from ownership diversification. On the effect of competition, this regression only reveals its significance. Its extent cannot be calculated because the contribution of competition to industrial growth still seems to be mainly through increased inputs. The cost-reduction effect can be partly offset by inefficient allocation of resources among different ownership groups at an aggregate level.

TABLE 5.5   **EFFECTS OF COMPETITION AND OWNERSHIP ON TOTAL FACTOR PRODUCTIVITY** (DEPENDENT VARIABLE (LNY): LN OF INDUSTRIAL VALUE ADDED)

Explanatory variables	Estimated coefficients	P-value
Intercept	1.056	0.543
LnL	0.038	0.867
LnK	0.685	4.93E-06
Number of industrial enterprises	1.36-E04	0.043
Share of state-owned enterprises in gross industrial output value	0.310	0.671
Share of collectives	2.022	0.030
Share of enterprises with other ownership types	3.967	0.017
Adjusted R^2	0.999	

This regression is the first trial of the quantitive evaluation. To get a more accurate evaluation of the contribution of competition and ownership diversification to industrial performance, product industry-specific studies are needed. Better measures for competition are required. Endogeneity of ownership shares should be considered as well.

CONCLUSION

During China's two-decades of economic reform, a hierarchical and networking market system has been forming. Although the market can yet be improved, competition based on the market mechanism has significantly contributed to China's industrial growth. Even though there was no large-scale privatisation of SOEs, the introduction and development of enterprises with diversified ownership types has increased industrial total factor productivity due to more clearly defined property rights within these enterprises. A primary estimate is that about 10 per cent of the average annual industrial growth comes purely from ownership diversification excluding embodied technology changes.

China's accession to the WTO is bringing in more FDI and stronger international competition. How the industrial structure will evolve depends not only on past government policies and regulations toward enterprises with different ownerships types, and the present ownership structure in different industries and industrial character, but also on the differentials in production efficiency of enterprises with different ownership types, the financial and liquidity constraints different enterprises face, and future industrial policies and regulations. Although various industries will face different challenges, improving the efficiency of the domestic industrial sector is crucial for domestic firms. As the cost reduction effect of market competition can be partly offset by misallocation of resources among different ownership sectors at aggregate level. To enhance the efficiency of the domestic industrial sector, further development of collectives and domestic private enterprises is desirable, together with the ownership transformation of SOEs.

Measures to improve market conditions and allow competition to exert its full function, such as equal treatment of enterprises with different ownership types in bank loans, more effective exits for insolvent firms and further development of the market system including the development of markets for secondary assets, may bring more efficiency gains.

Notes

[1] In the case where insolvent firms face a soft budget, and increase in output is from loss-making firms, social surplus can decrease.

[2] The general consumer price index was 18.8 per cent and 18.0 per cent in 1988 and 1989, respectively.

[3] A typical example of the establishing information market in the 1980s was the increase in small businesses that collect and provide information on the route of empty trucks and the demand for trucks for road commodity transportation.

[4] Data provided in this paragraph are from the Editorial Office of China Economic System Reform Yearbook, *Yearbook of China's Economic System Reform 1999*.

[5] Refer to the 'Guiding list of industries for investment by foreign businessmen' (issued on 20 June 1995 by the Ministry of Foreign Trade and Economic Cooperation, amended in December 1997) in the *Gazette of the State Council of the People's Republic of China 1997 (40)* for past regulations on foreign entry into China's industries. The legal documentation for World Trade Organization accession signed by China can be considered as the new regulations. There were restrictions in dometic private entry into industries which use very scarce resources; which are vital to national economy; or whose products are certain public hazards. See Garnaut et al. (2001) for some sample industries in which domestic private entry was limited.

[6] A very recent survey reveals that some domestic private enterprises have used R and D to win market compatition (see Garnaut et al. 2001), such examples are not common in the economy.

[7] See Wen and Zhang (2001) for the contribution of township village enterprises in ab¯

sorbing surplus labour and in gross industrial output value.

[8] The designated size of enterprise refers to annual sales of five million yuan.

[9] Data are calculated from *Statistical Yearbook of China 2001*.

[10] The better measures can be the industrial–concentration ratio and the Herfindahl index although they are not perfect measures when firms are not profit-maximisers or when there is a large proportion of transactions outside the market.

[11] Statistics by ownership group provided in *Statistical Yearbook of China* and *Industrial Statistical Yearbook of China* after 1997 changed the classification of ownership groups, hence consistent data for 1998, 1999 and 2000 are not available.

6

The WTO challenge to agriculture

Xiaolu Wang

A REVIEW OF CHINA'S AGRICULTURAL SECTOR

Agriculture is very important in China because it is still the major source of income for half of the country's 1.26 billion people. From 1952 to 2000, the share of agriculture in GDP decreased from 51 per cent to 16 per cent, whereas the share of agricultural workers in China's total employment only decreased from 84 per cent to 47 per cent.[1]

The disparity between the share of agriculture in GDP and the share of agricultural workers in total employment indicates how low agricultural labour productivity is when compared with other sectors. In 2000, rural per capita net income (similar to disposable income) was only 2253 yuan (US$272), or just 36 per cent of the average urban per capita disposable income. Agricultural income accounted for 50 per cent of rural per capita net income, and income from farming accounted for 39 per cent. Thanks to rapid rural industrialisation over the past 20 years, non-agricultural activities provide 44 per cent of farmers' incomes.

Grain output, yields and labour productivity

Grain production has been the most important component of agriculture. Rough calculations indicate that in gross value terms total grain output accounted for 65 per cent of total farm output and 38 per cent of agricultural output in 1998. China is the largest grain producer in the world; it accounts for over one-fifth of total world grain output. Grain output in China increased from 300 million tonnes to 512 million tonnes between 1978 and 1998 (but declined to 462 million tonnes in 2000). The large increase in grain output can be mainly attributed to four effects: market-oriented reforms and the adoption of the Household Responsibility System in the early 1980s; increases in domestic grain prices; technical progress (for example, development of hybrid rice); and continued increases in inputs (see for example Sicular 1988; Lin 1992, 1996; Rozelle and Boisvert 1993; Huang, Rosegrant and Rozelle 1998; and Wang 1999).

The average grain yields for China as a whole reached 4.95 tonnes per hectare (measured by sown areas) in 1998–99, significantly higher than in most developing countries and close to that of industrialised countries.[2] Yield per cultivated land unit is much higher, because the multiple-cropping ratio is high, usually 1.5 to 1.6. On average, three farmers in China share one hectare of arable land. Labour intensity has been one of the highest amongst the world's major grain producers—60 per cent higher than the world average, 20 times higher than the United Kingdom, Germany and France, 50 times higher than in the United States, and 100 times higher than Australia and Canada (World Bank 1997a; International Labour Office 1998). Because of natural limitations to the arable land area and the huge agricultural population, labour productivity in the agricultural sector is very low.

Inter-sectoral transfer of agricultural labour

A major challenge to China's agricultural sector is to shift to its huge redundant labour force to non-agricultural sectors. Rapid rural industrialisation resulting from the market-oriented reforms of the past 20 years has caused 100 million rural labourers to move from the agricultural sector to the Township and Village Enterprise (TVE) sector. Total TVE employment was 128 million in 2000. Following the relaxation of policy restrictions, rural–urban migration has increased rapidly since the late 1980s. The numbers of so-called 'floating labour' are statistically unavailable, but based on data from surveys, the author estimates that there was 14 million in 1990 and around 47 million in 2000.[3]

During the period 1980–2000, the total rural labour force increased from 347 million to 519 million, and the agricultural labour force increased from 317 million to 344 million.[4] The growth rate of rural labour will now slow due to the family planning policy and urbanisation. Estimates by the author indicate that there will be a total of 530 million rural workers by 2010.

While the natural growth of rural labour is slowing, rural industrialisation has also stagnated since the mid 1990s. Total employment in the TVE sector grew at an annual rate of 12 per cent in the 1980s, but only 3 per cent in the 1990s (and was negative in 1996 and 1997). There seems no reason to believe that the growth rate will recover in the medium term. We may assume an average 1.5 per cent growth rate of TVE employment from 2001–10, to reach a total of 149 million by 2010. Due to the weaker demand for, and oversupply of, unskilled labour in urban areas, rural–urban migration is unlikely to grow faster in the near future.

After deducting those who have been employed by TVEs and those who migrated to urban areas, nearly all the remaining rural labourers are in the agricultural sector. This is because they are entitled to a small parcel of arable land under the House-hold Responsibility System (HRS), which provides them with a form of minimum insurance. Therefore, the agricultural sector hosts the majority of the underem-ployed labour. Table 6.1 shows the growth (and expected growth) of the rural labour force, TVE employment, estimated rural–urban migration, and estimated agricul-tural labour. Assuming that the speed of the transfer of agricultural labour to the urban sector between 2001 and 2010 will be slightly slower than in the 1990s (that

TABLE 6.1   **RURAL LABOUR, TVE EMPLOYMENT AND RURAL–URBAN MIGRATION (MILLION PERSONS)**

Year	Agricultural labour	Rural labour (statistics)	Rural labour (adjusted)	TVE employment	Rural–urban migration
1980	318	347	30	-	317
1990	473	473	93	14	366
2000	499	519	128	47	344
2010 (assumption 1)	n.a	530	149	77	304
2010 (assumption 2)	n.a	530	149	107	274

Notes: Rural labour is adjusted according to the national census data (see Wang 2000). The number of rural–urban migrants was estimated by the author based on MLSS and NBS (1999). Agricultural labour is calculated from rural labour after the deduction of TVE employment and rural–urban migration. For the period 2001–10, the growth rates assumed for rural labour and TVE employment are 0.2 per cent and 1.5 per cent, respectively. Rural–urban migration under assumption 1 is assumed be 3 million per year. Under assumption 2, it is 6 million per year, while other assumptions remain the same.
Sources: Department of Training and Employment of the Ministry of Labour and Social Security, and Rural Social and Economic Survey Team of the National Statistical Bureau, 1999. *The Situation of Rural Labourers' Employment and Flow in China, 1997-1998*, printed report, Beijing.; and National Bureau of Statistics, 1999, 2001. *Statistical Yearbook of China*, Statistics Press, Beijing; Wang, X., 2000. 'The sustainability of China's economic growth and institutional changes', in X. Wang and G. Fan (eds), *The Sustainability of China's Economic Growth*, Economic Science Press, Beijing; and author's estimates.

is, 3.0 million instead of 3.3 million per year), then the agricultural labour force in 2010 will be 304 million—a 40 million reduction from 2000. This will mean only a minor improvement in agricultural labour productivity.

More optimistically, if urbanisation can be significantly accelerated, with rural–urban migration increasing from 3 to 6 million per year between 2001 and 2010, then the agricultural labour force will be reduced to 274 million by 2010. Agricultural labour productivity will be further increased.

IMPORTS, EXPORTS AND PRICES OF GRAIN

Grain trade

In the 20 years from 1981–2000, there were net grain imports in 11 years and net exports in 9 years. From 1995–2000, average annual net imports were 0.79 million tonnes. Annual gross grain imports have never reached the WTO tariff quota of 22.2 million tonnes over the past half a century. Only in 1995 were imports close to the quota, although this caused a serious oversupply of grain in the domestic market.

Grain prices

Domestic prices of grain (farm-gate prices) took three forms in the past: the state quota price, the state above-quota price, and the rural market price. Between 1985 and 1993, state quota prices decreased in real terms by 20.3 per cent on average because the nominal price increased slowly while there was high inflation. Due to supply shortages, the state progressively increased its quota and above-quota prices from 1994–1996. Market prices also increased in 1994 and 1995 because market supplies were squeezed by the increased state purchases and increased state grain stocks. The weighted average of the state and market prices in real terms reached its highest level in 1996 (Table 6.2). At that time, major grain prices exceeded world market prices by 38–45 per cent, except for rice, which was 8 per cent lower (Wu, Liu and Ke 1997).

In 1997, quota prices increased even further despite market prices declining in 1996. This led to quota prices exceeding market prices in 1997 and 1998. In 1997, quota prices in real terms were 50.8 per cent higher than in 1993, and 20.2 per cent higher than in 1985. However, in real terms, market prices declined to their 1985 levels.

The increases in grain prices over the 1994–97 period resulted in historically high output levels (above 500 million tons) between 1996 and 1999. Together with the

84

large grain imports in 1995 and 1996 (20.8 and 12.2 million tonnes, respectively), this caused large surpluses in the domestic market. As a result, state purchase prices in real terms fell by 19 per cent from their highest levels in 1997 to the recent lows of 2000, and the real market price dropped by 43 per cent from its highest level in 1995 to the 15-year low in 2000, which was 20 per cent lower than its 1985 level (Table 6.2). Detailed discussion on the price fluctuations can be seen in Wang (2001).

There was a recovery in domestic grain prices in 2001. Up to September 2001, grain prices were 5.7 per cent above the levels at the end of 2000 (Center for News Gathering and Editing 2002). The recovery in prices has been modest, as total grain stocks were still large at the end of 2001.[5] If there is not a major increase in imports, further recovery in grain prices could be expected in the near future.

One may conclude that either the 1995–96 domestic market prices or the 1997 quota price significantly exceeded their intermediate internal equilibrium levels, whereas the 2000 domestic prices were far below equilibrium levels. To compare with world prices, we can use the average domestic market price level (in constant terms) during the period 1985–2000 to represent an intermediate internal equilibrium price level. This average level is equal to 110 per cent of 1985 market prices, 79 per cent of 1995 market prices, and 137 per cent of 2000 market prices. It happens to be equal to the mean of market prices between 1995 and 2000.

We should note that farm-gate prices are not comparable with world market prices because the former does not include the domestic purchase, transport and wholesale costs, and the latter does not include the transport, insurance and other costs when grain is imported to China. It would be better to compare domestic wholesale prices and the import C.I.F. prices; however, wholesale prices in the past were either similar to, or lower than, the rural market prices due to state subsidies in earlier years or supply surpluses in recent years.

In Table 6.3, the means of real rural market prices between 1995 and 2000 are compared with C.I.F. prices. Except for rice, the mean of rural market prices between 1995 and 2000 for all major grains is higher than the 2000 C.I.F. prices. If the domestic charges of purchase, transport and wholesale costs are added, the domestic prices would be even higher. Note that there are also quality differences between domestic and imported grains; for example, imported rice and wheat is usually of a higher quality than domestic rice and wheat.

In general, it is reasonable to accept the points of many Chinese experts, who believe that China has a comparative advantage in rice production, compared with

TABLE 6.2   REAL PRICE CHANGES: STATE AND MARKET (1985 PRICE = 1.00)

	State quota price	Market price	Average
1985	1.000	1.000	1.000
1990	0.784	1.158	0.909
1993	0.797	0.965	0.853
1994	0.929	1.140	1.000
1995	0.969	1.399	1.112
1996	1.090	1.290	1.157
1997	1.202	1.028	1.144
1998	1.140	0.964	1.081
1999	1.001	0.912	0.971
2000	0.975	0.802	0.917

Notes: Both the state and market price indexes are derived as a weighted average of the price index of rice, wheat, corn and soybean according to their output. The rural consumer price index is used as the deflator. For the average index, the weights are two-thirds and one-third for the state and market, respectively.

Source: Calculated from annual and monthly data from the Ministry of Agriculture (various years), and data from the Information Centre of Ministry of Agriculture; Wu, L., 2001. 'Price Comparison Between World and Domestic Grain Markets', prepared for the ACIAR project on China's grain market, The Australian National University and National Bureau of Statistics, various years; *Statistical Yearbook of China,* Statistics Press, Beijing.

TABLE 6.3   COMPARISON OF RURAL MARKET PRICES WITH C.I.F. PRICES, 1995–2000 (YUAN/TONNE)

	Rural market price	2000 C.I.F. price
Rice	2452	3859
Wheat	1477	1375
Corn	1265	976
Soybean	2341	1785

Note: Rural market prices are calculated as the mean of 1995 and 2000 rural market prices in 2000 constant prices. C.I.F. prices are derived from the imported volumes and values in 2000, converted from US dollars to renminbi. For corn, the C.I.F. price is for 1999 since the 2000 data are unavailable.

Source: Calculated from annual and monthly data from Ministry of Agriculture (various years), data from the Information Centre of Ministry of Agriculture, Wu, L., 2001. 'Price Comparison Between World and Domestic Grain Markets', prepared for the ACIAR project on China's grain market, Australian National University and National Bureau of Statistics, various years; *Statistical Yearbook of China,* Statistics Press, Beijing.

all other major grain products. Even for rice, due to the quality differences between domestic and imported products, a large volume of imports is still possible in the medium term. Thus, the WTO tariff quota will have a substantial impact on domestic grain production.

THE DIRECT IMPACT OF THE WTO QUOTA ON GRAIN IMPORTS

Major changes after WTO accession

The most important change in agriculture following from China's WTO accession is that China will adopt a tariff quota for total grain imports at a 1 per cent token tariff rate. The quota will be 18.3 million tonnes in 2002, 20.2 million tonnes in 2003, and 22.2 million tonnes in 2004 (Table 6.4). According to the accession agreement, the tariff quota is to be shared between the state and private trading enterprises, and all unused state quotas are to be transferred to private enterprises.

Other major commitments are

- above-quota tariff rates for the major grains will be 65 per cent. For soybeans the tariff rate will be 3 per cent
- the average tariff rate for all agricultural products is to be reduced from 22 per cent to 17.5 per cent
- the average rate of domestic support for agricultural products will be zero. There will be no export subsidies
- other non-tariff restrictions on imports of agricultural products, such as licensing, are to be eliminated. This includes restrictions on imports of wheat from the north-west areas of North America, which may have TCK disease.

The economic impact of the latter changes is not clear and the issues are strongly debated. More detailed information and analysis are needed. The above-quota tariff rate may not be important because past experience indicates that there is little likelihood of imports exceeding the quota.

Size of the import quota compared to domestic grain market

To assess the impact of the 22 million tonnes grain import quota on the domestic grain market, a calculation of the size of the domestic market (grain traded both by the state dealers and in the free market) is necessary. The domestic market is far smaller than the total output, because a substantial part of the grain output is

TABLE 6.4   **TARIFF QUOTAS FOR GRAINS,** 2002–04 (MILLION TONNES)

	2002	2003	2004
Wheat	8.468	9.052	9.636
Corn	5.850	6.525	7.200
Rice	3.990	4.655	5.320
Total	18.308	20.232	22.156

Source: World Trade Organization, 2001. 'Accession of the People's Republic of China, decision of 10 November 2001', cited from http://www.moftec.gov.cn/

TABLE 6.5   **ESTIMATION OF THE VOLUME OF NON-TRADED GRAIN, 2000, (UNPROCESSED GRAIN, MILLION TONNES)**

	Rural consumption	Self-consumption ratio	Non-market grain
Rural food grain	201.9	0.8	161.5
Feed grain	..	..	83.4
Meat	85.7	0.5	51.4
Poultry & eggs	22.4	0.5	13.4
Cultivated fish, etc.	13.0	0.3	3.9
Milk	9.2	0.3	0.8
Draught animals	17.4	0.8	13.9
Seed grain	16.3	0.6	9.8
Total			254.7

Note: Rural food consumption of grain is derived from household survey and rural population data. Feed grain is derived from livestock production data. The quantity of meat (pork, beef and lamb) is converted from the gross weight (with bones) at a conversion ratio of 0.5. The weight conversion ratios between feed grain and meat are assumed to be 2.8 for meat production, 1.0 for poultry, egg, cultured fish and shrimp, etc., and 0.3 for milk production. The feed consumption of draught animals is assumed to be 0.5 kg per animal per day. The consumption of seed grain is derived from the areas sown to grain in year 2000 and an estimated average 0.15 tonnes per hectare. Self-consumption ratios are the proportions of on-farm consumption of grain they produce on the farm themselves. They are based on the author's personal experience.
Source: Calculated from National Bureau of Statistics, 2001. *Statistical Yearbook of China,* Statistics Press, Beijing.

consumed by farmers and does not enter the market. There are no statistics on the quantity of grain sold in the domestic market, so that it has to be estimated following an estimate of the volume of non-market grain consumed by farmers in 2000 (see Table 6.5). The volume of traded grain is derived and converted to a trade weight as 186 million tonnes for 2000. From Table 6.6 it can be seen that the tariff quota for imported grain (2004) accounts for 5.5 per cent of total domestic demand and 12 per cent of total market demand.

The impact of the tariff quota on domestic grain prices

In estimating the impact of the WTO import quota on domestic prices, it is assumed that the 22 million tonnes of grain against the quota is an external shock at a time when the domestic market is in equilibrium. The domestic equilibrium prices are based on the calculation in Table 6.3 plus a 15 per cent increase to include the domestic purchase, transport and wholesale costs. Thus, the wholesale price of rice before the shock will be 27 per cent lower than the price of imported rice (but the average quality of domestic rice is also lower). Prices of wheat, corn and soybean before the shock will be higher than the imported prices by 24, 49 and 51 per cent, respectively. Thus, we may assume that the entire wheat and corn quotas, and 50 per cent of the rice quota will be used. These sum to 19.5 million tonnes. Together with other grain imports (soybean imports for example, may increase dramatically), total grain imports in 2004 will be above 21 million tonnes—that is, an 18 million tonne increase from an average of 3.5 million tonnes between 1998 and 2000 equal to 9.6 per cent of market demand and 4.4 per cent of total demand.

Grain consumption in China is price inelastic. Based on estimations of China's grain demand elasticity reported in the literature, the author used 0.37 as a weighted average elasticity of total demand for grain (alternatively, we can use 0.81 as the elasticity of market demand, which can be derived from the ratio between total demand and market demand).[6] On this basis, the price effect of the 18 million tonnes of imports will lead to a 12 per cent decline in prices in the domestic market.

Alternatively, we may assume that the external shock occurs when the domestic market is still in surplus (as is more likely to be the case). The domestic price level will be lower than in the first case, and imports will be less. However, because the remaining quota can be used at any time when domestic prices are rising, the effect of imports will be similar to that in the first case except that it will prevent the price from recovering instead of pushing the price level down. For simplicity, only the first case will be considered.

The impact of the tariff quota on domestic production

According to the estimate by Wang (2001), the total price elasticity of grain supply is 0.52, and the effect of price changes on output is fully attained in two years. Based on this, grain output will decline by 6.2 per cent in two years. There is likely to be a 'cobweb effect' because the price elasticity of demand is smaller than the price elasticity of supply. In this case, both production and price levels may

TABLE 6.6 **ESTIMATING THE SIZE OF THE DOMESTIC GRAIN MARKET, 2000, (MILLION TONNES)**

	Unprocessed weight	Trade weight
Total production	462	400
Non-traded consumption	255	221
Change in stocks	-20	-17
Net exports	12	10
Domestically traded	215	186
Total domestic demand	470	407
Tariff quota (2004 and later)	..	22.2
TQ as % of traded grain	n.a.	11.9%
TQ as % of total demand	n.a.	5.5%

Note: Trade weights are derived from the unprocessed weight. Rice is converted from paddy at a conversion ratio of 0.68, other grains are unprocessed. The change in grain stock is assumed.
Source: Calculated from Table 6.5 and National Bureau of Statistics, 2001. *Statistical Yearbook of China,* Statistics Press, Beijing.

fluctuate increasingly and never converge to the equilibrium. However, this effect may be reduced by the government operation of a price stabilisation scheme and improvement in information services to farmers. For simplicity, we may consider the case where, on average, the price level declines by 6 per cent and output falls by 3.1 per cent as an equilibrium result.[7]

Producer losses

The producer losses can be approximately derived from the following formula: (price before shock) x (percentage price reduction) x (volume of market grain before shock − net import) + (output reduction) x (domestic price after shock) − (material input cost) + (fixed cost that cannot be reduced) − (net incomes from new jobs after shock).

Using the 2000 production and consumption data, we can calculate:

[1815 x 6% x 215 + (462 x 3.1%) x 2006 x (1− 6% − 40% + 10%)] x (1 − 30%) = 28.0 (billion yuan),

where 1815 is the mean of 1995 and 2000 real grain price levels as a weighted average (constant yuan of 2000 per tonne), which is used for the assumed internal equilibrium price before the shock; 6 per cent is the calculated price reduction due to the import shock; 215 is the calculated volume (million tonnes) of market grain that is produced domestically before the shock; 3.1 per cent is the calculated

90

reduction in total grain output; 40 per cent is the ratio of material input costs derived from the ratio between gross output value and value-added of agriculture in 1998; 10 per cent is the assumed ratio of fixed costs to the reduced output, which cannot be proportionally reduced; and 30 per cent is the assumed proportion of farmers who can move to the non-grain sector in the short run and obtain the same income as before. In this calculation, farmers' self-consumed grain is excluded because it is offset by their own production.

The derived 28.0 billion yuan of net losses is equal to 0.3 per cent of GDP and 4.2 per cent of farmers' net income from farming. For those pure grain farmers who have no other employment opportunities, they would incur 9.1 per cent net income losses on average.

Producer losses could be much smaller if grain farmers could efficiently shift to non-grain production with the same available resources. Currently, the number of grain farmers (those fully or mainly engaged in grain production) is still very large, accounting for at least 60 per cent of the total of 350 million farmers, and they are concentrated in the less-developed central and west regions. Their productivity and incomes are very low, annually producing only 2 tonnes of grain per farmer. The transfer of these farmers to other sectors has been slow. The major obstacles are

- limited employment opportunities for unskilled and less educated labour
- poor information, telecommunication and transport services in the remote rural areas for access to domestic or world markets of non-grain products
- government quotas on grain production, although these have been relaxed in recent years.

Consumer gains

Consumer gains from increased imports can be approximately calculated from the difference in grain prices before and after the import shock times the market consumption of grain after the shock:

$$1815 \times 6\% \times 215 \times (1 + 9.6\% - 6.8\%) = 24.1 \text{ (billion yuan)}$$

where 9.6 per cent is the ratio of imported grain to domestic market grain before the shock, and 6.8 per cent is the ratio of output reduction to the market grain before the shock. Again, farmers' consumer gain is excluded for the reason mentioned earlier.

The 24.1 billion yuan of consumer surplus is equal to 0.27 per cent of GDP, and 0.83 per cent of urban residents' income.

Impact on employment

If we assume that the imported grain will proportionally crowd out farmers without reducing the remaining farmers' income, then 4.4 per cent of the grain farmers (9.2 million) will be forced off the farm; although the increase in imports can only marginally increase employment opportunities in the grain export countries due to their much higher labour productivity. Assuming that all these grain imports would come from the United States, for example, this would create only 40,000 new jobs in the US farming sector according to its average productivity per capita.

Summary of the direct impact of grain imports

The above results are summarised in Table 6.3. Although the results show some net losses in the short-run, this will not be the major problem. The major problem is the unbalanced distribution of losses and gains. The cost directly affects low-income farmers, resulting in a relatively large percentage decline in their income, whereas the benefit mainly goes to urban consumers who have a much higher income, and therefore accounts for only a small proportion of their income. In addition, due to the inelastic adjustment, job losses will exert pressure on the economy in the years ahead.

STRUCTURAL ADJUSTMENT

In the long run, inefficiencies in agricultural production must be addressed, and the opening of China's agricultural sector is unavoidable. The most important issue is how to adjust China's economic structure so that more efficient use is made of resources.

Adjustment in the agricultural structure

According to China's comparative advantage, rice production could expand to replace other grains. Some adjustment is already underway. From 1995 to 2000, the area sown to wheat decreased by 7.6 per cent whereas the rice area was only reduced by 2.5 per cent. Further adjustment can be expected but the capacity is limited, due to the lack of water resources in most wheat and corn producing areas in north China.

Grain may also be replaced by other agricultural products. The share of area sown to grain in the total sown area has fallen from 80 per cent to 69 per cent over the past 20 years, with grain being replaced by cash crops, vegetables, tea and fruits. The government has abolished grain quotas in the major grain importing coastal provinces. In fact, quotas to the major grain producing provinces have also been dropped, because of grain surpluses. Further market-oriented adjustment can be expected in the future.

Export-oriented agriculture has had limited development in most provinces. In 2000, exports of food and food animals from China accounted for only 4 per cent of the value of agricultural output. Future adjustment should be directed to increases in exports of labour-intensive products with low land intensity. To achieve this, major efforts are needed, especially for remote inland areas, to develop business connections with world markets, and also to develop related human resources, infrastructure and other facilities. These are long-run tasks, needed not only to overcome import shocks, but also as a means of modernising traditional agriculture.

Removing price supports

Past experience indicates that government protection of grain prices has had a negative impact on farmers' incomes, because it has distorted market prices and sent the wrong signals to producers. Government grain prices set at levels higher than market prices encourage farmers to produce grain in excess of market demand, eventually resulting in market surpluses and declines in prices. The inelastic government adjustment in prices has also resulted in large fluctuations in production and has seriously injured farmers (Wang 2001). Under the WTO commitments, price support is ruled out. This will have a positive effect on the agricultural sector.

To help low-income farmers, more effective measures may include improving information, technical and training services to farmers to promote their production adjustment towards more efficient production areas.

TABLE 6.7   **THE DIRECT IMPACT OF GRAIN IMPORTS**

Costs and benefits	Producer losses	Consumer gains
Value (billion yuan)	28.0	24.1
As % of GDP	0.31	0.27
As % of all farmers' income	4.2	n.a.
As % of pure grain farmers' income	9.1	n.a.
As % of all consumers' income	n.a.	0.52
As % of urban consumers' income	n.a.	0.83
Rural employment opportunities	Domestic losses	Foreign gains
1000 persons	9240	40

Note: Foreign gains in employment opportunities are calculated using labour productivity in US farming sector as an example.
Source: Author's calculations.

Industrialisation and urbanisation

A major structural adjustment that can be expected is the further transfer of agricultural labour to the industrial and service sectors, especially in urban areas. At present, only 36 per cent of the total population lives in urban areas. This ratio has been 10–20 percentage points lower than in other countries with the same level of per capita GDP. In the cities with a population of one million or more, the more developed services sector provides 41–45 per cent of employment opportunities, whereas the service sector in small cities of less than 200,000 only provides 23 per cent of job opportunities. The statistics imply that urban development in China—particularly development of medium and large cities—has been insufficient. In the long run, urbanisation will provide substantial opportunities for further transfer of the agricultural population (Wang and Xia 1999).

Under normal circumstances rural industrialisation and urbanisation could reduce the agricultural labour force by 4 million annually from 2001–10. To absorb the grain import shock fully, at least an additional six million farmers will have to be employed by the TVE and urban sectors between 2002 and 2004 (assuming that 3.2 million can move to non-grain agricultural production). However, over a longer period, urbanisation may be accelerated via policy adjustments, such as by removing restrictions on rural–urban migration, eliminating policy biases against medium and large-sized cities, and improving urban infrastructure. In this case, the grain shock may be fully absorbed and there will be greater improvements in agricultural productivity.

Notes

[1] Data are from the National Bureau of Statistics (NBS). The same source is used below unless specified otherwise.

[2] This is according to the official statistics. However, according to the 1996 National Agricultural census (and supported by satellite imaging data), the cultivated land area was understated by 27 per cent in the official statistics in the past (NBS 1999, 2001). Using the same ratio to adjust sown areas, the average yield becomes 3.61 tonnes per hectare, which is still higher than in most developing countries.

[3] 'Floating labour' includes rural labour working outside their hometown including those who have moved to urban areas without having urban residential registration. Major sources for the estimation were a surveys by the Department of Training and Employment of the Ministry of Labour and Social Security, the Rural Social and Economic

Survey team of the National Bureau of Statistical (MLSS and NBS 1999), and the 1990 national census data (NBS 1991).

4   These are the author's estimates. The official data for these two years are 318 million and 499 million, respectively, for rural labour. For agricultural labour, they are 291 million and 334 million, respectively. See Wang (2000b).

5   From a speech by Du Runsheng, the former director of the Rural Development Research Centre of the State Council, at the symposium 'Agriculture and Private Enterprises in China' in Guangzhou, 18 December 2001.

6   Lin et al. (2001) estimated the price elasticity of rural demand for wheat, corn, paddy rice and beans as −0.857, -0.044, -0.155 and −0.549, respectively. The fact that elasticities of wheat and beans are far higher than those of corn and rice, appears to be because that the former can be substituted by cheaper grains. This is not the case for rice because rice is the only major food grain in south China. The weighted average of these elasticities is 0.34, and it is adjusted to 0.37 to include urban demand.

7   The impact of price fluctuations on production and farmers' incomes would be far more serious if the government incorrectly responds to the price changes. For a description of past experience see Wang (2001).

7

Entry to the WTO and the domestic private economy

Ligang Song

China's entry to the WTO on 11 December 2001 began a new phase in China's economic transition as the terms of accession require further fundamental change in China's economic system. Existing studies have focused predominantly on the impact of China's WTO entry on different sectors of the economy or the economy as a whole. One area that has not been adequately discussed is how conforming with the WTO requirements will affect the development of the emerging domestic private economy in China.

The challenges facing domestic private enterprises in the wake of the WTO entry are particularly pronounced because domestic private enterprises have historically already faced unequal terms of competition with state-owned enterprises and foreign firms (including joint venture firms). Nevertheless, China's ability to face the challenges of WTO entry will depend to a great extent on whether the domestic private sector can successfully develop and expand. This is largely because the private sector has already played an important role in the economy, and further development of the private sector will influence the reform program in many areas, including reform of SOEs and state-owned banks (SOBs). Most importantly, vibrant development of the domestic private sector will require market-compatible institution building—the most fundamental task in meeting the requirements of the WTO.

Specifically, WTO entry requires transparent and formal procedures in the conduct of business and trade, property rights to enhance incentives and facilitate business transactions, level playing fields to fulfil the obligation for 'national treatment' and ensure fair competition, and rule of law to provide a legal environment in which businesses can operate. All these requirements have direct implications for the development of domestic private enterprises.

CONSTRAINTS, GROWTH TREND AND CONTRIBUTIONS

Private firms have emerged in several different ways, reflecting the complexity of a transitional process based on gradualist reform. These include spontaneous eruption of individually operated private businesses in urban and rural areas; the emergence or transformation of private enterprises from urban collectives and township and village enterprises (TVEs) in rural areas; private enterprises transformed from state-owned enterprises; and private foreign enterprises, including joint ventures and wholly foreign-owned firms (Figure 7.1).

In a partially reformed system, private enterprises face enormous difficulties and constraints imposed by various political, institutional, economic and social factors. The following are amongst the more important constraints requiring correction

- arbitrary fees and taxes imposed on private enterprises by local governments
- private firms' access to business finance, particularly from state financial institutions
- the absence of efficient and transparent bank lending systems to small and medium-size enterprises generally, and private enterprises in particular
- the weakness of the skill base in private enterprises, particularly those of medium and small size, at both managerial and employee levels
- the weakness and lack of transparency in accounting and auditing practices
- the weakness of the legal and regulatory environment
- the weakness of markets, particularly financial and labour markets
- the absence of a competitive environment in which all types of firms are competing on an equal footing.

Despite constraints, the private sector is now the most dynamic sector in the economy, and has, since the early 1990s, made important contributions to growth and reform. Growth in the number of formally registered private enterprises, including the *getihu* (individual businesses or enterprises), can be seen from Table 7.1. The average growth rate of formally registered private enterprises far exceeded that of both state and collective enterprises during the period 1989–98 in most respects, including in employment, registered capital, tax revenue, gross value of industrial output and retail sales.

FIGURE 7.1   **TRANSITIONAL PATHS TOWARD THE PRIVATE ECONOMY**

Development stages

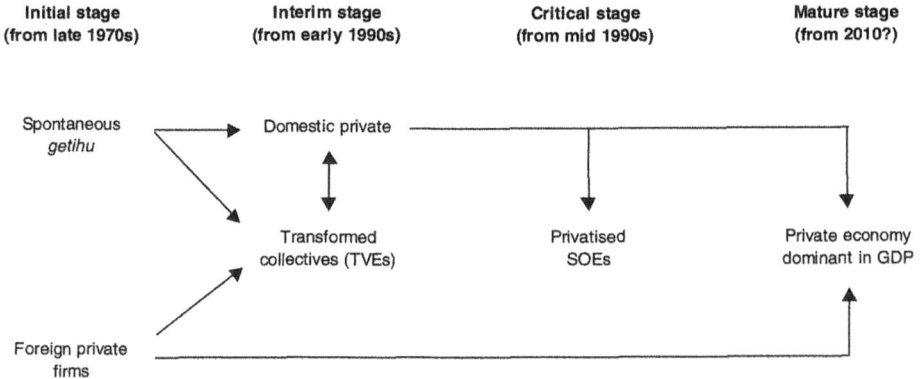

Initial stage	Interim stage	Critical stage	Mature stage
(from late 1970s)	(from early 1990s)	(from mid 1990s)	(from 2010?)

Spontaneous *getihu*

Domestic private

Transformed collectives (TVEs)

Privatised SOEs

Private economy dominant in GDP

Foreign private firms

The development of the private sector at this stage of economic transformation plays an important role in a number of areas. It increases employment, both by recruiting new workers into the non-farm economy and by absorbing workers laid-off by reformed SOEs. It creates competition, nurtures entrepreneurship and instigates innovation. It helps channel an increasing proportion of investment into more efficient uses and hence increases the overall efficiency of the economy. It helps drive the regulatory and institutional framework into becoming more compatible with a market system, thereby facilitating improved performance in state-owned and collective enterprises. It also accelerates growth with less risk to macroeconomic stability than would expansion of state-owned enterprises, since private firms are subject to hard budget constraints.

As a result, there has been a significant shift from the state to the non-state sector in the economy despite various constraints imposed on non-state, especially private, enterprises (Figure 7.2). The share of domestic private enterprises in total GDP, industrial outputs, employment, foreign trade and taxation revenues has increased phenomenally relative to similar shares for SOEs. In line with such a shift, the state has gradually withdrawn from the more competitive sectors of the economy, giving way to non-state enterprises in these industries. The state's share in total industrial output has fallen considerably, accounting for less than one-third

99

of the total by the end of the 1990s. Given the differences in their respective growth rates, the state's share in the total economy will continue to shrink in the face of private sector expansion.

Facing constraints because of the partially reformed institutional framework, the private sector has induced institutional changes to accommodate its development. In the process, the legitimacy of the private economy (property rights) has gradually come to be accepted ideologically, politically and, more importantly, constitutionally—a fact which has long-term implications for Chinese society. These institutional changes have been vital in enhancing the growth and development of private enterprise but also in prompting state-owned enterprises (SOE) reform. In contributing to progress in two crucial issues in economic transformation—the creation of incentives and the reallocation of resources—private enterprise has become the key for successful restructuring of the SOEs.

Many key reform issues remain. The building of market-compatible institutions is the most important factor for the continued development of private enterprise. Ownership and property rights need to be formalised and made more secure. Regulatory policies that affect, among other things, entry, exit, markets (especially financial markets) and government functions need to be enhanced. Reform in these areas will help overcome the remaining constraints on the development of the private sector, leading it to make an even greater contribution to the reform and growth of

TABLE 7.1   **GROWTH OF PRIVATE AND OTHER ENTERPRISE, 1989–98 (AVERAGE GROWTH RATE)**

	Average	State	Collective	FDI	*Getihu*	Private[a]
Number of firms		5.37	0.27	34.4	8.48	33.27
Employment	2.64	-0.01	-0.06	22.55	13.6	29.76
Registered capital		12.89	11.56	36.94	27.64	63.97
Tax revenue (89–97)	17.55	14.83	11.8	30.37[b]	60.79	73.15
Fixed capital investment[c]	24.2	21.6	28.2	11.73[d]	16.0	33.8
Gross value of output	16.61	5.39	18.3	27.84[c]	32.95	51.85
Retail sales	13.2	5.32	4.64		22.35	57.24

Notes: [a]Private here refers to formally registered private enterprises; [b]1994–97; [c]1990–98; [d]1994–98.
Sources: Constructed using the figures contained in various tables in Zhang, H. and Ming, L. (eds), 2000. *Development Report on Private Enterprise in China*, Social Sciences Literature Publishing House, Beijing; and Chinese Statistical Agency, *Statistical Yearbooks of China*, (1999).

FIGURE 7.2   **OWNERSHIP SHARES IN CHINA'S GDP, 1998**

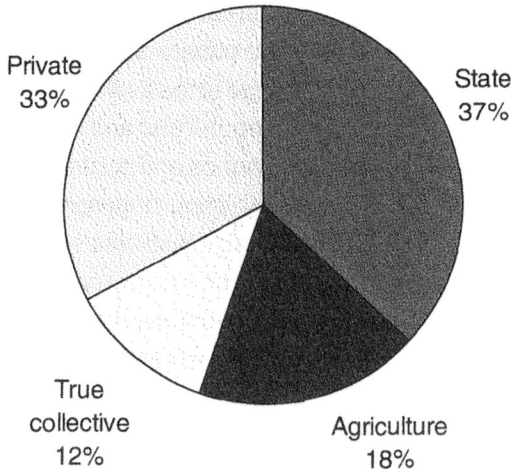

Source: Garnaut, R., Song, L., Yao, Y., and Wang, X., 2001. *Private Enterprise in China*, Asia Pacific Press, Canberra:19).

the Chinese economy and lay a more solid foundation for China's integration into the world economy.

INFORMALITY VERSUS FORMALITY

Informality can be defined as variations in social behaviour from formal rules, norms and practice (formality). Informalities are in principle inconsistent with the WTO requirements, which demand formal rules and procedures as the foundation on which member countries apply their policies and conduct business with each other. It is therefore important for the government to facilitate a rapid shift from informality to formality.

Informality, ranging from family-based management and reliance on trust rather than contracts to non-transparency in accounting and taxation systems and informal financial markets, has been a feature of private enterprise development. Informalities associated with the activities of private enterprises stem largely from the imperfect institutional changes resulting from various reform measures and cultural influences. The scale and depth of informality are determined by the extent of the market distortion and progress in reform and institution building. The existence of informality under certain circumstances brings about gains as well as costs to agencies who attempt to exploit it. A shift that increases the costs and reduces the gains of exploiting informality requires that certain conditions be met.

It can be argued that the informality of the private sector was a great strength during a period of uncertainty and rapid change since it allowed private enterprises to respond flexibly to changing policies and regulations and new market opportunities. These private gains, such as obtaining finance and contracts, securing the use of land and material, avoiding taxes, and violating copyright, often help private enterprises survive and expand in an unfavourable business environment. But these private gains are acquired at a cost to the firm and also carry social costs, including the worsening of bureaucratic corruption. For example, the survey of Chief Executive Officers in Chinese private businesses, reported in Garnaut et al. (2001), show that the cost of 'unproductive activities', including expenditure on maintaining and improving *guanxi* (connections), can reach 20 per cent of a firm's total profits, and can take up as much as 80 per cent of a CEOs' time and energy.

Institutional factors can also contribute to the widespread practice of informalities. For example, poorly defined and insecure property rights, burdensome government regulations and lack of law enforcement have seriously hampered private enterprises' adjustment to change and have created ample opportunities for exploiting informalities.

Informality now, however, poses serious obstacles to the further growth and development of private enterprises. Informality has resulted in opaque and unfocused companies with limited management capacity, which find it difficult to attract the finance and skills they need to grow (Gregory et al. 2000). More importantly, exploiting various kinds of informality to acquire private gains incurs costs (penalties) for entrepreneurs. From an economic point of view, entrepreneurs will pursue these activities so long as the gains are larger than the costs. A graphic approach is developed here to explain, (1) how the benefits from exploiting informality change over time with the deepening of reform (marketisation); and (2) how the relative payoff (benefits versus costs) shifts over time for the same reason (Figure 7.3).

Without a competitive market system and well-established market-compatible institutions, there are numerous opportunities, at certain stages of economic transformation, for entrepreneurs to exploit informality for private gain (shown by a precipitously rising *b* curve in Figure 7.3). When marketisation reaches a certain level as a result of a deepening of reform and institution-building, however, entrepreneurs

FIGURE 7.3   **REFORM, MARKETISATION AND CHANGES IN PRIVATE GAINS AND COSTS FROM INFORMALITY**

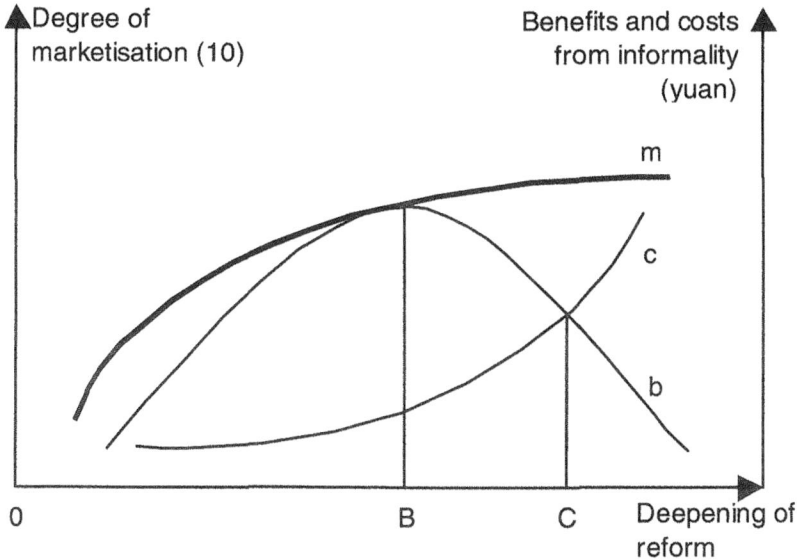

Source: Constructed from Song, 2001b. Behaviour of private enterprises in a partially reformed system—China, Paper presented at the 13th Conference of the Association for Chinese Economic Studies, (Australia), Wollongong University, Wollongong, 14–15 July: Figures 1 and 2.

are forced to change their behaviour. The private gains from exploiting informality reach their peak at point *B*. If economic transformation is to be successful, this peak level of private benefits from exploiting informality must be reached at some point in the process of reform.

After point *B*, even a small dose of reform that could only marginally raise the degree of marketisation (as shown by the shape of the *m* curve), could lead to a substantial (accelerated) fall in the benefits of informality (as shown by a decline of *b*). Another factor contributing to declining net benefit is the steadily rising costs (penalties) (represented by the cost curve *c* in Figure 7.3).

As market institutions are gradually established, the costs associated with unproductive entrepreneurial activities become higher (*c*). Furthermore, the probability of being caught for exploiting informality (for example, conducting unproductive activities illegally) becomes higher than before, causing the two curves to converge after point B. In response to these changes in the relative pay-off, entrepreneurs will pay more attention to the way they operate in order to minimise the costs associated with exploiting informality. From a dynamic point of view, a quickened reform program will lead to a faster convergence of the two curves as shown in Figure 7.3.

Eventually, the cost curve will intersect with the benefit curve at some point (point *C*). After that point, the costs associated with exploiting informality will surpass the benefits of conducting these activities. Not only that, after the intersection point, costs increase at a higher rate while benefits decelerate sharply (so even a small dose of reform at this stage can have profound effects).

The declining (increasing) trend of private gains (costs) resulting from a shift from informality to formality has become a mechanism in forcing entrepreneurs to direct more entrepreneurial resources away from unproductive to productive activities by changing their behaviour to be more in line with the requirements of a rules-based system. In reality, many enterprises, especially larger ones and those with foreign partners, have recognised the need for more formality to resolve the incentive problems that have plagued private entrepreneurs. A shift from informality to formality will help pave the way for more solid growth of private enterprises.

The evidence from China suggests that the development of private enterprise has exerted the strongest force for institutional changes (such as those to do with property rights, rules and regulations). This has occurred through an interaction between private enterprise development and government (institutional) adjustment, although the government's role has been fairly passive. Informal private enterprises have slowly become more formal as laws and regulations have been established. At the end of the 1990s, this transformation started to go beyond the private sector to affect SOE restructuring, fiscal policy and reforms of the financial and banking systems.

When further institutional changes occurred in response to this private sector development, including laws and regulations and ultimately a constitutional amendment acknowledging the role of private enterprise in the economy, a further burst of activity occurred in response to the changed social and economic environment. Institutional changes brought greater formality, leading to a rapid fall in the number of 'red hat' firms, a substantial increase in the number of private enterprises that has been transformed from collectives, a faster pace of SOE privatisation and increases in the number of private start-up private enterprises, especially in high-tech industries.

LEVEL PLAYING FIELD

The importance of the domestic private sector in meeting the challenges of WTO entry derives from a principle that is fundamental to the WTO, namely the requirement of 'national treatment'. In many areas, such as taxation treatment and market entry, domestic private enterprises have been treated less favourably than SOEs and foreign firms. One prominent area is bank lending to private enterprises, which requires fundamental reform of SOBs as well as development of the non-state banking sector in order to put private enterprises on an equal footing with others (Song 2001b).

The private sector's access to bank loans has been extremely limited. Table 7.2 shows that in the fourth quarter of 1999 private enterprises received only 0.6 per cent of all bank loans, and less than 0.5 per cent of all loans from state banks. This is despite the fact that private enterprises contributed nearly 35 per cent of industrial output in 1998.[1]

The discrepancy between the private sector's share of output and its share of bank finance suggests the extent of its latent demand for credit. Unable to obtain loans from the state banks and with limited access to equity markets, private enterprises have had to rely on self-finance or informal sources of financing, usually at much higher interest rates. A recent survey suggested that financial constraints may be influencing the investment behaviour of private enterprises—especially small and medium-sized enterprises (SMEs)[2]—in that firms tie investment demand to the availability of internal funds (Gregory et al. 2000; Garnaut et al. 2001).

Another obstacle to obtaining formal finance is that private firms find it difficult to communicate information about themselves to financial intermediaries.[3] Financial institutions, particularly SOBs, have little experience in assessing credit risk or the potential for profitable investment opportunities. And, even if banks do price risk correctly, the controls on interest rates prevent them from charging higher interest rates. Higher transaction costs are involved in lending to private enterprises because there is a need to monitor the competence of entrepreneurs and the return on the investment and there is a greater risk of default. For these and other reasons, long-term loans are not offered to private enterprises.

The distorted interest rate structure and bias toward lending to state enterprises has tended to reduce the net worth of non-state enterprises (which have paid much higher interest rates for informal financing) and has hampered their prospects of becoming creditworthy borrowers. This highlights the importance of developing a

TABLE 7.2   **BANK LENDING TO PRIVATE ENTERPRISES, 1999 (RMB 100 MILLION, PER CENT)**

Items	Jan–Mar	Apr–Jun	Jul–Sept	Oct–Dec
State banks				
Total loans	69,409.2	71,589.5	73,757.3	73,695.9
Loans to private sector	222.8	256.5	282.7	301.0
(per cent)	0.3	0.4	0.4	0.4
All banks				
Total loans	87,825.5	90,620.3	93,390.4	93,734.3
Loans to private sector	483.5	518.1	556.0	579.1
(per cent)	0.6	0.6	0.6	0.6

Notes: These figures are end-of-quarter balances. Loans made to private enterprises include loans to sole proprietors.
Source: Calculated from Tables 3.7 and 3.8 in *Quarterly Statistical Bulletin*, January 2001, Vol. XVII:89–90.

non-state banking sector and increasing competition to meet the needs of the large pool of unsatisfied borrowers. What is required is reform to build a financial system that can transfer the resources currently locked up in the state sector to the emerging private sector, which is better able to generate growth.

There are two main approaches to increasing competition in the financial sector in order to meet the demands of the private sector for funding. One is to privatise the SOBs, and the other is to allow more non-state, including private, financial institutions to enter the financial sector. The latter approach appears to be more feasible in China. The existing non-state banking sector can help resolve the lack of incentives for SOBs to act commercially. In order for this strategy to work, an effective institutional structure must be in place that imposes financial discipline on the decentralised banks. Financial institutions must be subject to tight prudential control by the financial authorities to ensure the safety and stability of the financial system.

The non-state banking sector consists of small and medium-sized banking institutions (joint-equity commercial banks, city commercial banks and the prefecture-level urban credit cooperatives), foreign banks, rural credit cooperatives, trust and investment corporations, and finance and leasing companies. At the end of 1999, there were 10 joint-equity commercial banks, 90 city commercial banks, 836 urban credit cooperatives, 41,755 rural credit cooperatives, 238 trust and investment corporations, 70 finance companies and 15 leasing companies in China (PBC 2000:24–5). China has no true private banks. The non-state financial institutions accounted for 31 per cent of the banking sector's total assets at the end of 1999 (see Figure

FIGURE 7.4   **ASSETS DISTRIBUTION OF FINANCIAL INSTITUTIONS**
              (END OF 1999)

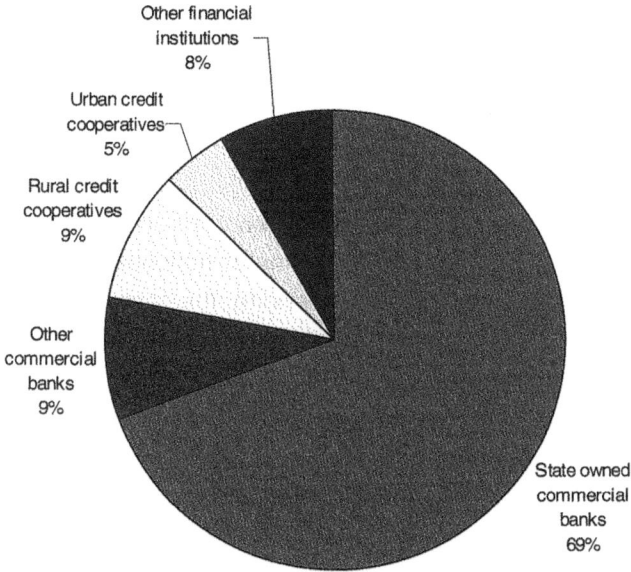

Source: Figure 9, in *Quarterly Statistical Bulletin*, January 2001, Volume XVII:64.

7.4). These institutions have played an important role in fostering more enterprise equality by enhancing competition and providing much-needed investment finance to the non-state sector.

After studying various countries' experiences with financial sector liberalisation, Zank concludes that

> much of the economic activity that should take place in developing countries does not occur because of the constraints placed on private sector activity or the preferences given to SOEs. If these constraints are removed, the playing field will be levelled, and new participants could begin to take part, leading to increased economic growth (1990:37).

China is facing exactly the same problem with market fragmentation, and a shift in the distribution of assets from state to non-state financial institutions is likely to result in a marked increase in bank lending to the private sector.

China has just begun the process of establishing a financial system that will allow borrowing and lending to be undertaken at market-determined interest rates. Price distortions will be gradually removed through an ordered program of interest rate liberalisation. Only when prices reflect the true economic scarcity of financial resources can resources (including foreign capital after the capital account is liberalised) be channelled into most profitable investment opportunities. The further development of the real economy, especially with regard to the private economy, therefore depends on the reform of the financial sector.

ROLE OF THE GOVERNMENT

The development of the private economy needs new rules and new roles for government. The old role of the government as a planner is no longer relevant. Realising the importance of the private sector in the economy, the government has adopted various measures to overcome the constraints facing the private sector. For example, it has tried to define and enforce property rights, and put SOEs on level terms with private enterprises in many areas. China's entry to the WTO helps with an understanding of what government should and should not do with regard to the development of the private economy.

In order to define clearly the role of government in supporting the development of private enterprises, especially small and medium-size enterprises (SMEs), Mousley (2001) distinguished three type of firms. Type I firms are small and labour-intensive firms. Government support to those firms should mainly seek to reduce the costs of formalisation in terms of getting permits, licensing and taxation, while increasing the cost of corruption. Type II firms are labour-intensive firms. Government support for these firms should be in the areas of eliminating corruption and anti-competitive behaviour. Type III firms are knowledge-intensive and fast-growing firms. Government support for these firms should be in the areas of the trade and foreign investment regime, removing barriers to entry, providing telecom infrastructure, and guaranteeing intellectual property rights.

Mousley further distinguished three stages of development: entry, operation and exit. At the entry stage, registration, licences and permits, taxation, and unofficial fees and levies are the most important concerns. At the operation stage, financial policies, the legal system and regulation, property rights, trade, exchange rate and labour policies, inspections, government procurement, and unofficial fees and levies are the areas of concern. At the exit stage, when a firm is forced to stop operation, bankruptcy laws, equity markets, the judicial system, and unofficial fees and levies may be the most important areas for reform.

Government intervention is usually justified on the grounds that there are market failures. If market failure is caused by information asymmetry such as in the case of banking lending to private enterprises, however, it can not easily be remedied by government intervention. Evidence shows that there is a tendency for local governments to try to do too much by involving themselves in microeconomic management, resulting in low efficiency and larger government. For example, in response to the need for funding for private enterprises, especially SMEs, many loan guarantee funds have been established by local governments nation-wide. These guarantee funds should be carefully designed to ensure private agents take the central role in bearing risk. It is best if private owners are involved in management, as well as contributing to the funds. Here, the government should be a facilitator, not a substitute for private enterprises themselves.

The government should also avoid giving unequal treatment to different firms through extension of preferential treatment to some firms. The role of the government should be to level the playing field, not to create uneven competition. In proposing a role for government in supporting the development of private enterprises, especially SMEs, it should be kept in mind that the market works better than government most of the time because decentralised individual decision making is generally better informed and more efficient than government decision making (Yao 2001). The government's main job is to build a transparent and enforceable legal and regulatory system to ensure market order.

CONCLUSIONS

Although tremendous challenges lie ahead in carrying out the main reform, much progress has been made in institutional reform and this appears likely to continue. In recent years, there have been clear signs that the government is serious about implementing deeper institutional reforms to accommodate the development of private enterprise. More private enterprises have been given export and import licenses and access to loans, and have been allowed to invest in a greater number of sectors. Rules and regulations that impede private investment, such as those on taxation, land use, business registration, domestic and overseas listings, and imports and exports, are being phased out.

The reform measures adopted by the government in response to private sector demands have not been radical, but have been sufficient to make a substantial impact on the economic structure of the economy. With the mounting urgency of

SOE reform and the imperatives resulting from China's accession to the WTO, the government now needs to make radical changes to foster private enterprise. There is evidence that reforms have been accelerating.

Notes

[1] See Figure 5.2 and Figure 2.4 in (Gregory et al. 2000:46, 17).

[2] The latest estimate is that there are now 8 million SMEs in China and that they constitute 99 per cent of all enterprises. SMEs contribute 76 per cent of industrial output, 60 per cent of output, 40 per cent of tax revenue, 60 per cent of exports and 75 per cent of urban employment (*People's Daily*, Overseas Edition, 2 August 2001).

[3] This is partly due to the problems of private enterprises themselves, such as non-transparent reporting systems and lack of creditworthiness.

8

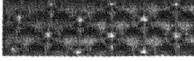

Services driving growth

Christopher Findlay and Mari Pangestu

China has made substantial commitments to liberalisation in the service sector. At the time of full implementation, these commitments are generally more extensive than those that any other group of economies made during the Uruguay Round. Even at the time of accession, China's commitments are substantial. Commitments of this extent suggest there will be substantial gains to liberalisation in the service sector and the dynamic effects of services liberalisation, we expect, will be an important driver of growth in China.

The extent and impact of China's service sector commitments are reviewed in this chapter. We outline the commitments made by China in the accession process and compare them to the GATS commitments by other countries. We illustrate some of these impacts by reference to particular sectors (although see other chapters for discussion of issues in the financial services sector).

We also comment on some of the key issues in the implementation of services sector commitments, including the capacity of local governments to meet the expectations created in the rest of the world by WTO accession, the problems of meeting domestic expectations of service obligations and the nature of the some of the key regulatory questions that might arise.

IMPEDIMENTS AND COMMITMENTS

China has made substantial commitments to liberalisation of the service sector in the accession process. Work comparing China's commitments in terms of the structure of the GATS shows that China's count coverage (the proportion of sectors and modes of supply in which commitments are made) is 'much higher than any other group of countries (including high income countries)' (Mattoo 2001). Mattoo reports a comparison of the extent of China's commitments based on a representative sample of service sectors as defined in the GATS. The comparison includes all four modes of supply for these sectors (that is, cross-border supply, consumption abroad, commercial presence, and the presence of natural persons).

The comparison of commitments includes consideration of commitments on market access and on national treatment. Market access in the GATS is defined in terms of types of policy which are prohibited, and by illustration of a number of limitations—on the number of suppliers, on the value of service transactions or assets, the number of operations or the quantity of output, the number of people that can be employed, and measures which restrict the type of legal entity which might be used to supply the service. These are measures affecting access to the market by both domestic and foreign suppliers. There is also reference under the market access provision to limitation of participation of foreign capital. The national treatment provision requires that Members accord suppliers of other Members treatment no less favourable than that accorded to its 'own like services and service suppliers' (Article XVII). Commitments only apply in sectors which are scheduled in the GATS commitments and in any such sector Members can record limitations on either market access or national treatment in each mode of supply.

China at the time of accession has made at least partial market access commitments of some kind in nearly all sectors sampled in the work reported by Mattoo for all modes (although less so for cross border supply). But if focus is the point in time when all the commitments are implemented (seven years after accession) then the extent of China's commitments is 'much higher than the commitments offered in the Uruguay Round by any other group of countries (including high income countries)'. The extent of commitments to full liberalisation was also higher than that of any other group of developing economies.

A further important component of China's commitments is the provision in its commitments of full national treatment. These are also wider (covering more sectors) and deeper (higher level of commitments to openness, that is, fewer limitations recorded) than those of all other country groups. For further detail of China's sectoral commitments in relation to commercial establishment in the services sector, and the treatment of foreign suppliers, see Chapter 9 in this volume.

Mattoo reviews the nature of the restrictions that do remain. He observes that China has adopted the standard commitments on the movement of natural persons, that is, entry is only guaranteed for managers or specialists (either intra-corporate transfers or people employed by foreign invested enterprises) or services salespersons on business visits. There is no commitment to other types of movement of natural persons, such as unskilled labour or movement of people which is not linked to a commercial presence.

With respect to commercial presence, Mattoo notes that restrictions imposed include rules on the form of establishment, on geographic scope, and on business scope. There might also be other regulatory requirements, such as a rule requiring a foreign establishment to have a certain amount of assets.

IMPACT

It is possible in the processes of the GATS that commitments made in international negotiation may have a relatively small impact, since as a result of the negotiating process, economies may be binding but not changing the current state of policy. This is not to deny that the process of binding has substantial value, including the reduction of risks of future policy changes, and the greater confidence among foreign entrants in the openness of the policy regime.

There is however a limited amount of evidence of the overall pattern of impediments in the service sector in China, which might be used to assess the extent of liberalisation implied by the difference between current policy and the commitments. There is some evidence from the telecommunications sector that China has been an outlier in terms of the high level of impediment (Warren 2000).

Building on joint work by the ANU and the Productivity Commission (Findlay and Warren 2000), and in preparation of a data base for modelling work, Dee and Hanslow (2000a) divided impediments into two types, those affecting establishing and those affecting the operations of services firms. They also identified impediments which applied to all firms and those which only applied to foreign firms. Both domestic and foreign firms in China were estimated to face high barriers to entry and significant restrictions on operations. The extent of these restrictions can be expressed in terms of a tax, either on output in the case of restrictions on operations, or on income from capital in the case of restrictions on entry. Their assessment is that for the services sector as a whole, domestic firms face a tax on output of 19 per cent, which is equivalent to the restrictions on operations, and a tax of 124 per cent on income from capital to reflect limits on rights of establishment. Foreign firms faced additional barriers, as evident in margins of discrimination equivalent to an

18 percentage point tax on output, due to restrictions on operations, and a 127 percentage point tax on income from capital, reflecting restrictions on establishment. The next highest set of margins is that for Indonesia, for example, a 40 percentage point tax on income from capital to reflect restrictions on establishment.

The size of the welfare gains associated with services liberalisation are large (Dee and Hanslow 2000b). They report that out of total worldwide gains from eliminating all post-Uruguay Round barriers, about 19 per cent are associated with agriculture, 31 per cent with manufacturing and 50 per cent with services. Of the global services gain in their model, just over three quarters is associated with the full liberalisation of the service sector in China. They stress that these gains are associated with the liberalisation of the FDI mode of supply of services as well as cross border trade, and not just the latter. This simulation applies to full liberalisation in China, not just China's accession offers.

Liberalisation commitments in services contribute direct gains to China, as noted above in terms of the modelling results, but a more open services sector also complements reform in other sectors. Access to cheaper intermediate services reduces the biases against other export-oriented sectors and facilitates the participation of other sectors in world markets.

The service sectors themselves are often noted for the intensity with which they use other sectors. Service sector commitments can therefore have significant effects in terms of the international orientation of the whole sector. For example, lower cost telecommunications services reduce the bias against the provision of some labour-intensive services (data entry for instance) in the cross border supply mode. An efficient transport and telecommunications system is a key element in the growth of the tourism sector in China. Dee and Hanslow (2000a) also show that the greatest unit cost impost from services trade barriers actually falls on the services sector itself. Therefore the benefits of services trade liberalisation are likely to be concentrated in that sector.

Services sector barriers inhibit entry and reduce supply, creating the scope to earn rents in this sector. An indication of the extent of this effect is available from Hoekman (1999) who reports estimates of average gross operating margins of 50 per cent for all services in China on average, compared to 28 per cent for manufacturing.

Dee and Hanslow report that, in the particular experiment they design, some large industrial economies actually lose from services liberalisation. They explain this result by pointing out that their welfare measure is based on national income, from whatever source (the home economy or the host economy of an offshore project). Services liberalisation leads to a relocation of the capital stock with consequent effects on income. It also affects the rents available in services markets. When liberalisation reduces those rents, then foreign investors can be made worse off. In this particular experiment the scale of these effects is large, because it is assumed that the effects of the barriers to create rents rather than lead to higher costs (that is, the tax equivalents are captured by firms operating in the protected markets).

A different specification would lead to a different set of welfare results. However this experiment does highlight the impact of protection on rents in this sector, the possibility that those rents will be captured by investors operating in these protected markets, and that those investors will include foreigners. Liberalisation which reduces the size of those transfers can lead to substantial welfare effects in the host economy. This consideration is important in the design of policy in China and the value of completing the transition to full implementation of services commitments.

Further evidence of the impact of reform can be illustrated from work in progress in particular sectors. Luo and Findlay (2001) have examined the extent of commitments in the group of activities that make up the logistics sector. They find that a more open market for logistics services in China which transfers the technology for the redesign and management of integrated services is likely to have significant effects on total logistics costs in China. The savings are associated not so much with the fall in the costs of transport (which has already experienced domestic deregulation) but to the application of systems which reduce the costs of warehousing, storage and damage to goods. They estimate that the savings could amount to as much as 10 per cent of the wholesale price of manufactured goods in China. The effect could be even larger for fresh food where the importance of logistics costs in prices at wholesale level is even higher.

In the logistics sectors, there is evidence already of substantial foreign presence in anticipation of further opening up of the market. Most of the major global players have some form of operation in China. In telecommunications, there is a different story. Foreign investors are likely to review and assess China's policy in this sector carefully. The caps on the extent on foreign ownership and the geographic limitations on foreign activities may not be the main problem. A major issue at this stage is reported to be the lack of specificity on the regulations for foreign investors in the sector. Meanwhile, foreign investment will be more likely concentrated at the high end or some special segment of basic telecom and value-added services, and as strategic partners, or in alliance with existing operators. Therefore it is unlikely that competition will flourish just because of WTO accession. Furthermore, there is no requirement that the licensing procedure currently used will need to be eliminated. Foreign entrants and their new ventures will still need to go through the licensing procedure, which will remain at the discretion of the government agencies.

Another issue related to entry into the markets is the dominance of the two market leaders, despite the recent mandates to provide entrants with access to leased lines. In fact, it is because this access was so expensive in the past that a number of other organisations developed their own internal networks for communication purposes. This includes the PLA, which developed Great Wall Communications ultimately transferred over to Unicom, and the Ministry of Rail, whose Railcom has recently become operational and begun offering services to the general public.

In addition to these, the State Power Commission, and other state ministries also have built their own internal networks throughout the decades and are eager to obtain licenses to enter the lucrative telecom service market. Many of these organisations realised that once the market does open up to foreign investment, they would be prime targets for capital injections that would facilitate their restructuring and reform processes, and create substantial potential for gains in the future if they were to become a viable network supporting telecom services.

In the goods sector, restrictions on foreign entry would lead to higher domestic prices and larger domestic production. The protected sector would then account for a larger share of domestic output. But despite these restrictions on foreign entry, the service sector in China appears to be relatively underdeveloped. China's services share of output is only 33 per cent, which is low compared to the standards of other developing APEC economies.[1]

A number of factors could contribute to the observation of a low services share of output. Services are delivered through the presence of the producer, so discrimination against foreigners also has the effect of reducing investment in the service sector in the economy applying that policy. Furthermore, there are also significant impediments which apply to all potential entrants into the services markets, not just foreign suppliers.

China has confirmed that WTO rules apply to SOEs. As a result, decisions by those enterprises on purchasing and sales are expected to be guided by commercial considerations. In the agreement with the United States, subsidies to an industry sector which are received predominantly by SOEs could trigger action under US unfair trade laws. While considerable progress has been made dealing with reform issues associated with the SOEs in goods production (Drysdale 2000), there remain many SOEs operation in the service sector. The services negotiations on market access will add to the competitive constraints on those firms.

The impact of reform in the service sector also generates extensive real gains. This is because the impacts on real incomes are greater than those of the removal of a tax, for example, the impact of which includes transfer effects. When logistics costs, for example, are reduced resources are saved (the rectangle effects are gains, not just transfers, see Deardorff 2001).

Services reform can also contribute to a wider distribution of the effects of and gains from liberalisation. In the logistics sector, for example, a more efficient transport system creates a more integrated domestic market, and reduces the costs of trading in to the world market. The consequence is that, as full implementation is reached, the degree of openness is increased across the whole of China. The distribution of the gains from liberalisation is also widened. However, this effect is not universal. Issues remain concerning access to telecommunications services which we discuss below.

LESS-DEVELOPED REGIONS AND LIBERALISATION

Luo and Findlay (2001) point out that logistics efficiency is vital to the development of the less-developed regions. Reducing the costs of doing business between the so-called poor areas and the outside areas (both the relatively developed coastal areas and overseas) will promote trade. It will also promote investment projects in the poor areas, either for manufacturing or resource exploitation.

People living in poor areas can benefit from a more efficient logistics sector in a number of ways. First their terms of trade will improve. The costs of items they buy from the rest of China will be less. The prices they receive for the items they export to the rest of China will be higher. Work in other developing economies suggests the orders of magnitude of these effects can be high (Limao and Venables 2001).

The opening up of markets due to improvements in transport and logistics services can also have effects on competition in the local markets. Competition has a number of effects.

One is the impact on the rents available. Suppliers who previously had monopoly power are constrained by the options of supply from outside the region. Thus regulatory reform not only lowers costs but its competitive effects forces the passing on of those cost reductions to consumers in business and in households. Firms which previously earned rents from their protected position are clearly worse off but overall the region will show a welfare gain from the introduction of competition. In term of the welfare of the group of people living in the poor area, this effect is even larger when those who captured the rents were not local firms.

Another effect of competition, and a greater 'foreign' (both out of the country and out of the region) presence in all markets within a poor area, could be a dynamic one, for example, on the transfer of technology and productivity growth. This effect is likely to be greater in those services markets where an establishment is required to deliver the activity, and where therefore there is more interaction between the new supplier and local firms.

These are the kinds of dynamic effects which, in addition to the real income gains available immediately from reform, will be important drivers of growth in China. Furthermore, the development of a more efficient set of services which link the now isolated and underdeveloped areas with other markets inside and outside China is essentially providing an alternative to more extensive relocation of people from those areas that might otherwise be required.

ISSUES IN IMPLEMENTATION[2]

There are some issues in the nature of the commitments and their application in China. As noted above, a number of types of restrictions are evident in China's commitments. One is the restriction on the form of entity used in commercial presence, particularly in terms of the requirements to use joint ventures, and the timing of permission to establish completely foreign owned enterprises.

These arrangements for a transition impose costs on China. They delay the benefits of reform. Some motivations for this approach could include an attempt to capture some of the rents created in the transition to full openness, to slow down the transition and therefore (it is hoped) reducing the costs of adjustment (the consequence may be to delay those costs and add to the risks of backsliding) or simply to limit for a longer time foreign ownership in sectors about which there is domestic political sensitivity related to foreign participation.

The commitments also restrain in some cases the geographic distribution of entry (in professional services, telecommunications, and insurance for example). These generally restrict foreign entry to areas already relatively well developed. The motivation is presumably to provide a longer transition to local firms which it is

118

judged are less able to face foreign competition. However the cost to consumers could be substantial and as Mattoo points out the policy could make worse existing regional inequalities. Mattoo is also concerned that some regions will not have the chance to develop as a regional hub since the sequencing of openness combined with the agglomeration effects important in some service activities might lead to particular irreversible decisions on location of operations.

Another issue is the difference between policy at national level and that at local level. There is some evidence that while commitments to openness are made at national level, a number of aspects of local administrative processes can be used to retain discrimination against foreign (including those from other parts of China) suppliers.

The sequencing of reform and the differences between the stages of reform across provinces and between levels of government adds to the chances that China will be drawn into more trade quarrels on the grounds that the application of policy was not consistent with China's WTO commitments. Once accession occurs, then these quarrels could be resolved in the WTO dispute settlement system, which following the Uruguay Round operates in a much more judicial manner. Worse, these quarrels could be the subject of bilateral actions, such as the US 'Special 301' cases. A review of issues in US–China trade highlights the significance of these issues. The author nominated this question as a 'major barrier', which was described in the following way

> China's trade laws and regulations are often secretly formulated, unpublished, unevenly en-
> forced, and may vary across provinces, making it difficult for exporters to determine what
> rules and regulations apply to their products. In addition, foreign firms find it difficult to gain
> access to government trade rule-making agencies to appeal new trade rules and regulations.
> (Morrison 2001:6).

Clearly there is some value in considering strategy for developing processes to transit the commitments made at national level to local government levels.

Another issue is the importance of the design of policy on universal service obli-
gations. Some areas may remain beyond the reach of the foreign suppliers—areas not well served by physical infrastructure will not gain from world class logistics services in fresh food markets. Similar issues arise in the telecommunications sector. There is value in attention to the design of policy on service obligations in these areas. Experiences in the rest of the world will be valuable, and this work could be another focus in capacity building programs. These issues are especially

important in China with respect, for example, to road and rail transport and also access to the telecommunications system.

Box 8.1 includes material on the current situation with respect to this issue in telecommunications.

There has been discussion of a plan to set up a universal service fund that will be used for developing the western and rural regions that currently lag far behind its eastern coastal counterparts. However, it remains unclear who and how contributions to the fund will be made, and how they will in turn be disbursed.

In a recent presentation, Gruen (2001) has raised a number of questions and options for consideration of the management of these obligations. Gruen highlights the value of reconsidering the popular approach to a service obligation policy. Common is the use of cross-subsidies between consumer groups applied to provide specific services (for example, a rail link) to all residents in a particular area. An alternative is to provide services to well-defined target households so that the recipients have options for the manner in which they receive that support. Recipients might even be able to 'cash out' for example, or at least substitute between types of services. Gruen also discusses the value of broadening the funding base for service obligation policies, such as raising revenue in the general tax base. A further issue is introduction a competitive process that will generate new ideas about exploit-

BOX 8.1   **<u>UNIVERSAL SERVICE OBLIGATIONS IN TELECOMMUNICATIONS</u>**

Officially, the current rate of fixed-line phone ownership for China on average is still barely over 20 per cent of the population, while only 10 per cent of the population has access to mobile phones. However, some indicators point towards a much lower rate of teledensity in rural areas at around 6 per cent. The relevant authorities so far have not given any explicit universal service mandate to either of the two telecom companies who are the market leaders in China. They are more concerned at this point with creating a globally competitive industry than with providing universal service. Their aim, apparently, is to popularise the services through significant reductions for both calling and connection fees, as well as by eliminating installation costs altogether.

Yet, there remain large areas of the country in which the basic infrastructure for telecommunication connectivity still do not exist. In many remote areas out west, telephone poles have been set up along side roads, but remain unconnected. At the same time, mobile stations are limited to serving only the large cities. And while Internet can be very reasonably priced in the cities (averaging about RMB4 per hour in internet cafes in western cities) illiteracy remains the chief obstacle to their uptake in many of the western regions where Chinese is still the second language. There has been discussion of a plan to set up a universal service fund that will be used for developing the western and rural regions that currently lag far behind its eastern coastal counterparts. However, it remains unclear who and how contributions to the fund will be made, and how they will in turn be disbursed.

ing technological change to provide services or bundles of services at lower cost.

Finally, the capacity to implement new domestic regulatory arrangements consistent with the goals of the liberalisation program is another important question. Again, the experience in the rest of the world in the design of access regimes will be valuable. An important reference point will be the set of principles specified in the WTO's Telecommunications Reference Paper[3] which refer to prevention of anti-competitive practices, the terms on interconnectivity, the right to develop a universal service policy, processes for managing licensing and the allocation of scarce resources like frequencies. The principles also refer to the importance of having a regulatory body which is independent of any supplier of basic telecommunications services. Mattoo points out that China has accepted these principles for telecommunications and, of most note so far, is establishing an independent regulatory body. He also argues that similar approach should be taken with respect to energy services and transport infrastructure.

CONCLUSION

China stands to reap substantial gains from services reform. The implementation of liberalisation will also have significant intersectoral effects, given the intensity with which other goods and services sectors consume services as an intermediate input. As these effects emerge, the services liberalisation is making an important indirect contribution to the liberalisation program. It does so by removing impediments to growth in new areas of specialisation and providing options for employment of resources displaced from other sectors in the adjustments that occur during implementation in all sectors of WTO commitments. The services commitments also have important implications for removing impediments to the integration of people now located in relatively poor areas in the domestic and the international markets. Access to markets which services liberalisation supports is a critical driver of development.

China's commitments on services are extensive and there is some evidence that policy is shifting from a relatively high starting level of impediments. The reforms will have both immediate effects on prices and the distribution of gains between producers and consumers, but also services reform stands to generate important longer term dynamic effects. The result will be an important contribution to the drivers of growth in China.

However, there are substantial issues in implementation. We illustrated some of the difficulties of moving from a high-level impediments to more open markets by reference to the telecommunications sector. The impact of reform, on the other hand, appears to be more predictable in the logistics sector. While in principle reform in the services sector will generate significant real income effects and make contributions to growth through the sorts of dynamic impacts noted above, there are also likely to be significant differences in the rate and effectiveness of the implementation of the commitments between sectors. Disappointed expectations among foreign suppliers will lead to further discussion or even dispute with China over the implementation process.

These are not the only concerns about implementation of the commitments. Some additional implementation issues include the resistance to change that might be found at local government level, the operation of policy with respect to meeting universal service obligations, and the design of the necessary institutions for domestic regulation. With respect to the institutional development required to respond to these issues, there are clearly valuable inclusions in the development of any capacity building programs designed to facilitate the implementation process in China.

Acknowledgments

Findlay's contribution to this chapter was supported in part by a grant from the Australian Research Council

Notes

[1] The low share could also be due to recording problems, for example, the lack of access to data on the activities of small firms in rural areas, and to the role of state owned enterprises in the provision of services to staff.

[2] There are also important issues in the application in some cases of grandfather provisions. See the chapter on insurance by Ken Waller in this volume.

[3] Availalable at http://www.wto.org/english/tratop_e/serv_e/telecom_e/tel23_e.htm

9

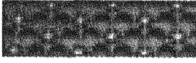

The impact of WTO accession on FDI

Chen Chunlai

FDI in China has been one of the most significant features of China's economic reform and opening up to the outside world. The gradual liberalisation of restrictions on FDI since 1979, and the government's commitment to further opening, have greatly improved the investment environment. Foreign firms have been attracted by the huge domestic market and pool of relatively well-educated, low-cost labour, making China one of the most attractive destinations for FDI in the world. By the end of 2001, China had attracted a total of over US$390 billion in FDI inflows, making it the largest FDI recipient among developing economies and the second largest FDI recipient in the world.

In the WTO negotiation agreements, China agreed to reduce tariff and non-tariff barriers to trade in agriculture, manufactured goods, and services, remove a number of restrictions on FDI particularly in services, and improve protection of intellectual property rights.

Very few studies have incorporated investment or financial liberalisation in their estimation of FDI inflows after China's WTO accession. The most common results of these studies are that China's WTO accession would have a positive impact on its GDP growth, mainly through efficiency gains resulting from trade and investment liberalisation, and China's WTO accession would accelerate FDI inflows into China and increase the foreign ownership share in China's assets.

WTO AGREEMENTS RELATING TO FDI AND CHINA'S FDI POLICY

The Agreement on Trade-Related Investment Measures (TRIMs) was achieved in the Uruguay Round multilateral negotiations of GATT. The overriding objective of the TRIMs Agreement is to promote the expansion and progressive liberalisation of world trade and to facilitate investment across international frontiers so as to increase the economic growth of all trading partners, particularly developing economy members, while ensuring free competition.

Because of the difficulties associated with bringing discipline to investment into the international trading framework, the TRIMs agreement has emerged as the shortest and most limited of the WTO agreements, with only nine Articles plus an Illustrative List. The TRIMs agreement applies to investment measures related to trade in goods only. TRIMs themselves are not defined. Instead, the Illustrative List of measures which are deemed to be WTO-inconsistent refers to measures which are mandatory or enforceable under domestic law or administrative ruling, or compliance. A TRIM may fall into at least one of the following five categories

- a firm is required to source a specified minimum proportion of its purchases from local sources (local content requirement
- a firm is required to achieve a specified import–export ratio in relation to local product embedded in the exports (trade balancing requirement)
- a firm's level of imports in relation to its export or local production (trade balancing restriction)
- a firm's access to foreign exchange is restricted (foreign exchange balancing restrictions)
- a firm's level of exports is restricted (export restrictions).

The most significant provisions of the TRIMs agreement relate to national treatment, elimination of quantitative restrictions, notification and transparency, and transitional arrangements. The TRIMs agreement has a number of positive elements. First, the adoption of specific investment-related disciplines should help to bring a greater degree of predictability into international investment flows. Second, it will improve the level of certainty for investors abroad by limiting the scope for governments to attach onerous conditions to investment approvals or to link them to the receipt of other advantages. Investors will also have the certainty that the notified TRIMs will be eliminated within a specified time period. Third, the agreement provides a greater level of transparency in investment rules through notification of

WTO-inconsistent rules and through advice of publications in which information on TRIMs at both the national and sub-national level may be found. Fourth, the agreement reinforces the interrelationship between trade and investment, by noting the possible need for more work in the future in investment and competition policy, thereby emphasising the interconnected nature of government policy, and enhancing consistency between policies. Finally, the TRIMs Agreement provides that the principles of national treatment and most-favoured nation (MFN) apply to the use of trade-related investment measures.

However, there are also limitations to the TRIMs agreement. The main limitation is that it does not provide a comprehensive list of WTO-inconsistent TRIMs but is instead limited to a subset of what are generally referred to as performance requirements. It is unclear just how complete the Illustrative List is, and whether other measures not on the list could be held to be inconsistent within TRIMs obligations. In addition, the agreement is limited to goods and so does not include services.

Although the TRIMs agreement is the most relevant part of WTO agreements for FDI, it is not the only WTO instrument which has a bearing on investment measures. Other relevant WTO agreements include the General Agreement on Trade in Services (GATS) and the Agreement on Trade-Related Aspects of Intellectual Property Rights (TRIPs).

The GATS sets out the rights and obligations for non-discriminatory services trade. While it does not explicitly refer to investment measures, it does implicitly include provisions on investment through references to commercial presence. Commercial presence is one of the four modes of supply identified in GATS (the other three are cross-border trade, movement of suppliers, and movement of natural persons). Commercial presence is defined as any type of business or professional establishment, including through the constitution, acquisition or maintenance of a juridical person or the creation or maintenance of a branch or a representative office, within the territory of a member for the purpose of supplying a service. Member countries are required to schedule their commitments to liberalisation in particular sectors (that is, to provide market access and national treatment) in terms of the four modes of supply. In addition, countries are required to apply the principle of MFN in all sectors. This means that even where countries do not specify greater liberalisation in particular sectors, the MFN obligation will still apply. Given the direct link between investment and establishing commercial presence, it is clear that further liberalisation will directly influence investment flows.

The agreement on TRIPs does not refer directly or even indirectly to investment. However, to the extent that foreign investment is related either to investment in products or process with an intellectual property content (that is, the value of the product is in part determined by the legal protection accorded to the intellectual property) or to licensing arrangements for technology transfer, decisions to invest may be affected by the level of intellectual property protection offered by the host government. The TRIPs agreement, which provides for minimum standards of protection and enforcement of intellectual property, may have some influence on the direction of investment flows.

FDI in China was prohibited prior to 1978. In order to achieve new objectives of economic growth and development, however, China began to relax restrictions on FDI into its domestic economy in 1979. Since then, the FDI regime has been liberalised gradually, especially since the early 1990s. Admittedly, China has achieved substantial progress in its FDI policy reform within a relatively short period. However, China's FDI policy regime still needs further liberalisation. On the one hand, China's current FDI policy is still relatively restricted in terms of FDI entry forms, foreign ownership shares, industry restrictions and performance requirements. On the other hand, China still extensively uses fiscal and other incentive policies to encourage some specific types of FDI; for example, export-oriented and technologically advanced FDI, and to induce FDI flows into some targeted regions and industries.

Table 9.1 presents an indicative list of China's current FDI policy relating to the key provisions of the TRIMs agreement. China's current FDI policy needs to be further improved in all aspects.

China has made substantial commitments in trade and investment liberalisation, especially in the automobile industry and services sector, and has agreed to comprehensively implement the TRIMs agreement after entering the WTO. Undoubtedly, the reduction in foreign investment barriers and liberalisation of the FDI regime will provide great opportunities for foreign investors to invest and operate business in China. Therefore, China's accession to the WTO will have a positive impact on China's FDI policy regime, particularly in the aspects of national treatment and transparency. Meanwhile, it will also help China to improve its competition policies, industrial policies and intellectual property rights protection and enforcement.

IMPACT ON FDI INFLOWS TO CHINA

FDI inflows into China grew steadily during the 1980s, but increased very rapidly in

TABLE 9.1   **KEY PROVISIONS OF TRIMS AGREEMENT AND CHINA'S CURRENT FDI POLICY**

Provisions of TRIMs agreement	China's current FDI policy
National treatment	Extensive restrictions in various sectors, particularly in services. Moving toward national treatment for incentives, which still favour foreign investors.
MFN status	Gives no preferences relating to the establishment, expansion and creation of foreign investment.
Performance requirement and restrictions	Requires local content in some industries. Requires technology transfer and a certain level of technology content in some technologically advanced industries. Requires research and development activities in some industries. Requires foreign exchange balancing for all foreign-invested firms. Requires export performance for export-oriented foreign invested firms. Prohibition from foreign investment in some industries. Restrictions on types of entry and ownership shares in various sectors. Business scope restrictions in most service sectors. Geographic restrictions in most service sectors.
Transparency	Extensive laws, regulations and guidelines relating to FDI. Requires significant documentation in the application process.

Source: Author's compilation.

the 1990s (Table 9.2). From 1979 to 2001, China attracted over US$390 billion in FDI inflows, making it the largest FDI recipient among the developing economies and the second largest FDI recipient in the world. However, FDI inflows into China slowed after 1997 and actually declined in 1999 and 2000. There was a moderate recovery in 2001.

The slowdown of FDI inflows into China in recent years could be explained by several factors. First, it is likely that high FDI inflows into China during the early 1990s were exceptional and will fall back to a more sustainable level in the long run. Second, there has been a slowdown from the surge in transfers of labour-intensive activities from neighbouring Asian economies. In addition, the East Asian financial crisis substantially weakened capability for outward investment of the Northeast and Southeast Asian economies. As a result, FDI flows into China from the

TABLE 9.2   **FDI INFLOWS INTO CHINA, 1979–2001**

Year	FDI inflows (US$ billion)	Year	FDI inflows (US$ billion)
1979	0.1	1991	4.4
1980	0.2	1992	11.0
1981	0.4	1993	27.5
1982	0.4	1994	33.8
1983	0.6	1995	37.5
1984	1.3	1996	41.7
1985	1.7	1997	45.3
1986	1.9	1998	45.5
1987	2.3	1999	40.3
1988	3.2	2000	40.7
1989	3.4	2001	46.9
1990	3.5	Total	393.4

Note: Data for 2001 are from the Ministry of Foreign Trade and Economic Cooperation (MOFTEC).
Source: State Statistical Bureau, various years. *Zhongguo Tongji Nianjian* (China Statistical Year-book), Zhongguo Tongji Chubanshe, Beijing.

Northeast and Southeast Asian economies have declined substantially since 1997. Third, market rates of return to investment in China have not been as high as foreign investors expected. In many cases foreign investors' high hopes for China's market have been slow to materialise. Informal relationships and corruption still hinder many business transactions by foreigners. In addition, inefficient SOEs still dominate many key sectors of the economy. Finally, there are still restrictions on FDI, such as on ownership shares, modes of FDI entry, and regional and sectoral restrictions.

Therefore, China's accession to the WTO comes at a very critical time when China is facing difficulties in sustaining a high level of FDI inflows. Could China's accession to the WTO revive the trend of a high level of FDI inflows and bring greater inflows?

McKibbin and Wilcoxen (1998) explored the impact of trade liberalisation and financial liberalisation on China's economy by using a dynamic intertemporal general equilibrium model (DIGEM). According to their study, under the trade liberalisation scenario, China's tariff cuts would improve economic efficiency and raise the overall return to capital, which would in turn increase foreign investment. Under the financial liberalisation scenario, financial flows into China would increase very quickly.

Walmsley and Hertel (2000) estimated the economic effects of China's WTO accession by using a dynamic GTAP model, which incorporates international capital mobility and ownership data. In their simulation, China's accession raises the rate of return to capital, thereby increasing foreign investment and capital stock, particularly in the first rive years following accession. Overall foreign ownership of China's capital increases relative to the baseline as a result of accession.

The United Nations Conference on Trade and Development (UNCTAD 2000) estimated that in the short term, China's WTO accession would have only a small effect on FDI flows into China, as investors adopt a wait-and-see attitude while reforms are being implemented. However, in the medium term, UNCTAD predicts FDI flows into China could increase from current levels of about US$40 billion to US$60 billion and possibly US$100 billion annually if cross-border mergers and acquisitions are allowed.

Goldman Sachs (1999) examined China's reported April 1999 offer to the United States and projected that China's WTO accession would significantly boost China's economic growth, foreign investment and trade. According to the study, trade liberalisation and greater openness would boost productivity, expanding GDP growth. China's total trade (exports plus imports) and FDI flows would nearly double by 2005.

How much FDI will flow into China after China's accession to the WTO? Obviously, no one knows the exact figure. However, a rough estimate would still be useful in a policy evaluation of the impact of WTO accession on FDI inflows into China. Chen Chunlai (2001), using an empirical model,[1] estimated future FDI inflows into China. According to the estimation (Table 9.3), after China's accession to the WTO, FDI inflows into China would increase moderately in the first two years, with annual FDI inflows around US$45 billion. Then inflows would increase rapidly and considerably. In the medium term (2005), annual FDI inflows into China would reach over US$60 billion, and in the long term (2010) roughly US$100 billion.

In summary, China's WTO accession would have a positive impact on FDI in China. It would accelerate FDI inflows into China and increase the foreign ownership share in China's assets. However, the answer to whether China will benefit from WTO entry and realise its potential in attracting FDI inflows after accession to the WTO, largely depends on how China implements the WTO agreements, fulfils its WTO commitments, further reduces and eliminates trade and investment barriers and opens up more domestic markets, manages internal economic reforms (particularly the reform of SOEs), and enforces the protection of intellectual property rights.

TABLE 9.3   **ESTIMATION OF FUTURE FDI INFLOWS INTO CHINA**

	Baseline scenario (US$ billion)	WTO scenario (US$ billion)	WTO over baseline (%)
2000	40.1	40.1	-
2001	42.1	43.9	4.2
2002	44.2	48.1	8.7
2003	46.5	' 52.7	13.4
2004	48.8	57.8	18.4
2005	51.2	63.3	23.8
2006	53.7	69.6	29.7
2007	56.3	76.6	35.9
2008	59.1	84.3	42.7
2009	62.0	93.0	50.1
2010	65.0	102.7	58.1

Source: Chen Chunlai, 2001. 'The implications of China's WTO accession for foreign direct investment in China', in *The Implications of TIL for China's Domestic Economic Development and Policies*, OECD, Paris.

IMPACT ON THE COMPOSITION OF FDI SOURCES

FDI in China comes from more than 100 economies across the world, but FDI into China has been overwhelmingly dominated by the developing economies, particularly the Asian newly industrialised economies (NIEs). In terms of individual investors, FDI in China has been dominated by four investors—Hong Kong, Taiwan, the United States and Japan.

As Table 9.4 shows, during the period 1983–2000, investment from developing economies dominated FDI in China, accounting for 74.2 per cent of the total accumulated FDI inflows. Among the developing source economies, as a group, the NIEs have been the largest investors, accounting for 64.7 per cent of the total. Within the NIEs, Hong Kong has held the dominant position, accounting for 49.6 per cent, followed by Taiwan (7.5 per cent). In contrast, in the same period, the accumulated FDI inflows from industrial source economies accounted for only 25.8 per cent of total FDI inflows into China. Among the industrial economies, the United States and Japan are the most important investors, each accounting for 8.6 per cent and 8.1 per cent respectively, while the combined share of the other industrial economies is 9.1 per cent. Apart from the United Kingdom, Germany and France, no other individual industrial economy has contributed more than 1 per cent of the total accumulated FDI inflows to China.

TABLE 9.4   **ACCUMULATED FDI INFLOWS INTO CHINA BY SOURCE ECONOMIES**

Source	Total FDI inflows 1983–2000 (US$billion)	Share 1983–2000 (%)
NIEs	222.3	64.7
Hong Kong	170.3	49.6
Taiwan	25.6	7.5
Singapore	16.3	4.8
South Korea	10.0	2.9
ASEAN	5.9	1.7
Japan	27.7	8.1
United States	29.7	8.6
West Europe	26.6	7.7
UK	8.5	2.5
Germany	5.7	1.7
France	4.1	1.2
Other industrial economies	4.6	1.3
Other Asia	4.7	1.3
East Europe	0.5	0.1
Latin America	14.7	4.3
Africa	0.8	0.2
Others	6.1	1.8
Developing economies	254.9	74.2
Industrial economies	88.5	25.8
Total	343.4	100

Note: Calculations are based on 1995 constant US dollar prices.
Sources: State Statistical Bureau, various years. *Zhongguo Tongji Nianjian* [China Statistical Yearbook], Zhongguo Tongji Chubanshe, Beijing.

Obviously the current composition of FDI sources in China needs to be diversified if China is to benefit more from FDI. The diversification of FDI sources is not only necessary for China to attract a greater quantity of FDI inflows, but is also important in order for China to attract high quality FDI inflows. China's accession to the WTO provides a great opportunity for China to improve and diversify its FDI sources and therefore will have a significant impact on the composition of FDI sources in China.

In general, with the implementation of trade and investment liberalisation after China's accession to the WTO, both developing and industrial economies would increase their investments in China as a result of the improvement of the overall investment environment and the reduction of trade and investment barriers in China.

For developing economies (mainly the NIEs), because they have moderate technological and innovative capabilities and are at a middle stage of economic development, the ownership advantages possessed by their enterprises are more concentrated in the forms of labour-intensive production technology, standardised manufactured products and well-established export market networks. Obviously, China, being relatively abundant in labour resources and having a comparative advantage in labour-intensive activities, is a very attractive location for developing economy investors, particularly for export-oriented FDI. After China's accession to the WTO, on the one hand, China will reduce trade and investment barriers and improve the investment environment; on the other hand, China's export markets will also be greatly enlarged as the member economies—particularly the industrial economies—will open more domestic markets for China's exports. Therefore, there are great incentives for developing country investors to increase total FDI in China in general and to increase export-oriented FDI in China in particular. It is expected that China will remain an important host economy for investment from developing economies, particularly the NIEs, after China's accession to the WTO.

In general, enterprises from economies with high technological and innovative capabilities and high overall economic development, will possess more ownership advantages in the forms of high technology, product differentiation, managerial and entrepreneurial skills, and knowledge-based intangible assets. Because of these firms' specific ownership advantages, FDI from industrial economies is more market-oriented. The general implication is that host economies with larger market size, faster economic growth and a higher degree of economic development will attract more market-oriented FDI. China's huge domestic market, fast economic growth and increasing per capita income are very attractive for industrial economy investors, particularly for market-oriented FDI. Therefore, China's accession to the WTO will provide great opportunities for industrial economy investors to explore China's huge domestic markets. It is expected that with the implementation of WTO agreements and fulfilment of its commitments to the WTO in trade and investment liberalisation (particularly in the areas of strengthening intellectual property rights protection, opening more economic sectors, especially the services sector, to FDI, and allowing and encouraging cross-border mergers and acquisitions [M&As]), China will become an increasingly important host economy for FDI from industrial economies. This will not only increase total FDI inflows from industrial economies, but will

FIGURE 9.1   **REGIONAL DISTRIBUTION OF ACCUMULATED FDI**
              INFLOWS INTO CHINA, 1983–2000

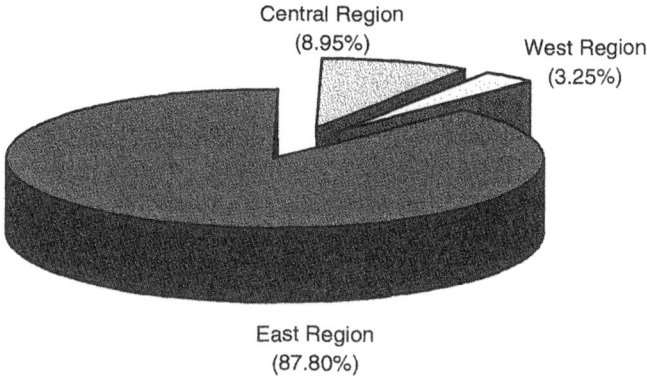

Central Region
(8.95%)   West Region
                           (3.25%)

East Region
(87.80%)

Note: Calculations are based on 1995 constant US$ prices.
Source: State Statistical Bureau, various years. *Zhongguo Tongji Nianjian* (China Statistical Yearbook), Zhongguo Tongji Chubanshe, Beijing.

___

also increase the quality of FDI inflows into China.

IMPACT ON THE REGIONAL DISTRIBUTION OF FDI IN CHINA

Since China began to attract FDI into its economy, the regional distribution of FDI within China has been very uneven. FDI inflows into China in the 1980s were overwhelmingly concentrated in the four special economic zones and the two municipalities of Beijing and Shanghai. With the development of overall economic reform and the nationwide implementation of open policies for FDI in the 1990s, FDI inflows into China gradually spread from the initial concentrated areas to other provinces. Increasingly the most important areas for hosting FDI are the Yangzi River Delta including Jiangsu, Shanghai and Zhejiang, and the Bohai Gulf including Shandong, Hebei, Tianjin and Liaoning. Several provinces, such as Jilin, Heilongjiang, Anhui, Jiangxi, Henan, Hubei and Hunan in the central region, and Sichuan and Shaanxi in the west region, also experienced relatively large increases in FDI inflows in the 1990s.

Comparing the three province groups of the east, central and west regions,[2] the east region provinces have overwhelmingly dominated the other two province groups in attracting FDI. For the period 1983–2000 the percentage shares in the national total of accumulated FDI inflows were 87.8 per cent for the eastern region provinces, 8.9 per cent for the central region provinces, and only 3.3 per cent for the western region provinces (Figure 9.1). This uneven regional distribution of FDI has to a certain extent helped to enlarge the gap in income levels between the east and the central and west regions.

With China's accession to the WTO, it is expected that trade and investment liberalisation will bring more benefits to the east region than to the rest of the country, especially than to the west region. As a result, after accession, economic growth in the east region will be higher and faster than in the west region. Consequently, it is expected that more FDI will flow into the east region.

The attractiveness of the east region for FDI is its relatively more liberalised and industrial economy, closer connections with the outside world, better infrastructure, a higher level of scientific research and technical innovation, and a higher quality labour force. Therefore, with further liberalisation in trade and investment after China's accession to the WTO, the east region will attract more FDI inflows. Labour-intensive export-oriented FDI in the manufacturing sector is likely to maintain a positive and important role in export promotion, economic growth and employment creation. Market-oriented FDI is expected to continue to show an upward trend in the years following China's accession to the WTO, especially in the east region.

To boost economic growth and therefore reduce the gap of economic development between the east region and the central and west regions, the Chinese government launched the West Development Strategy in 1998.[3] The Strategy emphasises infrastructure development, environmental protection, industrial structural readjustment, the development of sciences and education, and economic reform and openness. To realise these goals, four concrete measures are to be implemented. First, the central government will dramatically increase investment in the central and west regions, and increase transfer payments from the central government budget. Second, the central and west regions will increase the degree of openness and implement more open policies, in particular by opening more areas and sectors to FDI. Third, enterprises—especially foreign-invested enterprises (FIEs)—in the east region are encouraged to invest and to do business in the central and west regions. Fourth, the central and west regions will enhance the development of

134

sciences and education in order to attract and improve human resources.

To improve the investment environment and accelerate economic growth in the west region, China will need to invest heavily in infrastructure development in the west region. According to the West Development Strategy, the major infrastructure projects include investing 120 billion yuan in highway and road construction from 2000–2020; investing 100 billion yuan in large and medium-size railway projects from 2000–2005; creating a hydro-electricity generation base in the west region and constructing a national electricity supply network in order to transport electricity from the west region to the east region from 2000–2015; investing 300 billion yuan in gas pipeline construction to transport natural gas from the west region to the east region from 2000–2007; and constructing more airports in the west region (Office of the Leading Group for West Development of the State Council 2000).

Undoubtedly, the West Development Strategy and the further opening of the central and west regions have provided great opportunities for foreign investors. The comparative advantages of the central and west regions are rich natural resources, low labour costs and growing markets. In addition, there are many SOEs in the central and west regions, with a huge amount of idle capital stock. Currently China is stipulating relevant laws and regulations on cross-border M&As and foreign investors are encouraged to participate in SOE reform and transformation through M&As. With the deepening of SOE reform and the participation of foreign investment through M&As, it is expected that in the medium and long run more foreign capital will flow into the central and west regions.

It is most likely that in the short run following China's accession to the WTO, regional economic development will be uneven, and as a result, the uneven regional distribution of FDI between the east region and the central and west regions will be reinforced. However, in the medium and long run, with the implementation of the West Development Strategy, and economic development in the central and west regions, it is reasonable to expect a greater flow of FDI to the central and west regions.

IMPACT ON THE SECTORAL DISTRIBUTION OF FDI IN CHINA

The sectoral distribution of FDI in China is characterised by the concentration of FDI in the manufacturing sector. At the end of 2000, the primary sector attracted 2.2 per cent, the manufacturing sector 61.0 per cent, and the services sector 36.8 per cent, of total contracted FDI inflows into China (Figure 9.2). However, in the services sector most FDI was in the real estate industry, which accounted for 24.0

FIGURE 9.2   **SECTORAL DISTRIBUTION OF ACCUMULATED FDI**
               INFLOWS INTO CHINA, 1983–2000

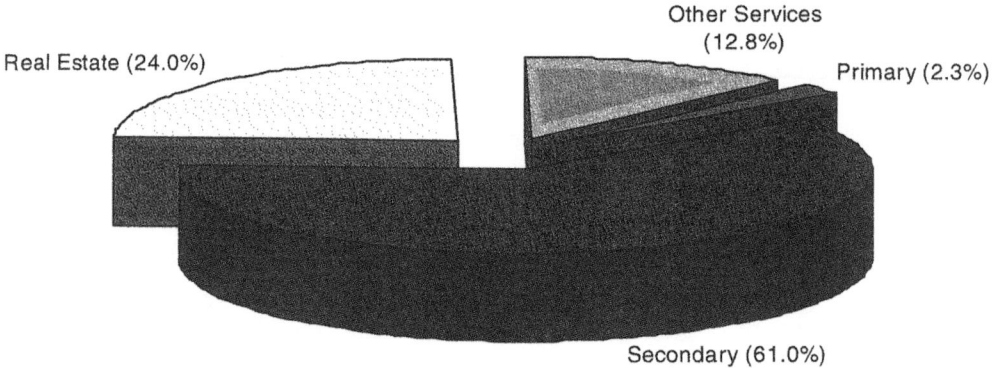

Other Services (12.8%)

Real Estate (24.0%)

Primary (2.3%)

Secondary (61.0%)

Note: Calculations are based on the contracted value of FDI.

Source: State Statistical Bureau, various years. *Zhongguo Duiwai Jingji Tongji Nianjian* [China Foreign Economic Statistical Yearbook] and *Zhongguo Tongji Nianjian* [China Statistical Yearbook], Zhongguo Tongji Chubanshe, Beijing.

per cent of total FDI inflows to China. As a result, the other services industries attracted only 12.8 per cent of total FDI inflows.

The current sectoral distribution of FDI in China is biased towards the manufacturing sector. Although FDI inflows into the primary and services sectors have been increasing since the mid 1990s, the volume of FDI inflows into these sectors is still low when compared to FDI inflows to the manufacturing sector.

Following China's accession to the WTO, the sectoral distribution of FDI inflows will experience some changes. The general trend will be for the proportion of FDI in the manufacturing sector to decline, while the proportion of FDI in the services sector—particularly in finance, insurance, commerce, telecommunications and auxiliary services—will increase. However, changes to the sectoral distribution of FDI will primarily depend on the successful implementation of China's WTO commitments and the degree of market opening to foreign investors.

Primary sector

Of all the sectors of the Chinese economy, the primary sector has received the smallest amount of FDI. By the end of 2000, FDI in China's primary sector was around US$7.9 billion, of which US$4.7 billion was in agriculture and US$3.2 billion was in ocean oil and natural gas exploration, mining and other primary industries. It should be noted that most foreign investments in ocean oil and natural gas exploration are recorded as other foreign investments which are not included in China's FDI statistics.

Agriculture was one of the earliest sectors to open up to FDI. However, the success of agriculture in attracting FDI has not been impressive when viewed in the context of the large volume of FDI inflows over the last two decades. There are many reasons for the poor performance of agriculture in attracting FDI, but there are two that are probably most important. First, China's agricultural land tenure system, and hence, the traditional small-scale family-based agricultural production method has greatly limited the inflows of agricultural FDI and large-scale production and advanced technology. Second, government controls over production, pricing, purchase, storage, transportation, domestic sales, and international exports of grains and other major agricultural products have been a significant disincentive for foreigers to invest in China's agricultural sector. Therefore, China will not attract large FDI inflows into its agricultural sector without fundamentally changing its land tenure system and dramatically reforming and liberalising its grain and major agricultural products marketing system. China's accession to the WTO provides a good opportunity for China to reform and restructure its agricultural sector in a new environment of international competition.

In general, China has no comparative advantage in land-intensive grain production. However, with its abundant and cheap labour resources, China has a comparative advantage in labour-intensive horticultural and animal husbandry production. After accession to the WTO and the restructuring of China's agricultural production structure, China will have the potential to expand its production and exports of horticultural products and animal products. Therefore, the horticultural and animal husbandry industries have great potential to attract FDI inflows after China's accession.

However, China's potential to expand exports of horticultural products and animal products is limited by deficiencies in its technologies, capital and marketing networks. Therefore, there is also a great opportunity for foreign investors to invest in areas such as horticultural products and animal products quality upgrading, processing, fresh preservation, packaging, storing and transportation. In addition, with the development of the animal husbandry industry, the feed processing industry is also a very attractive sector for FDI.

The oil and natural gas exploration, and mining industries will have great potential to attract foreign investment if China removes the restrictions on foreign ownership shares, types of investment and operation scopes on FDI in these industries. It is expected that after China's accession to the WTO, the oil and natural gas exploration and mining industries will attract more FDI inflows as China gradually reduces and eventually eliminates the restrictions on FDI in these industries. In addition, China's west region is well-endowed with natural resources, particularly oil, natural gas and mines. With the implementation of the West Development Strategy and the improvement of the overall investment environment, particularly in infrastructure and open policies in the west region, it is expected that the west region will attract more FDI inflows into its resource-based primary industries.

Manufacturing sector

The manufacturing sector is the largest FDI recipient sector in China. By the end of 2000, the manufacturing sector had attracted US$210.9 billion in FDI, accounting for over 60 per cent of total FDI inflows to China. In terms of the industrial distribution of FDI in the manufacturing sector, 40.7 per cent of total manufacturing FDI went to labour-intensive industries, while capital-intensive industries and technology-intensive industries accounted for 24.4 per cent and 34.7 per cent, respectively (Figure 9.3).

Studies of the impact of China's accession to the WTO predict that after accession, labour-intensive manufacturing industries—especially textiles and clothing industries—will grow rapidly, led by a large expansion of China's exports. This expansion will follow from industrial economies' reduction of import tariffs and elimination of quotas on imports of China's labour-intensive manufactured goods. However, to realise this potential, China needs to introduce foreign capital, technology and advanced equipment to help upgrade its relatively backward labour-intensive industries, in order to compete in global markets. Therefore, there are great opportunities for foreign investors to invest in China's labour-intensive and export-oriented manufacturing industries. It is expected that with trade and investment liberalisation after accession to the WTO, China will attract more FDI inflows into its labour-intensive and export-oriented industries. While the southeast coastal region will still be the

FIGURE 9.3 **COMPOSITION OF FIES BY INDUSTRY GROUPS OF FACTOR INTENSITY** (END 2000)

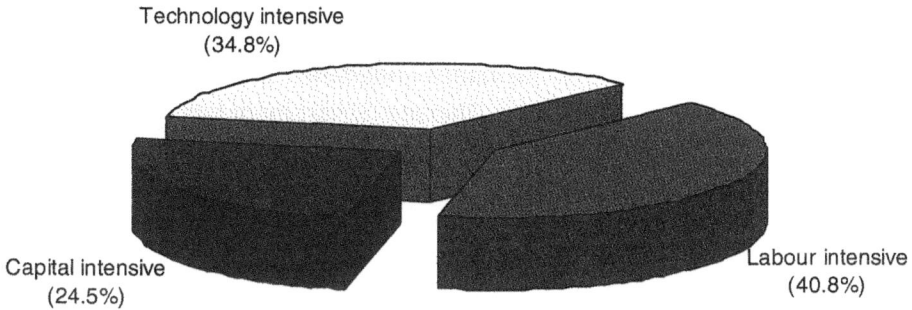

Technology intensive
(34.8%)

Capital intensive
(24.5%)

Labour intensive
(40.8%)

Note: Calculations are based on the total assets of FIEs at the end of 2000.
Source: State Statistical Bureau, 2001. *Zhongguo Tongji Nianjian 2001* (China Statistical Year-book 2001), Zhongguo Tongji Chubanshe, Beijing.

main receipt of labour-intensive and export-oriented FDI, following the implementation of the West Development Strategy and the improvement of the investment environment, especially the breakdown of regulatory barriers and reduction of tranport and transaction cost to internal trade, the central and west regions will become increasingly attractive to foreign investors. Thus, more labour-intensive FDI is expected to flow into the central and west regions in the medium and long run, causing a gradual shift of labour-intensive FDI from the southeast coastal region to the central and west regions as these regions' comparative advantages change in the process of economic development.

Generally speaking, China's capital-intensive and technology-intensive manufacturing industries have no international comparative advantage. Therefore, after accession, China's capital-intensive and technology-intensive manufacturing industries will face significant competition from foreign companies. On the one hand, the enhanced competition can pressure China's domestic enterprises to improve their management and technology and, therefore, to increase efficiency. On the other hand, more domestic enterprises might face the possibility of being forced out of business. This is especially critical for those loss-making SOEs in the traditional capital-intensive industries.

SOE reform is essential to ensuring smooth accession to the WTO and is also very important for the successful implementation of China's WTO commitments. Currently, China's capital-intensive and technology-intensive manufacturing industries are still overwhelmingly dominated by SOEs. The successful reform of China's state sector will depend greatly on the means undertaken and the tools made available to foreign investors. Although the Chinese Government has allowed private capital participation in the restructuring and modernisation of SOEs, controls over foreign ownership and the forms of foreign investment, such as cross-border M&As, still exist.

Foreign companies in capital-intensive and technology-intensive industries have superior ownership advantages over China's domestic enterprises, and therefore have more advantages in investing and competing in China's capital-intensive and technology-intensive industries. If the Chinese Government further relaxes the controls over foreign ownership, allows direct transactions of cross-border M&As of China's enterprises (especially SOEs) by foreign companies, and effectively protects intellectual property rights, greater volumes of FDI—especially large multinational enterprises (MNEs) from industrial countries—will flow into China's capital-intensive and technology-intensive manufacturing industries. The most promising industries will be the new and high-technology industries, such as electronics, telecommunications equipment, synthetic materials, new-type building materials, pharmaceuticals and automobiles.

The automobile industry is the only manufacturing industry in which China has made specific commitments in investment liberalisation in the WTO agreements. The industry was one of the earliest industries opened to foreign investors in China. In 1984, two joint ventures were set up: Beijing Jeep Corporation LTD (Beijing/United States) and Shanghai Volkswagen Automobile Corporation (Shanghai/Germany). By the end of 1998, more than 400 Sino–foreign joint ventures had been approved in the automobile industry. The largest joint ventures are in Shanghai (Shanghai Volkswagen, Shanghai General Motors), Changchun (FAW–Volkswagen), Wuhan (DongFeng–Citroen) and Guangzhou (Peugeot, Honda).

China is a potentially large market for an automobile industry. Currently, China's annual production of motor vehicles is around 1.7 million. With rapid economic development and the increase of per capita income, demand for motor vehicles in China will increase rapidly. With China's accession to the WTO, import tariffs on motor vehicles will be reduced from the current level of 80–100 per cent to 25 per cent by 2006, and tariffs on auto parts will be cut to an average of 10 per cent by 2006. Undoubtedly, after China's accession to the WTO more motor vehicles will be imported to meet China's rapidly increasing domestic demand. However, domestic producers of motor vehicles will still be the main supplier for domestic automobile demand. Therefore, foreign automobile companies with superior technology, advanced production techniques, high managerial skills and rich experiences in international competition have tremendous advantages to invest in China's automobile industry. Furthermore, direct participation in local auto production will also be the most efficient way to secure foreign auto companies' shares in China's domestic automobile markets.

Currently, FDI in China's automobile industry faces some policy restrictions. For example, there are restrictions on the share of foreign ownership. Wholly foreign-owned enterprises are not allowed. There are also restrictions on production range and local content requirement. Furthermore, foreign investors are not allowed to invest and operate in motor vehicle distribution and maintenance.

China has made some specific commitments in investment liberalisation in the automobile industry after its accession to the WTO. The key points include: allowing non-bank foreign financial institutions to provide auto financing; commitments regarding importation, distribution, sale, and maintenance and repair of automobiles; freedom to determine product range within two years of accession; reduction of red tape, as provincial authorities will be empowered to authorise investments in the sector worth up to US$150 million (currently US$30 million) four years after accession; and allowing wholly foreign-owned enterprises to compete in engine manufacturing.

China's commitments in investment liberalisation in the automobile industry provide great opportunities for foreign investors to invest in the industry in China. It is expected that foreign investment in China's automobile industry will increase significantly after China's accession to the WTO.

Services sector

Service is the most restricted economic sector and the latest to be opened to foreign investors. To date, the Chinese Government has opened some services industries to FDI, mainly in the east region, in an experimental fashion, such as finance, insurance and commerce. By the end of 2000, the services sector has received FDI of US$127 billion, of which US$83 billion was in the real estate industry and only US$44 billion in other services industries. Therefore, the other services industries (excluding the real estate industry) accounted for only 13 per cent of the total FDI in China due to very limited openness and the tight restrictions on FDI in these services industries.

China's services sector is underdeveloped in the national economy. For the last half-century, the share of the services sector in China's GDP has been around 30 per cent. By international comparison, the development of China's services sector is also relatively low. According to the purchasing power parity (PPP) calculation, China's current per capita GDP is around US$3000. At the global level, the average share of the services sector in national GDP is around 50 per cent when per capita GDP is around US$3000 (based on PPP). However, the share of China's services sector in national GDP is 20 percentage points lower than the world average. Therefore, China's services sector not only lags behind the overall development of its national economy, but is also underdeveloped by international standards. Although the Chinese Government issued the 'Decisions on Accelerating the Development of the Services Sector' in the early 1990s, the targets set for the development of the services sector have not been achieved. The slow development of the services sector may well become a bottleneck, affecting the future overall development of China's economy.

There are many reasons for the slow development of China's services sector, but two stand out. One is closedness and the other is monopoly. During the last two decades of economic reform and opening up to the outside world, China's services sector has actually been relatively closed to foreign direct participation. Although the Chinese Government has gradually opened some services industries to foreign investors in a very restricted and experimental fashion, many services industries are still closed to foreign investors. The closed nature of the services sector to foreign competition has effectively protected the state monopoly in the services sector. At present, China's many services industries are monopolised by SOEs, especially in the industries of finance, telecommunications and in international trade.

Opening the services sector has been one of the most important issues in the bilateral negotiations of China's accession to the WTO. China has made some important and concrete commitments to the WTO in opening its services sector to foreign investors. Undoubtedly, after China's accession and with the implementation of the commitments, there will be a surge of FDI inflows to China's services sector. In the services sector, the following industries are likely to attract foreign investment.

Finance. China started to allow FDI in the finance industry in an experimental fashion in a number of selected cities in 1982. At present, China has eliminated the geographical restrictions on setting up operational branches by foreign financial institutions. By the end of 2000, there were 177 operational foreign-invested financial institutions and 238 representative offices set up by foreign banks in China. Foreign-invested financial institutions are mainly engaged in foreign currency business. However, 32 foreign-invested financial institutions in Shanghai and Shenzhen are permitted to engage in renminbi business. At the beginning of 2000, the People's Bank of China announced that foreign-invested banks in Shanghai can extend their RMB business to Jiangsu and Zhejiang provinces, and foreign-invested banks in Shenzhen can extend their renminbi business to Guangdong, Guangxi and Hunan provinces.

By mid 1999, total assets of foreign-invested financial institutions were US$32 billion, accounting for less than 2 per cent of the total assets of Chinese financial institutions. Total outstanding loans of foreign-invested financial institutions were US$24 billion, also accounting for less than 2 per cent of the total outstanding loans of Chinese financial institutions. Undoubtedly, there are great business opportunities for foreign investors in China's financial industry. China has committed upon accession to the WTO to further open its financial markets, eliminate regional and geographical restrictions, and permit more foreign-invested financial institutions to engage in renminbi business. Therefore, China's financial industry will attract a large volume of FDI inflows after China's accession to the WTO.

Insurance. In 1992, China conditionally opened its insurance markets, allowing foreign insurance institutions to set up two types of foreign-invested insurance institutions in an experimental fashion in Shanghai; branches of foreign insurance companies, and joint venture insurance companies. In 1995, the experiment was extended to Guangzhou. By the end of 2000, there were 26 foreign-invested operational insurance companies and institutions in China. In addition, the People's Bank of China has also approved two foreign insurance intermediary institutions and 196 representative offices. Currently, China is stipulating 'Management Provisions on Foreign-Invested Insurance Institutions'.

The main policy constraints to FDI in China's insurance industry are market access, regional and geographical restrictions, restrictions on business scope, and controls over foreign ownership. However, China has made some concrete commitments to opening its insurance industry to foreign investors after accession to the WTO.

China's insurance industry has registered double-digit revenue growth for several consecutive years. Total income from premiums is likely to top US$18 billion in 2001. As predicted by the China Insurance Regulatory Commission (CIRC), total insurance revenues will reach US$30 billion in 2004. Therefore, China's insurance industry has great potential to attract FDI provided China implements the WTO agreement and further open its insurance industry.

Telecommunications. China's regulations currently prohibit FDI in the operation and management of the telecommunications industry. In the 'Industrial Guidance on Foreign Direct Investment', the telecommunications industry is listed as a prohibited sector for foreign investment. However, China has made some commitments to the WTO to open its telecommunications industry to foreign investors after the accession.

China's telecommunications industry has been monopolised by state-owned companies. Foreign companies with advanced equipment and technology have shown great interests in investing in China's telecommunications industry, especially in value-added services investment. Therefore, China's WTO accession will not only provide an opportunity for foreign investors to enter China's huge telecommunications market, but also will increase domestic competition in the telecommunications market, thus increasing the industry's efficiency and benefiting consumers.

Domestic commerce. In 1992 China decided to set up several Sino–foreign joint ventures engaging in domestic commercial retail business at an experimental base in each of the following cities and areas: Beijing, Tianjin, Shanghai, Guangzhou, Qingdao and the five special economic zones. Later, China decided to set up two Sino–foreign joint venture chain retail stores in Beijing and Shanghai and to set up a number of mainland and Taiwan joint ventures engaging in domestic commercial retail business in inland areas, also in an experimental fashion. In June 1999, the State Economic and Trade Commission and the Ministry of Foreign Trade and Economic Cooperation (MOFTEC) under the approval of the State Council jointly issued 'The Experimental Methods for Foreign-Invested Commercial Enterprises'. The experiment on joint ventures engaging in domestic commercial retail business was extended to all provincial capital cities, and at the same time, an experiment on setting up foreign-invested enterprises engaging in domestic commercial wholesale business was implemented.

At the end of 2000, there were 27 foreign-invested commercial retail enterprises and one foreign-invested commercial wholesale enterprise approved by the central government.[4] There were about 277 foreign-invested commercial retail enterprises approved by local governments at the provincial level.

The current policy restrictions on FDI in the domestic commerce industry mainly include controls over foreign ownership, the degree of market access, business scope and geographical restrictions.

China has committed to increase the number of foreign-invested commercial enterprises, to expand the geographical areas for FDI in domestic commerce, to release restrictions on FDI in wholesale business, and to eliminate the limit of 50 per cent equity participation for large retailers.

China's huge domestic commercial markets, with annual retail sales of 3 trillion yuan, are very attractive to foreign investors. However, due largely to the policy constraints, foreign-invested commercial enterprises account for only 1 per cent of the total value of retail sales in China. With China's accession to the WTO and the further opening up of China's domestic commercial markets, foreign investors will have a great opportunity to invest in China's domestic commercial industry.

International trade. Foreign investors are allowed to set up trading enterprises in the 13 tax-bounded zones to conduct entrepot trade and serve as import and export agents for the enterprises in the tax-bounded zones. In September 1996, MOFTEC issued 'The Provisional Methods on the Experiment of Setting up China and Foreign Joint Venture International Trading Company'. China allowed foreign investors to set up Sino–foreign joint international trading companies in Shanghai Pudong area and Shenzhen special economic zone in an experimental fashion. The joint international trading companies can engage in commodity and technology import and export business except for 16 export commodities and 14 import commodities that are subject to state trading and control. At present, the experiment has approved five foreign-invested international trading companies outside the tax-bounded zones, of which three are in Shanghai and two in Shenzhen.

Currently, there are many restrictions on foreign investors setting up international trading business in China. However, with China's accession to the WTO and further trade liberalisation, restrictions on foreign investors conducting international trading business will slowly be lifted. Foreign trading companies with their rich experiences and well-developed international market network will certainly play a very important role in promoting China's international trade. Currently, MOFTEC is reviewing the regulations and policies governing FDI in the international trade sector, preparing to further open the sector to foreign investors, and extend the experiment of FDI in the international trade sector to the central and western areas of China.

CONCLUSION

In terms of investment liberalisation, China's commitments are mainly in the automobile industry and some key industries of the services sector. WTO negotiations will have an impact on China's FDI policy regime, but the WTO accession agreements have not significantly affected China's FDI policy regime. The limitations are mainly due to the limited effect the WTO has on investment policies. Therefore, unilateral reduction and elimination of investment barriers would still be the main task of further investment liberalisation in China.

WTO entry will have a positive impact on FDI inflows to China. However, whether China benefits from WTO entry and realises its potential to attract FDI inflows after entering the WTO, largely depends on how China implements the WTO agreements, fulfils its WTO commitments, further reduces and eliminates trade and investment barriers and further opens domestic markets, manages internal economic reforms (particularly the reform of SOEs), and enforces the protection of intellectual property rights.

China's accession to the WTO provides a great opportunity for China to improve and diversify its FDI sources and, therefore will have a significant impact on the composition of FDI sources in China. In general, with the implementation of trade and investment liberalisation after China's accession, both developing and industrial economies are likely to increase their investments in China as a result of the improved investment environment and the reduction of trade and investment barriers in China. However, while China will remain a very important host for investment from developing economies—particularly the NIEs—China will become an increasingly important destination for industrial economy investments as China progressively strengthens intellectual property rights protection, opens more economic sectors (especially the services sector) to FDI, and encourages cross-border mergers and acquisitions (M&As). This will not only increase total FDI inflows, but also the quality of FDI inflows into China.

In terms of regional distribution of FDI inflows after China's accession, the study reveals that in the short run, uneven regional economic development, and hence, the uneven regional distribution of FDI between the east region and the central and west regions in China will probably be exacerbated. However, in the medium and long term, with the implementation of the West Development Strategy, and economic development in the central and west regions, it is reasonable to expect that more FDI will gradually flow into the central and west regions.

The study also reveals that the sectoral distribution of FDI in China will experience some major changes after China's accession. The general trend will be for the share of FDI inflows into the manufacturing sector is gradually to decline while the share of FDI inflows into the services sector increases significantly. Opening the services sector has been one of the most important issues in the bilateral negotiations of China's accession to the WTO. China has made some important and concrete commitments to the WTO in opening its services sector to foreign investors. Therefore, it is expected that after accession, there will be a surge of FDI inflows to China's services sector, especially into finance, insurance, telecommunications, domestic commerce and auxiliary services industries.

Notes

[1] The empirical model is a multi-regression model with pooled data. The data set contains 32 developing countries (including China) for a period of 12 years from 1987–98. The dependent variable is FDI inflows into developing countries, and the independent variables include market size (GDP), GDP growth rate, efficiency wage (defined as the real wage rate adjusted by labour productivity), labour quality (approximated by illiteracy rate of the population), and economic distance (defined as the weighted average distance of a developing economy to the rest of the world, where the weights are the shares of the economies' GDP in total world GDP). In the regression the independent variables are lagged by one year. All the independent variables are statistically significant at the 1 per cent significance level, and the Buse–R^2 is 0.55, which indicates the relatively high explanatory power of the estimated equation. For more details of the model, see Chen Chunlai (2000).

[2] The east region includes Beijing, Tianjin, Hebei, Liaoning, Shanghai, Jiangsu, Zhejiang, Fujian, Shandong, Guangdong, Guangxi and Hainan. The central region includes Shanxi, Inner Mongolia, Jilin, Heilongjiang, Anhui, Jiangxi, Henan, Hubei and Hunan. The west region includes Sichuan, Guizhou, Yunnan, Tibet, Shaanxi, Gansu, Qinghai, Ningxia and Xinjiang.

[3] According to the Strategy, the areas include 12 provinces, municipalities and autonomous regions: Sichuan, Chongqing, Guizhou, Yunnan, Gansu, Shaanxi, Qinghai, Ningxia, Xinjiang, Tibet, Guangxi and Inner Mongolia; and two prefectures: Enshi of Hubei Province and Xiangxi of Hunan Province.

[4] Each enterprise may have several operating stores.

10

Insurance sector following WTO accession

Ken Waller

Under the WTO accession agreement, China has undertaken to implement significant reforms contributing to the further liberalisation of the insurance sector over a five-year period. This will allow increased foreign participation in ownership in the sector and in the scope of business that foreigners may engage in—geographic limits on foreign operations will be eased considerably.

One hundred per cent foreign ownership of a non-life subsidiary will be permitted within two years of accession; majority foreign ownership (51 per cent) of brokerages for insurance of large commercial risks, reinsurance and international marine, aviation and transport insurance will be permitted three years after accession; and wholly foreign-owned subsidiaries will be permitted five years after China's accession. Upon accession, a foreign life insurance company will be permitted to own 50 per cent of a joint venture with a Chinese partner of its choice (the same percentage has been applied in the recent period). Requirements for an insurance business to cede 20 per cent of its reinsurance needs to China Reinsurance will reduce in tranches to zero, four years after accession.

In the protocols of the Working Party involved with China's accession to the GATs, it is noted that China confirmed that on accession to the WTO, its licensing procedures and conditions would not act as a barrier to access; that for services, China will ensure a transparent procedure for applications for licences; that applications will be open without individual invitation; and that decisions on all applications will be taken promptly.

If an application is refused the applicant will be informed in writing and without delay of the reasons. Approved applicants will also be notified without delay and notice of approval will enable the applicant to start commercial operations upon registration of the company's name with the SAIC for fiscal and other administrative purposes. The registration processes will be completed within two months of submission of a complete application, as required by public SAIC regulations and in accordance with China's Schedule of Specific Commitments under the GATs.

These undertakings represent a significant and welcome change in the approach to the treatment of foreign applicants for licences to undertake insurance business in China. Another and important aspect of China's commitments under the relevant GATs schedule is that upon accession, foreign life insurers—which as noted above will be permitted 50 per cent equity in a joint venture—will be allowed to enter into the venture with a partner of their choice, and those joint venture partners can freely agree the terms of their engagement provided they remain within the limits of the commitments contained in the schedule. This in effect means that while the 50 per cent ownership limit will apply, it will be a matter for decision by the partners, without any legal impediment, as to who will control the enterprise.

Before authorisation, a foreign insurer will need to have 30 years experience in a WTO member country, total assets of more than US$5 billion and to have had a representative office in China for two years. Insurance brokers will be required to have assets of more than US$500 million and two years after accession, brokers will be required to have assets of more than US$200 million.

Upon accession, foreign life and non-life insurers will be permitted to provide services in Shanghai, Guangzhou, Dalian, Shenzhen and Foshan and two years after accession more cities will be open to foreign service providers—Beijing, Chengdu, Chongqing, Fuzhou, Suzhou, Xiamen, Ningbo, Shenyang, Wuhan and Tianjin. Within three years after accession, there will be no geographic restrictions.

The business scope for foreign insurers will be extended on a graduated basis. After accession, foreign non-life insurers will be permitted to provide 'master policy' insurance/insurance of large-scale commercial risk, with no geographic limitation. Foreign non-life insurers are permitted to provide insurance of enterprises abroad as well as property insurance, related liability insurance and credit insurance of foreign-invested enterprises in China. Within two years after accession, foreign non-life insurers can provide the full range of non-life services to both domestic and foreign clients. Within three years after accession, foreign life insurers will be permitted to provide health insurance, group insurance and pension/annuities insurance to foreigners and to Chinese.

The measures that China has agreed to undertake in the insurance sector as a condition of accession to the WTO do represent a major, if graduated, step in the liberalisation of the sector. Within a period of five years after accession, competition for the delivery of insurance services across China by wholly foreign-owned non-life companies will be possible and the total range of life insurance services will be available by entities which may involve up to 50 per cent foreign equity but which may well be effectively controlled by the owners of the foreign equity.

The impact of these undertakings will reinforce changes already underway toward a more market-oriented insurance sector. These changes are reflected in the broad range of reforms which China has been implementing over most of the last decade or so, aimed at deepening and widening its capital markets and modernising the financial system. The changes that will occur over the next five years will almost certainly include the restructuring of the state-owned insurance sector in China.

Since the insurance sector in China became open to foreign participation, the world's major insurance/finance firms have expressed strong interest in accessing the market. The reasons for this derive from the underdevelopment of the market and the major growth prospects on offer as China continues its economic and social modernisation.

STRUCTURE OF THE INSURANCE MARKET AND GROWTH OUTLOOK

In 2000, the aggregate premium income in China amounted to 1.8 per cent of GDP with an average per capita premium of just over US$15. Comparable figures for global insurance activity were 7.5 per cent and US$387, respectively, in 1999. The total national premium expenditure in 2000 in China represented only 2.3 per cent of the deposits in the nation's savings banks and only 25 per cent of the Chinese population held insurance policies. These figures indicate that insurance in China is in its early stages of development and insurance penetration is relatively low—particularly when compared to industrial economies generally and some major regional economies such as Japan, Korea, Australia and Taiwan.

Most business revenues of domestic insurers derive from internal distribution channels with only a small proportion of business so far generated through brokers. In some developed markets, intermediaries account for a significant majority of insurance business. Reinsurance has largely been channeled through the state-owned China Reinsurance and this near-monopoly position is a significant market impediment. In the period following China's accession, the role of intermediaries/ brokers is expected to develop into a more significant aspect of the market structure and greater competition in the reinsurance market will follow as new players enter the market.

Since the opening of the economy in the 1980s, the insurance sector has grown rapidly at an average annual rate of 37 per cent—much higher than GDP growth. Notwithstanding this, the market, is underdeveloped compared with other economies. The prospects for the industry are for continuing strong growth. This is so for all sectors—life, general and reinsurance—as the modernisation of the Chinese economy continues apace, and per capita income levels move along an upwards growth path.

Under the current 10th Five Year Plan, the economy is predicted to grow by around 7 per cent annually; GDP for 2005 is expected to reach around RMB 12.5 trillion. GDP per capita should reach about RMB 9,400, with disposable income growing annually by 5 per cent. Over the next five years, property and life premium in China is estimated to increase annually by 15 per cent and 20 per cent, respectively. Over the longer term, the growth of property premium income is forecast to moderate, but still to grow by above 10 per cent annually, while life premiums income is forecast to maintain high strong growth.

FOREIGN PARTICIPATION

Foreign insurers' share of the Chinese domestic market is extremely low—around 1.6 per cent of the life market and 0.5 per cent of non-life. Of the existing 33 insurers in China, fewer that 20 involve foreign participation, and these are concentrated mainly in Shanghai and Guangzhou. A limited number of wholly foreign-owned enterprises have been permitted in both the life and non-life sectors. AIA is by far the dominant foreign-owned enterprise in the life, accident and health insurance market and in the non-life market, AIU, Tokio Marine and Fire, and Winterthur are the dominant players, followed by Royal and Sun Alliance and Allianz Dazhong. Since 1998, six foreign insurance groups have entered China; four as minority partners with Chinese firms in the life insurance sector and two as wholly-owned foreign businesses in the non-life sector. In addition, four foreign insurers have made small strategic investments in Chinese life insurance businesses.

Many foreign insurance companies are known to be interested in investing in the Chinese market, attracted by potential rapid growth of the market over the medium to long term. There is no other market in the world where the prospects of growth are so great.

CHANGING MARKET AND REGULATORY ENVIRONMENT

Market opening is being accompanied by a changing regulatory environment. The insurance regulator, the China Insurance Regulatory Commission (CIRC), is applying international standards and codes in an increasingly objective way. This approach will contribute to the prudential strengthening of the sector and will add confidence in the sector for those investing in the insurance market.

CIRC and businesses in the sector now consult about the professional aspects of the insurance business—concerning, for example, actuarial and auditing functions—and in understanding the development of new products such as unit-linked products.

CIRC has reduced the level of 'guarantees' that life companies are required to set aside, and this reflects concerns of the local industry that it was unable to maintain the level required, at a time when interest rates and profitability were falling sharply and the industry was facing solvency problems. The approval process by which new products may enter the market is much less onerous than previously and the scope for product innovation is significantly better than it was only two or three years ago. Unit-linked, wealth accumulation products are now prominent innovations in the market. Premiums are increasingly determined by the market.

Professional standards are improving and those involved in the industry—including importantly in agency work forces—are now required to pass professional examinations. CIRC is developing its capacity for on-site inspections of insurance firms.

These developments point to a very serious upgrade in the regulatory approach as China faces the challenges posed by a rapidly changing financial environment.

THE IMPACT OF THE WTO

In many senses, the insurance sector has been adapting to a changing competitive environment for most of the last decade. A number of new foreign firms have entered the market, as well as some domestic privately owned firms, and the regulatory environment is undergoing major reforms. The main impact of WTO accession will be to accentuate these changes. WTO accession will reinforce the policy direction that China has already embarked on rather than mark a sharp change in direction. This is also the case for other segments of the financial services sector.

No doubt the prospect of WTO accession over the last 5 years or so has been a factor in influencing the adjustments that have occurred in the sector, but the deeper reason for the reform program has been internally driven, the key driver being the imperative for China to modernise the financial system to contribute to the continuing growth process that is vital to securing China's future.

CHALLENGES POST WTO ACCESSION

Significant challenges lie ahead and in a sense WTO accession will focus attention on meeting those challenges. The issues confronting the insurance sector are generally common to other parts of the financial sector. A primary issue derives from the segmented nature of the financial sector and this is reflected in a segmented regulatory system.

Reducing financial system segmentation

There were sound reasons why, during the last two decades, the ever-widening credit creation activities of financial institutions in China were reined in. Credit growth by institutions outside the state owned banking sector—but often undertaken by affiliates of those institutions—created the genesis of the financial crisis that developed in China in the late 1980's and early 1990's. The more rigorous control of credit and the more effective supervision of non-bank intermediaries within a reformed and segmented regulatory system evolved in the second half of the 1990's. Success in this area was of fundamental importance in contributing to price and economic stability.

The challenge for China over the coming period is to encourage competitiveness in the financial system so as to satisfy the burgeoning financial needs of a modernising economy, while at the same time continuing to develop a responsive and flexible regulatory system which provides for a stable financial environment. These challenges are a constant factor facing all economies; but they are particularly intense for China as it seeks to maintain a high growth rate but with an as yet underdeveloped financial system.

Pressures will be placed on the regulatory system to reduce regulatory segmentation and to facilitate the convergence of financial services and products. For this to occur, a next phase of regulatory reforms will be needed to allow for the integration of financial intermediaries. This process would not follow from any obligation

154

arising from WTO accession (no provisions of this kind exist in the GATS). Rather, it would arise as a consequence of an imperative on China to develop a competitive and efficient economy to maintain strong growth momentum and to develop its competitiveness in world terms. This imperative will come more sharply into focus as a direct consequence of China's accession to the WTO and as China becomes more closely integrated into the global economy.

Competitive impact on markets and products

Over the next five years, China will provide increased opportunities for foreign participation in the insurance sector (and in banking and other services) in more geographic areas of China. But, given the overwhelming domination of the state-owned insurance institutions, the impact of WTO accession will be only marginal, in terms of market penetration—at least for the next 5 years.

However, as is already apparent in the Shanghai and Guangzhou markets—where foreign players are most prominent in the insurance market—competition will intensify sharply in other cities as they are opened to foreign participation. This will manifest itself in a widening of the range of insurance products—particularly unit-linked, wealth accumulation products; in pricing; and in improvements in the quality of agency sales forces. Competition will intensify, and to respond insurers need to develop new distribution channels, and sales through bank branches and other retail outlets will intensify.

Implementing WTO undertakings

It remains to be seen how China's regulatory authorities will invoke the WTO accession agreement, in terms of allowing increased foreign participation. A large number of foreign insurers are known to have a strong interest in gaining an equity interest in the China market. Over the last decade or so, China has allowed foreign access—to foreign banks and insurers—on a gradual and controlled basis. WTO accession provides for increased opportunity but the regularity by which new entrants may come into the market will be determined by the processes invoked by the regulatory authorities in issuing new licenses. As noted earlier, regarding the protocols associated with accession, China has indicated that it will provide for a transparent process of the notification of procedures and will approve applications from those firms that meet the formal entry requirements within a two-month period. This aspect of WTO accession marks a major and welcome development in the process of market liberalisation.

Protectionist tensions

While some domestic interests will be more concerned with protecting the state-owned institutions from increasing foreign competition, others will see the need to force the pace in the modernisation of the financial system. These tensions have been a factor in Chinese policymaking during the economic reform era, and the reformists have generally been successful. One indication that the insurance sector will embrace more foreign participation would be signalled by a decision to introduce private equity into state-owned insurance businesses.

Depending on the business structures that would flow from such a decision, participation in the major part of the market now serviced by the state insurance firms could involve foreign companies. Such a development would involve the creation of new legal entities, and would mark a very important move by the Chinese government in the drive to create a modern financial system. Once such a policy is implemented there would be no basis to continue to protect the local industry from new foreign entrants.

It may well be the case that by the time the phasing-in of the WTO accession undertakings has been completed, China's major domestic insurers will have been restructured into stronger operational and profitable businesses, involving foreign equity. If that scenario were to unfold, the period beyond the 5 years after WTO accession would be one where foreign access to the Chinese market by new foreign insurers would be essentially dependent on the assessment of profitability by those foreign firms, and their capacity to meet capitalisation and other regulatory requirements.

Improving insurance sector performance and profitability

There is an urgent need to improve the profitability of China's insurance sector. The sector has gone through a period of very poor profitability, partly associated with the level of 'guarantees' required to be provided to policy-holders. More recently, the returns on premium income invested have been low and competition in the industry has reduced prices. Profitability is a fundamental concern to industry—state and privately-owned firms are similarly affected by the problems just outlined—but given the predominance of state-owned institutions in the life sector, state institutions have been particularly affected. It is partly as a consequence of these developments that the policy moves noted earlier—to privatise the state-owned sector—are now under consideration.

Clearly, the infusion of new capital into the state-owned institutions in the insurance sector (but also in the banking sector) will be of fundamental importance to ensuring the long-term stability of those sectors which are integral to the efficient functioning of the economy. And clearly, the benefits that should flow from market opening—the *raison d'etre* of WTO accession—will not be fully realised if major domestic components of those sectors do not have the capital base on which to conduct profitable and efficient businesses.

The development of risk-based products and investment liberalisation

Of long-term importance to the insurance industry will be the growth of risk-based products in which policy-holders share in the profit or loss on earnings of invested premium income. Greater flexibility in the area in which insurance companies can engage would also help companies improve their profitability and reduce the risk that arises from over-concentration of investments in a limited range of instruments. Investment guidelines applying to insurance firms were recently widened to include investment in stocks.

CONCLUSIONS

To ensure that the benefits of WTO accession are fully realised, it is important that the regulatory and financial policy environment promote profitable industry growth and development to improve provisioning against future claims, to meet regulatory solvency standards and to provide more acceptable returns to shareholders. To improve competitiveness in the industry, would involve the diminution and, ultimately the phasing out of 'implicit' official support for the state-owned sector of the industry. As noted earlier, China is adopting international regulatory standards for the prudential supervision of the insurance sector. This will greatly enhance the stability of the insurance sector and benefit those investing in the sector.

The infusion of new capital into the sector is also a pressing requirement and while some part of this will be provided by foreign insurers as they enter the market, capital for the privatisation of the state-owned insurance sector—given the dominant role it plays in the market—is critical. This would provide for the upgrade of the technical base of the industry and for the introduction of new systems and skills. The devolution of ownership and control to private sector interests—both domestic and foreign—which can best supply those needs will be highly important in ensuring that the insurance sector in an aggregate sense can develop efficiencies to meet the challenges ahead.

As the capital market develops—a key objective of the financial system reform program—investment opportunities will widen. Major reforms in the securities sector and in the social security and pensions system are foreshadowed in the near term and these will not only contribute to the deepening of the capital market but also to the integration of the financial system. The insurance sector can expect to find significant opportunities arising from pension system reform and the development of securities markets.

11

Securities market development: assessing and improving market efficiency

Michael Hasenstab

In 1978, China began a financial reform process that continues to grow in extent and impact, reducing the role of direct government credit allocation in favour of a market-driven allocation system (Table 11.1). While still in their infancy, these markets are providing an important means of channeling savings into productive economic uses. Under this new system, China's securities markets take on an increasingly important role and within this framework foreign financial institutions have the opportunity to hasten the development of domestic financial markets and improve efficiency in the allocation of capital.

These reforms have laid the initial groundwork for the development of securities markets in China and the effects of such reform on the recent growth of China's tradable securities markets is well summarised by Hale (2002).

> The number of listed companies has grown from 14 to nearly 1100. Market capitalisation now exceeds US$525 billion or a sum just over 50 per cent of GDP compared to numbers in the 20–60 per cent range for many developing countries. China also has developed markets for treasury bonds and corporate bonds. In 1999, the T-bond market was worth 401 billion Yuan (US$48.4 billion). The corporate bond market is much less developed. At the end of 1999, there were only 10 listed bonds with a market value of 50 billion Yuan (US$6 billion). But bond issuance during 1999 rose to 20 billion Yuan (US$2.4 billion), so there is potential for the market to expand more rapidly in response to both institutional and retail investor demand.

By March 2001, China's daily stockmarket turnover reached 25 trillion yuan, or 3 trillion US dollars (*China People's Daily* 2001).

TABLE 11.1   CHRONOLOGY OF KEY FINANCIAL MARKET REFORMS

Period[a]	Key reforms	Major implications
1978–84	1. Agricultural reform: creation of the Agricultural Bank, emergence of Town and Village Enterprises (locally funded) and formation of rural credit cooperatives. 2. Unofficial operation of inter-bank market among east coast banks. 3. Ministry of Finance (MOF) issues treasury bonds to finance the central government deficit. 4. People's Bank of China (PBC) allows select companies to issue share certificates on a very limited basis and undertake trial profit-sharing schemes in select firms. 5. PBC and MOF officially separated. 6. Trust and Investment Companies (TICs) and urban credit cooperatives permitted. 7. Foreign banks permitted to open representative offices.	China begins to dismantle administrative economic controls and sets the groundwork for the development of a market and increasingly private economy. The use of treasury bond issuance to finance the fiscal deficit creates the need for a formal treasurybond market in the future. Increased reliance on this market will later force the government to allow market pricing of debt and secondary trading. PBC begins first stage in what will prove to be a very long process in establishing a real central bank able to implement independent monetary policy, an object still unattained by the end of the century.
1985–88	1. Emergence of a money market and secondary market in certificates of deposit (CDs). 2. Local bank branches allowed to take in local deposits and no longer receive full funding from head offices. 3. Industrial Commercial Bank of China Shanghai branch issues the first financial bond. 4. Inter-bank market formalised in 55 major cities. 5. TICs expand in number and in total assets under management. 6. PBC transfers commercial banking operations to Industrial and Commercial Bank of China.	Informal markets emerge to take the place of previously government-controlled means of capital allocation. The growth of such markets and institutions will later force the government to formalise such markets. Financial sector becomes increasingly dependent on market forces.
1989–91	1. Shanghai and Shenzhen Securities Exchanges opened. Domestic and foreign share ownership segmented between A and B shares, respectively. 2. Banks and financial institutions begin underwriting bonds.	Securities markets are increasingly standardised and the level of sophistication in capital markets increases.
1992–95	1. Three new policy banks (State Development Bank, Agricultural Development Bank and Export–Import	Framework established for the separation of commercial and policy bank lending. Elimination of the

Period[a]	Key reforms	Major implications
	Bank) created. 2. PBC stops direct lending to MOF. 3. Elimination of two-currency system as Foreign Exchange Certificates (FEC) are converted into renminbi (local currency).	two-currency system is a crucial step toward greater internationalisation of the Chinese financial system.
1996–99	1. Foreign banks permitted to engage in renminbibusiness, and on a limited scale, trade local bonds. 2. Reorganisation of PBC into nine regional centres. 3. New securities regulations (Article 214) passed by central government. 4. Inter-bank market centralised out of Shanghai. 5. Banks prohibited from secondary trading of government bonds in Shanghai. 6. Overseas share listing of domestic firms and issuance of global sovereign bonds. 7. Current account liberalisation. 8. Collapse of Guandong International Trust and Investment Company (GITIC). 9. MOF places first of several global bonds in international capital markets.	Equity issuance in local and global markets increases. Securities markets take on an increasingly important means of fund raising while the GITIC bankruptcy motivates overhaul of securities and issuance regulation. Reform of PBC and inter-bank market helps set groundwork that will allow the PBC to manage monetary policy better in the future. Trading volume of secondary government bonds in Shanghai decreases late in this period. Overseas share and debt issuance and foreign participation in domestic banking increases Chinese financial internationalisation.
2000–01	1. Establishment of personal credit system in Shanghai on 1 July 2000. 2. Adoption of WTO-consistent laws and abolition of outdated and WTO-inconsistent laws and regulations (to date, 6 batches of such laws have been abolished and more are underreview). 3. 2001–05 five-year plan calls for swift development of the service sector (including banking and insurance).	Continued financial market deepening at the consumer level. New laws to make China WTO-compliant are moving China to allow increased access by foreign financial institutions to provide expanded commercial and retail foreign exchange and renminbi, fund management, and insurance services.

Note: [a]Period divisions from 1978–91 are taken from Xu (1998).
Source: Author's compilation.

While the increased size of China's securities highlights the elevated role of these markets in the allocation of capital, questions remain over the efficiency of such markets. This chapter will first outline the importance of efficiently operating securities markets for China. Second it will discuss empirical tests of the efficiency of these markets. Finally, it will assess policy reform efforts to date and suggest possible future policy innovations to further improve the efficiency of China's securities markets.

THE ROLE OF FINANCIAL MARKETS IN CHINA

More efficient securities markets will allow the government to finance its fiscal deficit more efficiently and for companies to raise much-needed finance. Properly functioning government bond markets are also important for the central bank's execution of monetary policy through open market operations. A well developed and well functioning government bond market also provides the capital market with information on sovereign risk, inflation and interest rate expectations, a benchmark for pricing new corporate debt issues in global markets, and efficient pricing of new government bond issues to minimise government financing costs.

Conversely, inefficient or dysfunctional markets threaten to raise government and company capital financing costs, misallocate capital to low productivity uses, and misprice sovereign and corporate risk. At the aggregate level, the close and positive link between the scale and depth of the financial sector and overall macroeconomic performance means that poorly functioning securities markets would be likely to seriously inhibit China's economic growth.

As China moves towards capital account liberalisation, the efficiency of China's securities markets is of paramount importance. Inefficient domestic capital markets do not allocate capital inflows to the most efficient uses and inflows with an open capital account, could create large-scale price disequilibria which would adversely affect government and company fundraising efforts and direct capital to inefficient sectors of the economy.

EVALUATION OF EQUITY AND DEBT MARKET BEHAVIOUR

While the size of securities markets has grown, questions remain over the efficiency of such markets. Hasenstab (2001) tested several components of market efficiency in debt and equity markets to help evaluate China's securities markets, which in turn can help assess China's readiness to open its capital account. Tests show that domestically-traded stocks and bonds are a random walk process which implies that they are efficient; at times an underlying common trend is present across various benchmark bond yields, creating a yield curve; and the yield curve has often reflected expectations of falling rates with a short end yield curve inversion.

Conversely, the equities markets show characteristics of market inefficiency and underdevelopment in several instances; the secondary bond market does not behave as a cointegrated system in periods of low trading volume; and the expectations hypothesis has extremely weak predictive power in the bond market. Such empirical analysis suggests that these markets lack the level of efficiency and development required to deal with the large foreign capital inflows likely to accompany full capital account convertibility.

China has control over the timetable of its formal and official movement to capital account convertibility, but there are already instances of integration between China's domestic and international equity markets, despite official segmentation. The presence of integration in the equities market, despite official controls to segment the domestic market from the international market, indicates that China's integration with global capital markets is moving ahead. With China increasingly dependent on additional sources of finance, this global integration is not contrary to Chinese interests, but China faces a time constraint. With integration developing on its own, the onus is on China to improve the efficiency of its domestic markets to prevent instability emerging from widespread integration without the support of domestic market efficiency.

Debt markets

In line with behaviour witnessed in developed markets, Hasenstab (2001) finds that the behaviour of domestic bond yields in this market imply efficiency. Furthermore, cointegration testing indicates that there is an underlying trend between the various benchmark yields, justifying the claim that China has a 'yield curve'. Error correction tests regarding the relationship between different parts of the curve were far less conclusive. The expectations hypothesis on the term structure of interest rates proved to have low predictive powers in China. It appears that the bond market behaves differently over different periods and is segmented between benchmark bonds with varying maturities.

The answer to the question 'is China's bond market sufficiently developed to operate with open capital controls?', is 'not yet'. When the government promoted secondary market activity on the Shanghai exchange before 1999, the market operated with an underlying common trend; that is, there was a yield curve and the outlook for the ongoing development and deepening of this market appeared optimistic. Budding characteristics of a more developed bond market should have been nurtured. Instead, reductions in institutional participation limits in this market reduced trading volume and reversed these trends. Without a liquid and transparent

TABLE 11.2   EVALUATION OF CHINA'S SECURITIES MARKETS

Requirements [a]	Evaluation of progress in China
Standardised contracts	Centralisation of trading markets to Shanghai and Shenzhen has helped significantly and numerous efforts to standardise the treatment of cash and pay-in-kind dividends to various classes of shareholder have improved overall standardisation. On the other hand, multiple share markets and multiple classes of equity holder greatly inhibit progress. Credit claims on assets are still unclear.
Grading of risk via underwriting	Essentially non-existent. The government still controls the listing process. A lack of independent investment banks or private banks hinders this process. More foreign bank underwriting activity would greatly improve this situation and transfer the necessary technology and skills to domestic market participants. Increased capabilities of new rating agencies could help provide some level of risk grading.
Database of historic statistics	Greatly improved in the past few years. Historic prices for most equities—listed domestically and internationally—are readily available. Comprehensive government bond price data are far more difficult to obtain. Inter-bank data is not publicly available—even to domestic financial players. Furthermore, many corporate bonds are traded over the counter without publicly available prices.
Standardisation of applicable laws	Securities laws are often 'on the books' as mandated in the 1998 Securities Reform Act, but few are enforced. Ownership remains unclear and the lack of clear bankruptcy laws inhibits credit restructuring—see, for example, the Guandong Enterprises (GDE) and GITIC cases.
Standardisation of service quality	Weak but gradually improving. Newly-gained experience in debt work-outs will help in the future if standardised measures can be built from the process.
Technology to handle complexity analysis	Arguably better in China than most developing countries. of The Shanghai Stock Exchange is nearly fully automated and the trading floor provides more of a public relations showcase than an actual market function. There are concerns about the oversight of the systems responsible for settlement and clearing of trades. Analyst skill levels in domestic Chinese financial institutions are improving dramatically. Foreign participation in the market will help facilitate 'technology skills transfers'.

Notes: [a]The China Chengxin Credit Rating Company, which is the newest joint venture rating agency in China, is an example.
Source: Author's compilation.

secondary government bond market that trades as a 'yield curve', China lacks a necessary building block towards developing an efficient securities market.

In addition to the domestic bond market, China issues global government bonds on the international market. These parallel markets are officially segmented by China's capital control restrictions regarding Chinese ownership of financial assets issued in foreign markets. Tests by Hasenstab (2001) of domestic and global relationships of Chinese government bonds confirmed that these two markets are completely segmented; that is, capital market controls are complete and effective for the time being. There are several explanations as to why these two markets have remained segmented. They include official capital controls, the small total amount of Chinese global bonds on issue, the lack of significant profit incentives for investors to circumvent capital controls, the institutional nature of bond ownership making illegal circumvention of capital controls very difficult, and suspected intervention by Chinese government-directed financial institutions with offshore investment capacities to hold up the value of China's global bonds in periods of global financial turmoil.

Equity markets

While similar capital controls affecting the parallel global and domestic bond markets apply to parallel domestic and international Chinese equity markets, the greater total issuance size, the higher potential profits from circumvention of capital controls, and the diverse ownership of both institutions and individuals create a significantly different market environment.

Extending empirical testing of debt market global integration to the equity markets and building upon the growing literature on Chinese stockmarket behaviour and efficiency, Hasenstab (2001) explored the relationship between mainland Chinese and Hong Kong equity markets. Econometric analysis of individual stock returns of Chinese companies dually listed in the Hong Kong H share and mainland Chinese A share markets, finds evidence, not yet reported in the literature, of both partial integration between these two markets and a significant uni-directional price effect going from the Hong Kong to the Chinese equity markets for some of the sample's dually listed companies. This evidence of partial integration in over 50 per cent of dually listed stocks is in direct contrast to observation of the segmentation of the Chinese bond market. Furthermore, tests confirm that the stock prices are first difference stationary, an important indicator of random walk behaviour.

The operation of parallel but officially-separated markets trading securities written on the same underlying companies also allowed the testing of the efficient market hypothesis. Error correction modelling identified a significant number of cases of uni-directional price transmission relationships from the Hong Kong market to the main-land Chinese market that violate this hypothesis. If China were to open its capital accounts while its markets remained inefficient, there could be inefficiencies in the allocation of capital if market efficiency dynamics identified in this sample apply to China's capital markets in general.

EVALUATION OF CHINA'S SECURITIES MARKET REFORM

While China has moved a long way towards building securities markets, concerted policy reforms must continue in order to complete this process. An evaluation of China's securities market reform effort is summarised in Table 11.2. The left-hand column outlines some of the basic requirements for the successful development of China's securities market. China's progress towards meeting these requirements is then assessed in the right-hand column.

Policy innovations

China's future economic success and stability will rest largely on the ability of the PBS and the MOF to continue their proactive reforms and to mobilise capital to fund the real economy better through a private, market-driven financial sector. The state-owned sector will also increasingly rely on private capital markets to fund its recapitalisation efforts. The following are possible policy initiatives that could help develop such markets.

- **Delay capital account convertibility until both the bond and equity markets trade efficiently; that is, until the efficient market hypothesis is broadly satisfied.** Until internationally and domestically-listed Chinese government bond and equities trade efficiently, full capital account convertibility risks allowing initial capital to flow into an inefficient domestic Chinese market and thus exacerbate price disequilibria. This would direct capital to low efficiency uses.
- **Open the domestic market to foreign banking and securities firms and permit these firms to source yuan funds from domestic institutions and investors and allow them to invest in domestic assets.** Despite the growth in tradable securities markets, Hale (2002) estimates that the ten officially licensed fund-management companies control only US$6.8 billion spread across 33 closed-end mutual funds. To expand the share of mutual fund assets, China

has recently begun to introduce open-ended funds. There are currently six joint ventures between Chinese and foreign asset managers; however, joint venture regulations requiring foreign asset mangers to partner with local firms will limit the growth of the asset management industry in China. Furthermore, Hale (2002) reports that foreign banks only have a 1 per cent market share in China and are constrained by geographic barriers to expansion. Foreign firms will bring competitive bidding and risk valuations to the domestic market to determine real prices. Prices that fully reflect risk are a critical information component missing from the Chinese market at present and the longer prices remain distorted, the greater the potential for asset bubbles. These firms will help facilitate financial services technology and skill transfers and create future distribution links to foreign client markets for future placement of Chinese securities. Japanese and Latin American historical examples suggest that allowing domestic banks to compete directly in deposit-taking activity will not lead to the immediate collapse of Chinese firms. The development of an advanced domestic capital market necessary to finance future government spending and assist in the recapitalisation of the state sector will take considerably longer in isolation.

- **Regularised and standardised government debt issuance**. Forced debt issuance only perpetrates circular debt (or triangle debt) and marginalises the legitimacy of the government bond markets as real institutions for long-term fund raising. Developing a regular auction timetable, pre-announcing volumes, issuing standardised treasuries available to multiple classes of investor, and pricing these instruments via public bidding would allow China to develop a deep and liquid bond market while minimising speculative behaviour. This developed government bond market would give real prices to government debt serving as an important feedback mechanism for government policy, providing a real benchmark for pricing other fixed income instruments. It would allow for better risk management through standard risk management hedging techniques and help end the ongoing cycle of non-transparent circular debt finance between the government, state banks and the state-owned sector. Ultimately government debt financing costs will be lowered by reducing market uncertainty.
- **Current efforts to move government bond trading away from the Shanghai exchange to the inter-bank market should be stopped and a unified treasury bond market should be promoted.** Given the lack of transparency of bond trading in the inter-bank market and the fact that the secondary spot

market on the Shanghai exchange exhibits a number of signs of behaving in an efficient form, this efficient trading arena should be capitalised on and trading activity should be returned to the Shanghai exchange.

The periods in which secondary government bond trading volume on the Shanghai exchange is highest correlates to periods when the presence of a yield curve is indicated by statistical testing of this market. If the market were massively inefficient, it would make more sense to correct the trading rules and regulations before increasing issuance. It appears, however, that given sufficient volume, the secondary bond market exhibits several important characteristics of market efficiency. Obviously rules and regulations need to be improved, but this longer-term reform requirement should not impede the continued operation of Shanghai treasury bond trading. If the government follows through with its intention to move all trading activity to the inter-bank market, every effort to create an open and transparent market must be made.

- **Increase stock and bond issuance to effect changes in corporate governance.** Bottlenecks in the approval process for share issuance continue to hamper market development. The current rate of domestic company listings averages 8.5 per month. At this rate it will take approximately two years to deal with the current backlog of companies that have registered an interest to list in 1999 (Neoh 2000). Furthermore, the quota issuance system, whereby local governments nominate which companies are permitted to list, takes the decision away from the market and puts it into the hands of administrators. Without an active underwriter market, the veil of secrecy is perpetuated and lack of transparency creates information asymmetry problems that raise overall market risk levels. Neoh (2000) observes that local governments tend to put forward for listing companies in which they have an equity stake. Expanding total issuance through changes to the underwriting system is a first step.

While continued stock issuance and thus the transfer of ownership rights could dramatically change corporate governance in both state-owned and non-state-owned companies, the state's dominance in tradable and non-tradable shares has largely prevented the development of a new political economy in corporate ownership. On the one hand, ongoing issuance of cash dividends to state holders and share dividends or rights offerings to non-state equity holders has helped decrease the state's once unequivocal majority ownership stake in listed firms. On the other hand, even new stock issuance does not necessarily change

168

corporate governance. Xu and Wang (1997) found official managers and party officials hold key board and supervisory positions in many incorporated firms with high levels of state ownership. Therefore, the ongoing issuance of shares in conjunction with the issuance of shares to non-state investors and the de-emphasis on government-appointed managers will increasingly empower share-holders to place pressure on firms to maximise corporate profits.

- **Total corporate bond issuance needs to increase to close the gap with total equity issuance so as to prevent an unbalanced capital market and provide firms with longer-term debt finance options.** Secondary markets need to be promoted in corporate bonds to allow the market to find real prices and limit the liquidity premium required by voluntary investors to hold such corporate securities. Furthermore, both issuance markets—but especially the corporate debt issuance market—need to be based more on objective financial criteria and to be subject to less political influence.

- **Utilise the Hong Kong market.** China is the only developing country that has a developed financial market within its borders, namely Hong Kong. Given Hong Kong's possible importance in facilitating price discovery superior to mainland markets, increased use of the Hong Kong markets for future funding needs until the mainland Chinese markets are more developed could facilitate more efficient fund raising. If the results found in the data reported in this chapter are true for the broader market, Hong Kong's better price discovery could help lower information asymmetry problems and thus lower the risk premium placed on Chinese securities. A lower risk premium will thus lower the price at which companies can raise capital through share issuance. Recent proposals to is-sue Chinese treasury government bonds via the Hong Kong Stock Exchange should indicate some willingness and interest by Chinese central government officials to capitalise on Hong Kong's existing financial market infrastructure, and further pursuit of such efforts would complement the domestic develop-ment of mainland exchanges.

- **Invest heavily in technical trading systems and vigilantly continue to up-grade financial reporting standards and legal rights of share and bond-holders.** The lack of a simultaneous payments system, the lack of a corporate bond repo market, inefficient settlement systems, and the lack of unified real time price sources will dramatically hinder the development of both corporate and government securities markets. China has been upgrading its trading systems rapidly but additional investments are needed to keep pace with the increasing volume of total debt and equity issuance as well as to expand the scope of distribution.

Without full financial disclosure, proper enforcement of market regulations and an extension of Article 214 to the bond and derivatives markets, the mechanism for shareholders to exert positive changes on corporate governance will be marginalised, poor firm investment decisions will go unchecked, and insider trading will dominate the exchanges.

While the challenges of future reform remain great, few countries have moved so far in the development of tradable securities markets in such a short period as has China. Hopefully the issues raised in this chapter can be of use in continuing to build and reform what will be, later in this century alongside the United States and the Euro block, one of the world's three most important capital markets.

Notes

[1] These build upon the policy recommendations of Hasenstab (1999).

12 ▓▓▓▓▓▓

Radical economic reform and income distribution

Xin Meng

Economic reform has experienced two stages—a modest reform stage, and a radical reform stage. Before the mid 1990s the Chinese economic reform followed a gradual approach. During this period inequality in urban areas widened but the Chinese people as a whole were made better off (Zhao and Li 1999).

Since the mid 1990s, however, economic restructuring has accelerated. The state and collective employment share has reduced from 76 per cent of total urban employment in 1995 to 49 per cent in 1999 and unemployment has increased significantly. Although official unemployment figures have been kept very low, at around 3 per cent, several different estimates suggest that as many as 15–27 million state sector workers were laid off in 1999—an additional 7–12 per cent of the urban labour force (Fan 2000 and Appleton, Knight, Song, and Xia 2001).

Questions naturally arise as to whether the acceleration of economic restructuring has changed the nature of the increase in income inequality in urban China, and whether any particular groups of households are badly affected. Using three comparable urban household surveys this chapter investigates these questions by comparing the change in income inequality between the periods 1988–95 and 1995–99 and identifying the different contributing factors to the changes in each period.

Previous studies on income inequality changes in China focused mainly on the period up to the mid1990s (Knight and Song 1991; Kahn, Griffin, and Zhao 1992; Aaberge and Li 1997; Gustafsson and Li 1997, 1998, 1999; Knight and Li 1999; Yang 1999; Khan and Riskin 2000; Riskin, Zhao, and Li 2001). Due to the lack of available data, there are, as yet, no published studies on recent developments. In early 2000, however, the Institute of Economics at the Chinese Academy of Social Sciences, with assistance from the China Statistical Bureau, conducted a new household income distribution survey, collecting information on household income and expenditure in 1999 in 6 provinces. This chapter utilises this new survey together with two other comparable surveys conducted by the same Institute for the years 1988 and 1995.

BACKGROUND

China has experienced rapid economic growth since economic reforms began in the late 1970s. Over the period 1982–99, urban household per capita real income increased by 7.4 per cent per annum (China State Statistical Bureau (SSB) 2000). The rate of increase, however, varied from period to period. The annual increase in urban household real income was 5.6, 8.3, and 7.3 per cent for the periods 1982–88, 1988–95, and 1995–99, respectively. Income inequality also increased and this increase also varied across different periods of economic reform (Figure 12.1).

In the period before the early 1990s, economic reform was mainly concentrated on product markets and little was changed in terms of the compressed wage structure, immobility of labour, and the domination of state sector employment (Meng 2000). Correspondingly, income distribution changed very slightly. This is shown in Figure 12.1, where the income ratio of the tenth to the first decile was not very large, changing only from 259 per cent in 1981 to 295 per cent in 1991.

Factor market reform proceeded gradually from the early 1990s. By the mid 1990s, labour mobility across urban regions and between rural and urban areas increased (Meng 2000; West and Zhao 2000) and the rate of return to different levels of labour market skills widened (Knight and Song 1999). Accompanying this reform process, income inequality increased sharply (Kahn, Griffin, and Zhao 1992; Aaberge and Li 1997; Gustafsson and Li 1997, 1998, 1999; Knight and Li 1999; Yang 1999; Khan and Riskin 2000; Riskin, Zhao, and Li 2001). The ratio of the tenth to the first income decile increased from 295 per cent in 1991 to 378 per cent in 1995. The increase in income inequality in this period was mainly the result of increased regional dispersion (Gustafsson and Li 1999 and Khan and Riskin 2000).

Since 1995, urban economic reform has taken a sharp turn. Due to soft budget constraints and other property rights related problems, the Chinese state sector has been performing badly. In 1995–96, around 50 per cent of enterprises were

172

FIGURE 12.1   **CHANGE IN DISPERSION OF REAL PER CAPITA HOUSEHOLD INCOME IN URBAN CHINA, 1981–99**

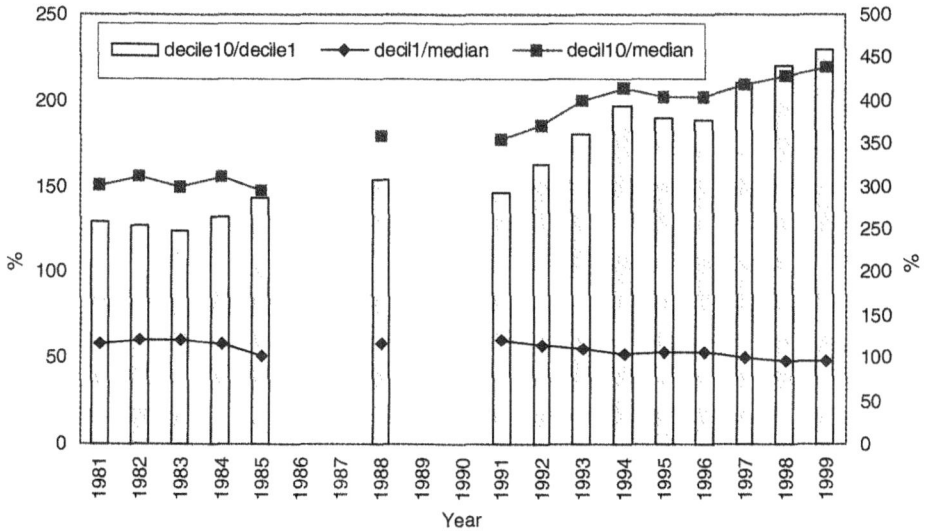

Source: State Statistical Bureau, *China Statistical Yearbook*, various years.

making losses. To vitalise the economy a policy of radical reform of SOEs was introduced in 1997 (Appleton, Knight, Son, and Xia 2001). Many small and medium-sized loss-making state enterprises were bankrupted as a result of this policy and the survivors began to take efficiency measures seriously. These two forces led to large-scale retrenchments.

Although official figures on urban unemployment only increased from 2.9 per cent in 1995 to 3.1 per cent in 1999, they do not include the majority of unemployed workers who were laid off from the state sector. The urban household surveys of 1995 and 1999 conducted by the Institute of Economics, Chinese Academy of Social Sciences, reveal that the urban unemployment rate when defined to include laid-off workers increased from 8 per cent to 17 per cent over this period.

Significant economic restructuring, leading to large increases in unemployment might be expected to widen income distribution. The effect of significant economic restructuring on income inequality during the period 1995–99 is apparent in Figure 12.1. The income ratio of the tenth to the first decile increased further from 378 per cent in 1995 to 459 per cent in 1999. More importantly, relative income at the bottom end of the distribution reduced from 54 per cent of medium income in 1995 to 47 per cent in 1999, while the average income at the top end of the distribution continued to increase.

CHANGES IN INCOME INEQUALITY OVER TIME

According to the survey data, average real household per capita disposable income grew from 1398 yuan in 1988 to 2125 yuan in 1995, and further to 2647 yuan in 1999. The average annual growth rate is 6.2 per cent for the period 1988–95 and 5.6 per cent for the period 1995–99. These growth rates are slightly lower than those reported in the national statistical data.

Table 12.1 presents a range of measures of income inequality. For the 1988 and 1995 data, the first column under each of the two years reports measures for the full sample (11 provinces) while the second column reports measures for the sample of 6 provinces consistent with those included in the 1999 data. Income inequality increased during the period of interest, regardless of the inequality measure, income measure, or sample used.

Using the Gini coefficient as an example, our estimates of the Gini for per capita household disposable income for the full sample increased from 23.4 in 1988, to 28.2 in 1995, and further increased to 31.3 in 1999.

Figure 12.2 plots the Lorenz curves for the three survey years (Panel A full sample, Panel B, 6 provinces sample). The solid curve indicates income distribution in 1988, the dash and dotted line indicates the 1995 situation, and the dashed curve presents the 1999 situation. If one Lorenz curve lies everywhere above another it is

TABLE 12.1   **VARIOUS INEQUALITY MEASURES OF INCOME, 1988, 1995, AND 1999**

	Real per capita HH income					Real HH income				
	1988		1995		1999	1988		1995		1999
	11 Prv.	6 Prv.	11 Prv.	6 Prv.	6 Prv.	11 Prv.	6 Prv.	11 Prv.	6 Prv.	6 Prv.
Relative mean Dv.	0.16	0.15	0.20	0.19	0.22	0.16	0.15	0.20	0.19	0.22
Coeff. Var.	0.49	0.45	0.60	0.59	0.63	0.49	0.44	0.59	0.54	0.65
Sd. Dv. of logs	0.42	0.39	0.51	0.50	0.60	0.43	0.40	0.50	0.48	0.61
Gini coefficient	0.23	0.22	0.28	0.27	0.31	0.24	0.22	0.28	0.26	0.31
Mehran measure	0.32	0.30	0.38	0.38	0.43	0.32	0.30	0.38	0.36	0.43
Piesch measure	0.19	0.17	0.23	0.22	0.26	0.19	0.17	0.23	0.21	0.25
Kakwani measure	0.05	0.04	0.07	0.07	0.09	0.05	0.05	0.07	0.06	0.09
Theil entropy measure	0.10	0.08	0.14	0.13	0.17	0.10	0.08	0.14	0.12	0.17
Theil mean log Dv.	0.09	0.08	0.13	0.13	0.17	0.09	0.08	0.13	0.12	0.17

FIGURE 12.2   **LORENZ CURVES FOR REAL PER CAPITA HOUSEHOLD DISPOSABLE INCOME, 1988, 1995, AND 1999**

Penal A: Full sample

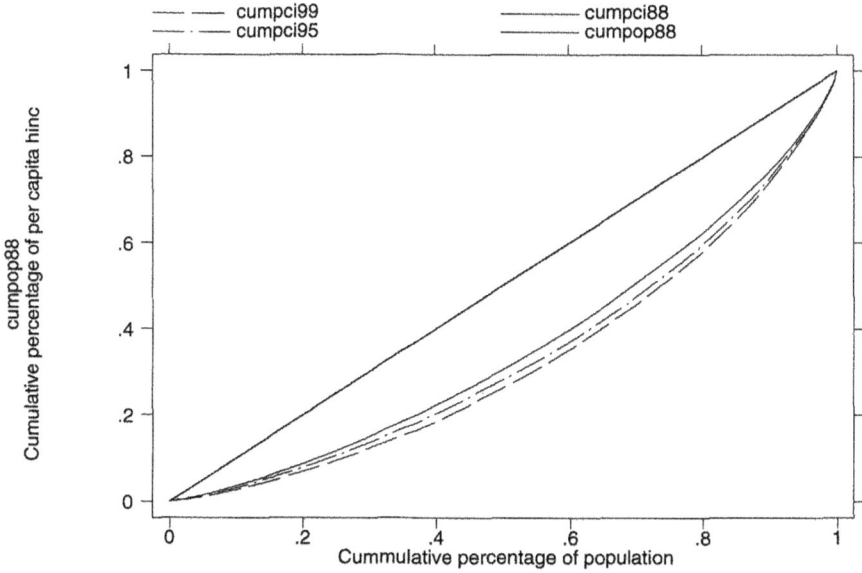

Panel B: Sample of consistent 6 provinces

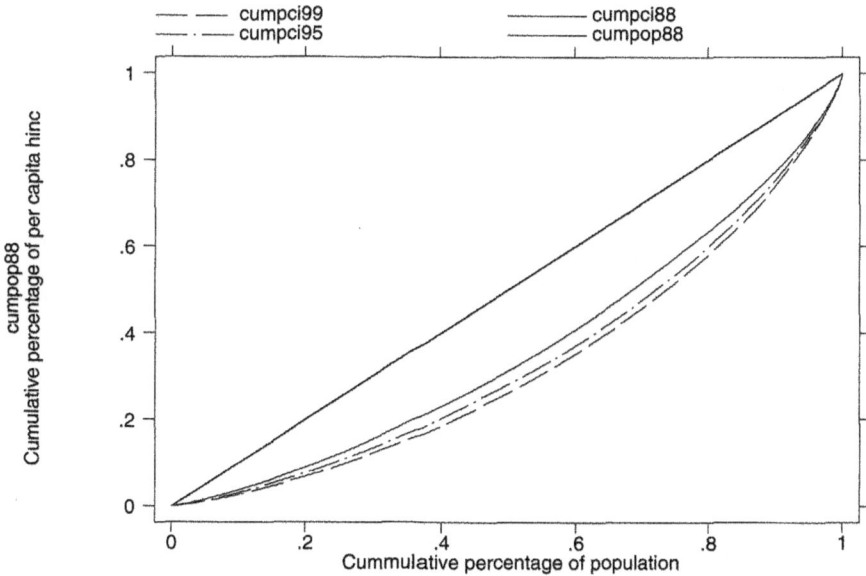

FIGURE 12.3 **AVERAGE PER CAPITA INCOME DISTRIBUTION, 1988, 1995, AND 1999**

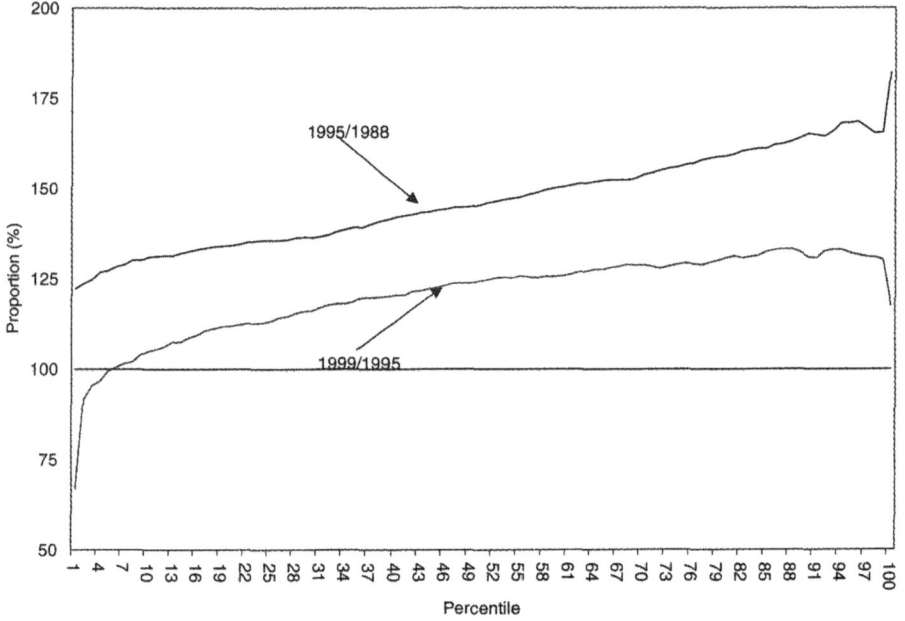

said to 'Lorenz dominate' the other curve and all inequality measures will show inequality to be lower for the higher curve. What is observed from Figure 12.2 is that the 1988 Lorenz curve dominates that of 1995, which in turn dominates that of 1999, confirming that income inequality increased over the period. The fact that there is no Lorenz-crossing enables an unambiguous conclusion that income inequality has increased, as a basis for study of its causes.

Figure 12.3 depicts the changes in the average income of each percentile of the real PCHI distribution. Over the 1988–95 period, both the top and bottom end of the income distribution gained income although the top end gained more. Whereas over the 1995–99 period strong income growth is observed for the top sixty percentiles (about a 20 per cent increase), a moderate growth for the lower middle income group (around a 10–20 per cent increase), a very slight increase for the fifth to the fifteenth percentile, and a reduction in income for the bottom five percentiles.

Why did household income at the lower end of the distribution fall while medium and high income families enjoyed significant income gains over the period 1995–99? As economic restructuring may be an important cause, Figure 12.4 presents the distribution of households with unemployed members across different income deciles in 1995 and 1999. It indicates that the number of households with unemployed members more than doubled for the lower two deciles while it hardly changed for the top two deciles.

If unemployment is an important cause of the reduction in income at the lower end of the distribution between 1995 and 1999, why is it that not all households with unemployed members fall into the lowest income group? Perhaps the reduction in household income from one member being unemployed can be offset by income earned by other employed members. Of course, households with more unemployed members are less likely to be able to compensate within the household and hence more likely to fall into the lower end of the distribution. Indeed, in 1999 around 50 per cent of the households with two or more unemployed members were located at the bottom ten percentiles of the income distribution, and about thirty per cent of these households were concentrated at the lowest five percentiles of the distribution.

IDENTIFYING CONTRIBUTING FACTORS TO THE CHANGE IN INCOME INEQUALITY

A regression analysis on the determinants of income variation reveals the following interesting results, especially when compared across the three survey years.

First, the effect of education on real PCHI has increased over time. One more year of education increased real PCHI by 1.9 per cent in 1988, 3.4 per cent in 1995, and 4.4 per cent in 1999. The increase in the return to education reflects the effect of market-oriented economic reform in the urban labour market.

Second, party members earn significantly higher earnings than non-party members. In 1988, a household where both husband and wife were party members received 10 per cent more per capita income than households without any party member, this ratio increased to 13 per cent in 1995, and 20 per cent in 1999.

Third, household residential location plays an important role in the determination in income variation in all three years. However, the effect is the most obvious in 1995.

Finally, the most important changes come about in variables representing economic restructuring. The effects on household income of unemployment and working in a loss-making firm have changed considerably, though the change in the

FIGURE 12.4   **DISTRIBUTION OF HOUSEHOLDS WITH UNEMPLOYED MEMBERS ACROSS INCOME DECILES**

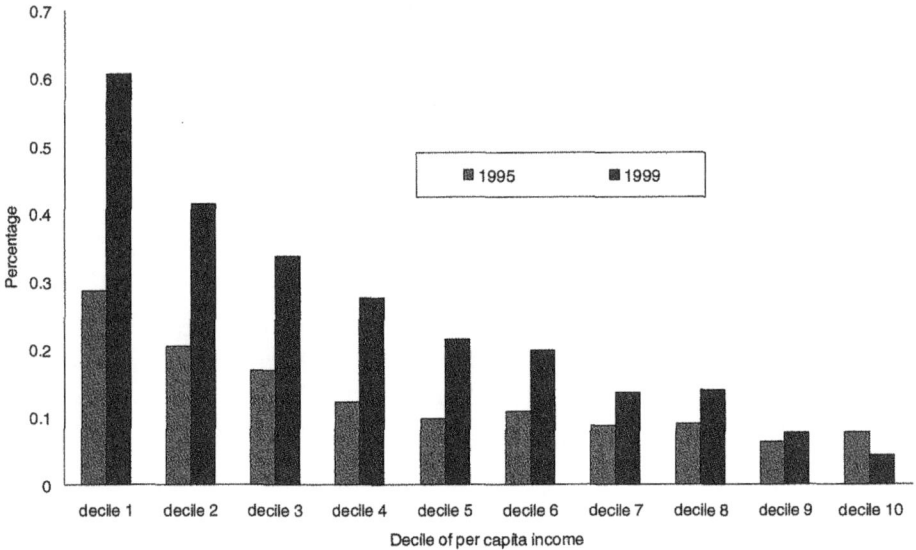

return to different sectors of employment have not been particularly significant.

In 1988, there were few unemployed individuals (only 3 per cent of the total labour force) and the effect of unemployment on household income was insignificant. By 1995 there was a significant change. A household with a husband who is unemployed has a 9 per cent lower PCHI than a household without the unemployed husband. The income reduction for households with wives or sons/daughters being unemployed is 10.5 and 7.5 per cent, respectively. In addition, working in loss-making firms also reduces income substantially. A household with both husband and wife working in a loss-making firm receives 17.7 per cent less income than otherwise. Working in a loss-making firm is a first step towards becoming unemployed.

By 1999, radical urban state sector reform had been in place for about 4–5 years and the effect on household income variation was even more severe than in 1995. Households with unemployed husbands, wives, or sons/daughters receive 29, 26, and 16 per cent less income, respectively, than households where these members were employed. These ratios are between double to triple those observed in 1995. The loss of income for households with husbands working in loss-making firms also increased. In 1995, the per capita income of these households was about 9 per cent less than households without husbands working in a loss-making firm. By 1999, this ratio had increased to 17 per cent.

To identify the contributing factors of income inequality further over the period studied, Fields' decomposition (1998) approach is employed to quantify the degree to which the variables included in the income-generating equation account for the level of income inequality. The variables included in the estimated per capita household income equation are grouped into 5 contributing factors.

- 'Economic restructuring' which includes the effect of household members (husband, wife, and sons/daughters) being unemployed, working in a loss-making firm, and their sector of employment.
- 'Regional effect' which is captured by the regional dummy variables.
- 'Party membership' which includes the two dummy variables indicating whether the husband or wife is a party member.
- 'Human capital' effect which is measured by the average age of household labourers, its squared term, and the average years of schooling of household labourers.
- 'Household composition' which covers the effect of the gender of the household head, the young and old dependency ratios, family size, and the number of labourers in the household.

This analysis shows that the most important contributing factor to income inequality changed from household composition in 1988 to regional effect in 1995, and to economic restructuring effect in 1999. In 1988 there is hardly any effect on income inequality from economic restructuring. In 1995, about 7 per cent of income inequality is due to the effect of economic restructuring, of which sector of employment accounted for about half. The effect of economic restructuring had increased to more than 20 per cent of the level of income inequality by 1999, of which the effect of unemployment contributed more than 9 percentage points.

The regional effect has always been significant, but only in 1995 is it identified as the single factor accounting for most of the income inequality. This result is consistent with that found in Gustafsson and Li (1999) and Khan and Riskin (2000). Other effects which have gained some grounds in 1999, relative to 1988 and 1995, are party membership and human capital effects but these do not play as significant a role as that of economic restructuring.

To what extent do different factors contribute to the increase in income inequality

TABLE 12.2   DECOMPOSITION OF THE CONTRIBUTING FACTORS TO THE CHANGE IN THE GINI COEFFICIENT, 1988–95, AND 1995–99

	1988 Gini=0.234 $S_j(lnY)$	1995 Gini=0.282 $S_j(lnY)$	1999 Gini=0.313 $S_j(lnY)$	Change 1988–95 $P_j(Gini)$	Change 1995–99 $P_j(Gini)$
Restructuring	0.39	2.02	6.35	33.96	139.55
Of which: unemployment	0.11	0.40	2.84	6.02	78.70
Loss-making firm	0.00	0.67	1.87	13.97	38.82
Sector of emp.	0.27	0.95	1.63	13.97	22.03
Regional effect	4.01	6.38	4.26	49.47	-68.60
Party	0.26	0.56	1.20	6.11	20.84
Human capital	0.67	1.81	2.23	23.65	13.53
Household composition	6.13	4.53	2.24	-33.40	-73.86
Residual	11.94	12.91	15.03	20.21	68.54
Total	23.40	28.20	31.30	100.00	100.00

over the periods? To quantify this the change in income inequality over the two periods are further identified. Table 12.2 summarises these results in terms of the change in the Gini coefficients between 1988–95 and 1995–99.

The results show that the regional effect contributed 50 per cent of the increase in the Gini coefficient between 1988 and 1995. Economic restructuring contributed around 34 per cent, of which unemployment accounted for 6 percentage points, while household members working in a loss-making firm or sector of employment each contributed to more than 13 percentage points. Another important factor that contributed to the increase in income inequality between 1988 and 1995 is the human capital factor, which accounted for about one quarter of the increase in the Gini coefficient. This finding is consistent with other studies indicating that the effect of labour market reform increased the rate of return to human capital in the 1990s (Knight and Song 1999; Meng 2000).

During the period 1995–99 the main contributing factor to the increase in the Gini coefficient is the factor of economic restructuring, which accounted for more than 100 per cent of such change[1] while the regional effect contributed to the reduction of the Gini coefficient. Of the economic restructuring factor, unemployment contributed 79 per cent of the increase in the Gini coefficient, while working in a loss-making firm and the sector of employment each contributed 39 and 22 per cent, respectively. Another important effect contributing to the increase in the Gini coefficient during this period was party membership. Around one fifth of the increase in inequality can be explained by this factor. The reason that the effect of party membership increased income inequality is due to a sharp increase in the rate of return to party membership as there has been little change in the proportion of households with a party member.

To conclude, the increase in inequality between 1988 and 1995 is mainly due to the increase in regional income variation, whereas the main contributing factor to the inequality increase between 1995 and 1999 is economic restructuring.

CONCLUSIONS

Income inequality has increased considerably over the period of economic transition from a planned to a market oriented economy in urban China. This study has investigated this change over two important phases of the economic transition: the initial stage of acceleration of the state sector and urban labour market reforms (1988–95) and the period of radical reform in the state sector and the urban labour market (1995–99).

First, although income inequality increased during each period, the nature of the increase is different. In the first period everybody was made better off and the increase in inequality was due to the relatively stronger income growth at the top end of the distribution. In the second period, however, households at the lowest 5 percentile income distribution experienced an income reduction, while households at the top end of the distribution enjoyed significant income gains. Thus, in terms of social welfare, the increase in inequality in the first period was compensated by an unambiguous increase in social welfare at every level of income distribution, whereas this was not the case in the second period. This may be a reason why the social stability issue has become more of a concern since the late 1990s.

Second, while the increase in income inequality in the first period was mainly due to the increase in regional income variations, this effect was dominated by the impact of economic restructuring in the second period. The increase in the number of households with unemployed members and the significant increase in income reduction for unemployed households contributed more than 78 per cent of the increase in the Gini coefficient over the period 1995–99. In addition, households with members working at a loss-making firm also contributed considerably to the increase in income inequality during this period.

The interesting issue, though, is that not all households with unemployed members fell into the low income group. While around 40 per cent of such households had income at or below the 20th percentile, nearly 11 per cent of households with unemployed members received income above the 70th percentile. This difference may be closely related to the concentration of unemployed members within each household. Indeed, although only 3.7 per cent of households in 1999 had more than one unemployed member, on average these households earned more than 50 per cent less real PCHI than other households, *ceteris paribus*. The significant effect of unemployment concentration on income reduction, and hence, on income inequality suggests that, to a large extent, some of the unemployment effect may have been cushioned by within household income transfers. Households whose members are unable to compensate each other are more likely to suffer from severe income reduction due to economic restructuring. Therefore, the households that deserve more government assistance may be those which have more than one member unemployed.

Acknowledgments

The author is grateful to the financial support from the Ford Foundation and the International Centre for the Study of East Asian Development, Japan.

Note

[1] This implies that, had there been no offsetting factors, the increase in the Gini coefficient would have been more significant.

References

Aaberge, R. and Li, X.,1997, 'The trend in urban income inequality in two Chinese provinces, 1986-1990', *Review of Income and Wealth*, 43(3):335–55.

Anderson, J.H., Lee, Y. and Murrell, P., 2000. 'Competition and privatization amidst weak institutions: evidence from Mongolia,' *Economic Inquiry*, 38(4):527–49.

Appleton, S., Knight, J., Song, L., and Xia, Q., 2001. 'Towards a competitive labour market? Urban workers, rural-urban migrants, redundancies and hardship in urban China', paper presented at American Economics Association Annual Conference, 2001, New Orleans.

Bao, S., Chang, G. H., Sachs, J. D. and Woo, W. T., 2001. 'Geographic factors and China's regional development under market reforms, 1978–98' memio, available online at http://www.utoledo.edu/gchang/publication/geo5.pdf, last accessed on 2 January 2002.

Carlin, W., Fries, S., Schaffer, M.E. and Seabright, P., 2001. *Competition and Enterprise Performance in Transition Economies: evidence from a cross-country survey*, Working Paper No. 63, European Bank for Reconstruction and Development.

Centre for News Gathering and Editing, 2002. 'Grain Price in China Continue to Increase in the Third Quarter of 2001', China Agriculture Web. Available online at: http://www.aweb.com.cn.

Chen, Chunlai., 2001. 'The implications of china's WTO accession for foreign direct investment in China', in *The Implications of TIL for China's Domestic Economic Development and Policies*, OECD, Paris.

——, 2000. *The Location Determinants of Foreign Direct Investment in Developing Countries: with special reference to comparing China's performance in attracting FDI with other developing countries*, Research Paper to the MOFTEC/OECD Cooperation Program on FDI.

Chen, Q., 2001. 'Issues on reform and development of large enterprise in China', *Management World*, Beijing, 1:2–6.

Countries: with special reference to comparing China's performance in attracting FDI with other developing countries, Research Paper to the MOFTEC/OECD Cooperation Program on FDI.

China People's Daily, 2001. 'Chinese debt market needs further reform', November 19. Available online at: http://english.peopledaily.com.cn/200111/19/eng20011119_84872.shtml.

Chuang, Y. and Hsu, P., 2001. 'International trade, foreign direct investment and industrial productivity: the case of China', *Academia Economic Papers,* 29(2):221–49.

Deardorff, A., 2001. 'International provision of trade services, trade, and fragmentation', *Review of International Economics,* 9(2): 233–48.

Dee, P. and Hanslow, K., 2000a. 'Multilateral liberalisation of services trade', Productivity Commission Staff Research Paper, March.

——, 2000b. 'Modelling the liberalisation of services', in Productivity Commission and Australian National University, *Achieving Better Regulation of Services,* Conference Proceedings, AusInfo, Canberra, November.

Démurger, S., 2001. 'Infrastructure development and economic growth: an explanation for regional disparities in China?', *Journal of Comparative Economics* 29(1): 95–117.

Démurger, S., Sachs, J. D., Woo, W. T., Bao, S., Chang, G. and Andrew. 2001. 'Geography, economic policy and regional development in China', *Working Paper NO.77,* Center for International Development at Harvard University, available online at http://www.cid.harvard.edu/cidwp/077.htm, last accessed on 2 January 2002.

Department of Industry, the State Economic and Trade Committee, 2001, 'The progress in loan-share conversion', *China Economic and Trade Herald,* Beijing, 1:12.

Department of Training and Employment of the Ministry of Labour and Social Security, and Rural Social and Economic Survey Team of the National Statistical Bureau (MLSS & NBS), 1999. *The Situation of Rural Labourers' Employment and Flow in China, 1997–98,* Beijing.

Drysdale, P., 2000. 'The implications of China's membership of the WTO for industrial transformation', Chapter 7 in Drysdale, P. and Song, L. (eds), *China's Entry to the WTO: Strategic Issues and Quantitative Assessments,* Routledge, London and New York.

Drysdale, P. and Song, L. (eds), 2000. *China's Entry to the WTO: strategic issues and quantitative assessments,* Routledge, London.

Editorial Office of China Economic Systems Reform Yearbook, 1999. *Yearbook of China's Economic System Reform 1999*, Golden Shield Printing, Beijing.

Fan, G., 2000. 'The dynamics of transition in China: change of ownership structure and sustainability of growth', paper presented at the International Conference of China Growth Sustainability in the 21st Century, Canberra, Australia.

Fan, G. and Wang, X., 2001. *NERI Index of Marketisation of China's Provinces*, Economic Science Press, Beijing.

Fields, G.S., 1998. 'Accounting for income inequality and its change', mimeo, Cornell University.

Findlay, C., 2001. 'China's admittance to the WTO and industrial structural adjustment in the world economy', *Pacific Economic Papers No.315* Australia–Japan Research Centre, The Australian National University, May.

Findlay, C. and Warren T., (eds) 2000. *Impediments to Trade in Services: Measurement and Policy Implications*, Routledge, London.

Garnaut, R., 1989. *Australia and the Northeast Asia Ascendancy*, Australian Government Publishing Service, Canberra.

Garnaut, R. and Song, L., (eds), 1999. *China: twenty years of reform*, Asia Pacific Press, Canberra.

Garnaut, R., Song, L., Yao, Y., and Wang, X., 2001. *Private Enterprise in China*, Asia Pacific Press, Canberra.

Goldman Sachs, 1999. *Global Economics*, Paper No. 14, 26 April.

Gregory, N., Tenev, S. and Wagle, D., 2000. *China's Emerging Private Enterprises: prospects for the new century*, International Finance Corporation (IFC), Washington D.C.

Gruen, N., 2001. 'Beyond the safety net: a view from outside', presentation to the APEC Telecommunications Working Group, Canberra, March.

Gustafsson, B. and Li, S., 1997. 'Types of income and inequality in China at the end of the 1980s', *Review of Income and Wealth*, 43(2):211–26.

——, 1998. 'Inequality in China at the end of the 1980s: locational aspects and household characteristics', *Asian Economic Journal*, 12(1):25–64.

——, 1999. 'A more unequal China? Aspects of inequality in the distribution of equivalent income', unpublished manuscript.

Hale, D., 2002. 'New opportunities for financial services firms in China', available online at: http://www.chinaonline.com/commentary_analysis/thiswk_comm/020109/C02011731.asp

Hasenstab, M., 2001. Tradable securities markets in the People's Republic of China: an empirical study of China's debt and equity markets, Ph.D. dissertation, The Australian National University, Canberra.

——, 1999. 'Financial system reform and implications', in R. Garnaut and L. Song (eds), *China: Twenty Years of Reform*, Asia Pacific Press, Canberra:117–48.

Hoekman, B., 1999. 'The next round of services negotiations: identifying priorities and options', paper presented at the Federal Reserve Bank of St. Louis conference on Multilateral Trade Negotiations: Issues for the Millennium Round, October 21–22, 1999 (revised 4 November 1999).

Huang, J. and Ma, H., 2001. 'Why is the difference in competition of agricultural products between China and the world so big? An international comparison of production costs.' *Working paper WP-oo-C21*, China Center for Agricultural Policy, Chinese Academy of Sciences, Beijing. In Chinese, available online at http://www.ccap.org.cn/cn/cn/research/discussc.htm.

Huang, J., Rosegrant, M. and Rozelle, S., 1998. *Public Investment, Technological Change and Reform: a comprehensive accounting of Chinese agricultural growth*, Department of Agricultural and Resource Economics working paper series, University of California, California.

International Labour Office, 1998. *Yearbook of Labour Statistics*; cited from National Bureau of Statistics, 1999. *Statistical Yearbook of China,* Statistics Press, Beijing.

Jefferson, G.H. and Singh, I., 1999. *Enterprise Reform in China: ownership, transition and performance*, Oxford University Press, Oxford.

Kendall, L., 1996. 'Securitization: a new era in American finance', in L. Kendall and M. Fishman (eds), *A Primer on Securitization*, MIT Press, Cambridge:1–16.

Khan, A.R., Griffin, and Zhao, 1992. 'Household income and its distribution in China', *China Quarterly*, 132:1086–100.

Khan, A.R. and Riskin, C., 2000. *Inequality and Poverty in China in the Age of Globalization*, Oxford University Press, Oxford.

Knight, J. and Li, S., 1999. 'Fiscal Decentralization, redistribution and reform in China', *Oxford Development Studies*, 27(1):5–32.

Knight, J. and Song, L. 1991. 'The determinants of urban income inequality in China', *Oxford Bulletin of Economics and Statistics*, 53:123–54.

——, 1999. 'Economic growth, economic reform and increase in income inequality in China' in Renwei, Z., Shi, L. and Riskin, C., (eds), *Re-Thinking Chinese House-*

hold Income Distribution (in Chinese), Beijing: Financial and Economic Press of China:167–211.

Kornai, J., 1980. *Economics of Shortage,* North Holland Publishing Co., Amsterdam.

Li R., 2001. 'Improving the comprehensive work for economic and trade', *China Economic and Trade Herald,* Beijing, 1:5.

Limao, N. and Venables, A., 2001. 'Infrastructure, geographical disadvantage and transport costs', *World Bank Economic Review,* 15(3):451–80.

Lin, J.Y., 1996. 'Dual-track price and supply response: theory and empirical evidence from Chinese agriculture', unpublished manuscript, Chinese Center for Economic Research, Beijing.

——, 1992. 'Rural reform and agricultural growth in China', *American Economic Review,* 82:34–51.

Lin W., Liu, G., and Wu, L., 2001. 'A research on food elasticity of China's rural residents', research report for the research project 'Chinese Food Supply and Demand Analysis', the Ministry of Science and Technology and the Ministry of Agriculture, Beijing.

Lin, Y. F. and Cai, F., 1997. *Sufficient Information and SOE Reform,* Sanlian Publishing house, Shanghai.

Liu, Z., 2001. 'The importance and urgency of carrying forward strategic restructuring of SOEs', *Management World,* Beijing, 2:5–7.

Lu, Z. Y., 2001. 'Achievement and problems of SOE reform, and suggestions on deepening reform during the '10th Five-Year-Plan' period', *Financial and Trade Economics,* 1:12–14.

McKibbin, W. and Wilcoxen, P., 1998. *The global impacts of trade and financial reform in China,* Asia Pacific School of Economics and Management Working Paper 98–3, The Australian National University, Canberra.

Mattoo, A., 2001. 'China's accession to the WTO: the services dimension', mimeo, World Bank, October.

Meng, L. and Wang, X., 2000. 'The reliability of the statistics on China's economic growth', in Wang and Fan (ed), *Sustainability of China's Economic Growth,* Economic and Science Press, Beijing:451–81.

Meng, X., 2000. *Labour Market Reform in China,* Cambridge University Press, Cambridge.

Ministry of Agriculture, China (MOA), various years. *China Agricultural Develop-*

ment Report, Beijing.

Ministry of Agriculture, China, Information Centre survey data.

Morrison, W. M., 2001. 'China–US trade issues', Congressional Research Service Issue Brief, IB91121, April 13, available online at http://www.cnie.org/nle/econ-35.html.

Mousley, P., 2001. The World Bank experience in building an enabling environment for SME development, Paper presented at the International Conference on Building Enabling Environment for SMEs, organised by International Finance Corporation (IFC) and State Economic and Trade Commission (SETC), Chengdu, 17–18 May.

Nathan, A. J. and Link, P., (eds) 2001. *The Tiananmen Papers,* Little, Brown and Co., London.

Naughton, B., 1994. *Growing Out of Plan: Chinese economic reform, 1978–1993,* Cambridge University Press, New York.

Neoh, A., 2000. 'China's domestic capital markets in the new millennium', Available online at: http://www.chinaonline.com/commentary_analysis/economics/currentnews/secure/c00082143.asp

Office of the Leading Group for West Development of the State Council, 2000. *Guojia Zhichi Xibu Dakaifa de Youguan Zhengce Cuoshi* [State's Relevant Policies and Measures on Supporting the Development of West Areas].

Pacific Economic Cooperation Journal, 2001. *2001 Pacific Economic Outlook,* available online at www.pacificeconomicoutlook.com.

People's Bank of China (PBC), 2001. *Quarterly Statistical Bulletin*, Volume XVII, January, People's Bank of China, Beijing.

——, 2000. *China Financial Outlook 2000*, People's Bank of China, Beijing.

Riskin, C., Zhao, R., and Li, S., 2001. *China's Retreat from Equality: income distribution and economic transition,* M.E. Sharpe, Armonk, N.Y.

Rozelle, S., and Boisvert, R., 1993. 'Grain policy in Chinese villages: yield response to pricing, procurement, and loan policies', *American Journal of Agricultural Economies*, 75, May: 339-349.

Sala-i-Martin, X., 1997. 'I just ran two million regressions', *American Economic Review 87* (Papers and Proceedings): 178–83.

Sicular, T. 1988, "Plan and Market in China's Agricultural Commerce", *Journal of Political Economy*, 96(2):283–305.

Song, L., 2001a. Behaviour of private enterprises in a partially reformed system—

China, Paper presented at the 13th Conference of the Association for Chinese Economic Studies, (Australia), Wollongong University, Wollongong, 14–15 July.

——, 2001b. Interest rate liberalisation in China and the implications for non-state banking, Paper presented at International Conference on Financial Sector Reform in China, John F. Kennedy School of Government, Harvard University, 11–13 September.

State Council of the People's Republic of China, (various issues). *Gazette of the State Council of the People's Republic of China*, General Office of the State Council of the People's Republic of China, Beijing.

State Statistics Bureau of the PRC, 1998. *Industrial Statistical Yearbook of China*, China Statistical Publishing House, Beijing.

——, 1997. *Market Statistical Yearbook of China*, China Statistical Publishing House, Beijing.

——, (various years). *Statistical Yearbook of China*, China Statistical Publishing House, Beijing.

——, various years. *Zhongguo Duiwai Jingji Tongji Nianjian* [China Foreign Economic Statistical Yearbook], Zhongguo Tongji Chubanshe, Beijing.

Sun, H., 2000. 'Economic growth and regional disparity in China', *Regional Development Studies* 6:43–66.

Sun, H. and Parikh, A., 2001. 'Exports, inward foreign direct investment (FDI) and regional economic growth in China', *Regional Studies* 35 (3): 187–96.

Tian, G., 2000. 'Property rights and the nature of Chinese collective enterprises,' *Journal of Comparative Economics*, 28:247–68.

United Nations Conference on Trade and Development (UNCTAD), 2000. *World Investment Report, Cross-border mergers and Acquisitions and Development*, United Nations, New York and Geneva.

Walmsley, T. and Hertel, T., 2000. *China's Accession to the WTO: timing is everything*, Centre for Global Trade Analysis, Purdue University.

Wang, X., forthcoming. 'The contribution of the non-state sector to China's economic growth', in R. Garnaut and L. Song (ed), *China's Third Economic Transformation: the Rise of the Private Economy*, Routledge, London.

——, 2002. 'The WTO impact on China's agricultural sector', mimeo, National Centre for Development Studies, Australian National University, Canberra.

——, 2001, 'Grain market fluctuations and government intervention in China', research report for the ACIAR project 'China's Grain Market Policy Reform', The Australian National University, Canberra.

——, 2000. 'The sustainability of China's economic growth and institutional changes", in Wang, X. and Fan, G. (eds), *The Sustainability of China's Economic Growth*, Economic Science Press, Beijing.

——, 1999. 'China's Rural Economy: sustainable development and population holding capacity', in F. Lo and Y. Xing (eds), *Sustainable Development Framework for Developing Countries: the case of China*, The United Nations University Publication, Tokyo.

——, 1996. 'Product, Management, and the Enterprise System: problems faced by firms', *Economic Research,* Beijing, 9.

Wang, X. and Xiaolin, X., 1999. 'Optimum city size and economic growth', *Economic Research*, 9, Beijing.

Warren, T., 2000. 'The impact on output of impediments to trade and investment in telecommunications services', in Findlay, C. and Warren, T., (eds), *Impediments to Trade in Services: measurement and policy implications*, Routledge, London and New York.

Wen, M., (forthcoming). 'Bankruptcy, sale and mergers as a route to the reform of Chinese SOEs', *China Economic Review*.

Wen, M., Li, D. and Lloyd, P., (forthcoming). 'Ownership and technical efficiency — a cross-section study on the Third National Industrial Census of China,' *Economic Development and Cultural Change*.

Wen, M. and Zhang, X., 2001. 'Capital allocation in China', in P. Lloyd and X. Zhang (eds), *Models of the Chinese Economy*, Edward Elgar, Cheltenham:135–48.

Wenping, L. and Findlay, C., 2001. 'Logistics in China: accession to the WTO and its implications', mimeo, World Bank, December.

West, L. A., and Zhao, Y., 2000. *Rural Labor Flows in China*, Institute of East Asian Studies, University of California, Berkeley.

World Bank, 1997. *World Development Indicators*, Washington DC, also available online at http://devdata.worldbank.org/data/query.

World Trade Organization, 2001. 'Accession of the People's Republic of China, Decision of 10 November 2001'. Available online at: http://www.moftec.gov.cn.

Wu, L., 2001. 'Price comparison between world and domestic grain markets', research report for the ACIAR project 'China's Grain Market Policy Reform', The

Australian National University, Canberra.

Wu, L., Liu, Q. and Ke, B., 1997. Monitoring and studying prices of major agricultural products: 1996 report, mimeo.

Wu, Y., 2000. 'The determinants of economic growth: evidence from a panel of Chinese provinces', Paper presented at the international conference of china: Growth sustainability in the 21st century, The Australian National University, Canberra, 9-10 September 2000.

——, 1999. 'Income disparity and convergence in China's regional economies', Discussion Paper 99-15, Department of Economics, University of Western Australia, available online at \urlhttp://www.econs.ecel.uwa.edu.au/economics/dpapers /DP1999/9.15.pdf, last accessed on 2 January 2002.

Xu, X. 1998. *China's Financial System Under Transition*, Macmillan Press, London.

Yang, D. T., 1999. 'Urban-biased policies and rising income inequality in China' *American Economic Review*, 89(2):306–10.

Yang, Y., and Huang, Y., 1997. 'The impact of trade liberalisation on income distribution in China', Economics Division Working Papers, China Economy 97/1, Research School of Pacific and Asian Studies, Australian National University, Canberra.

Yao, Y., 2001. The development of the private economy: the role of the government, Paper presented at the International Conference on Building Enabling Environment for SMEs, organised by International Finance Corporation (IFC) and State Economic and Trade Commission (SETC), Chengdu, 17–18 May.

Zank, N., 1990. 'Privatisation and deregulation in the LDC financial sector: an AID perspective', in D.J. Gayle and J.N. Goodrich (eds), *Privatisation and Deregulation in Global Perspective*, Quorum Books, New York:126–38.

Zhang, A., Zhang, Y. and Zhao, R., 2001. 'Impact of ownership and competition on the productivity of Chinese Enterprises,' *Journal of Comparative Economics*, 29:327–46.

Zhang, H. and Ming, L. (eds), 2000. *Development Report on Private Enterprises in China,* Social Sciences Literature Publishing House, Beijing.

——, 1999. *Development Report on Private Enterprise In China*, Social Science Literature Publishing House, Beijing.

Zhang, M. Q., 2001. 'What is Short in Annual-Salary System?', *China Reform*, Beijing 3:50–1.

Zhang, W., 1999. *Enterprise Theories and the Reforms of Chinese Enterprises*, Peking University Press, Beijing (in Chinese).

Zhao R. and Li, S., 1999. 'The analysis of increase in household income inequality in China' in Renwei, Z., Shi, L. and Riskin, C., (eds), *Re-Thinking Chinese Household Income Distribution* (in Chinese), Beijing: Financial and Economic Press of China:42–71.

www.ingramcontent.com/pod-product-compliance
Lightning Source LLC
Chambersburg PA
CBHW040143270326
41928CB00023B/3328